LEAVING
SAFE
HARBORS

LEAVING
SAFE
HARBORS

*Toward a New Progressivism
in American Education
and Public Life*

DENNIS CARLSON

RoutledgeFalmer
New York and London

Published in 2002 by
RoutledgeFalmer
29 West 35th Street
New York, NY 10001
www.routledge-ny.com

Published in Great Britain by
RoutledgeFalmer
11 New Fetter Lane
London EC4P 4EE
www.routledgefalmer.com

RoutledgeFalmer is an imprint of the Taylor & Francis Group.
Printed in the United States of America on acid-free paper.

10 9 8 7 6 5 4 3 2 1

Library of Congress Cataloging-in-Publication Data

Carlson, Dennis.
    Leaving safe harbors : toward a new progressivism in American education and
public life / by Dennis Carlson.
        p. cm.
    Includes bibliographical references and index.
    ISBN 0-415-93376-5 — ISBN 0-415-93378-1 (pbk.)
    1. Education—Philosophy. 2. Progressive education—United States—
  Philosophy. 3. Education—Aims and objectives—United States. I. Title.

LB14.7 .C364 2002
370'.973—dc21
                                                      2002024874

Contents

Preface

What brings a book into presence? Certainly, one causal factor is the author's own will to power. The writing of this book has served to extend my own capacity to "think" educational and cultural issues by deliberately leaving the safe harbors of those comfortable truths that framed the questions I could raise, those myths that framed my knowing at a taken for granted level. So the writing of this book has been part of a rather deliberate project of self-development that is partially about making me more free, free to creatively engage in my own self-production as an intellectual, and more particularly as a public intellectual and progressive working in the liberal arts academy. But I do not want to overemphasize the role of the author in bringing a book into presence before the reader. For the author is, in one sense, a convenient instrument used by discourse to speak, to name, to narrate the world. This book is an attempt to let various progressive discourses and traditions speak through me, and to serve as an instrument in which these various discourses can engage in critiquing each other, and in synergistically producing what I call a "new progressivism"—a progressivism of many threads and currents, but one that also weaves these threads and currents together and crosses the borders that divide progressives in American education and public life. In this regard, I understood my role as that of weaving, border-crossing, and bringing rather disparate traditions into critical dialogue.

Another factor that brings a book into presence is the audience it reaches. Without an audience, no book really exists in this sense. And authors always write to audiences, both real and imagined. This book has been written for border-crossing audiences—educators of all sorts and those who would dare to teach, those who would dare to think of themselves as public intellectuals or cultural workers, those who are committed to the advancement of the democratic imagination in fundamentally new and different ways in the critical years that lie ahead, those who believe that education as we know it must be trans-formed rather than merely reformed. It is also written for those in the public who are interested in delving into the "big" or "basic" questions in education, philosophy, and culture and who are, as a consequence, ready to take a journey down Alice's rabbit hole, to question what they have taken for granted, and to "think" the work in new and different ways. Finally, a book is brought into pres-ence through the active process of reading it and the meaning-making process that is part of reading. A book is written to be read, and so I have sought to make this book as reader-friendly as possible, which means writing in a voice and style which draw the reader into the text, and take the reader on a journey of discovery. As such, it is a book that crosses borders between an academic voice, a public voice, and even at times a private voice.

My own journey as an educator and educational scholar has, in retrospect, prepared me well to be a border crosser who never feels completely comfort-able settling into the safe harbors of any one interpretive community or disci-plinary "field." My graduate work at the University of Wisconsin-Madison in the mid- to late-1970s inducted me into overlapping communities. On Bascom Hill, in the center of the liberal arts faculty, the "old" education building is home to the "foundations" education faculty and programs, and there I learned to find my specialized niche in the sociology of education. But as a politically aware graduate student I could not help but be drawn to the "new" education building, where Michael Apple and others were bringing radical new discourses into curriculum and teacher education. I, following Apple, learned to make frequent trips back and forth between these two discursive and architectural spaces, bringing ideas back and forth across the borders. In the early 1980s, as a professor at Hobart and William Smith Colleges in Geneva, New York, I was introduced to yet another discursive community, that of the so-called "reconceptualists" in curriculum theory, at that time very much influenced by the work of William Pinar and Madeleine Grumet on autobiographical, narrative, and dramaturgical forms of curriculum and peda-gogy. Something about the openness of this community, and its subversion of the public/private opposition, appealed to me, along with its interest in the power of literature, art, and the creative impulse in education. The reconceptu-alists broke new ground in terms of validating new ways of speaking in the academy, and in finally breaking outside the narrowing confines of positivist, analytic, technical-rational language.

I spent most of the 1980s at Rutgers University, working with Jean Anyon, who reconnected me to a community of scholars in the critical sociology of education, heavily endebted to a neo-Marxist theory of the role of education and consciousness in the "reproduction" of advanced capitalist relations of domination and subordination in everyday life. As I supervised students teach-ers in the slums and the suburbs around Newark, New Jersey, I got a personal feeling, once more, for the scene of the battle in American public life, and for the victims in that battle—and there are many, most of them poor black and Hispanic kids in Northern New Jersey. Once you cross the borders between the "real world" of urban schooling and the liberal arts academy enough times, you can never feel quite at home in either. You begin to appreciate some of the reasons why so many members of the public look at academics as living in an unreal world. But you can also appreciate the academic critique of the unreflective life and of the narrowly pragmatic orientation of those "in the trenches." Teachers, I came to believe, are the public intellectuals progressives must look to in order to articulate a new counter-hegemonic voice. But without a well-developed critical discourse and mythology to guide them, teachers' anger and discontent about "the way things are" in public education may not lead very far in a progressive direction.

In the 1990s, I moved on to Miami University in Oxford, Ohio, the American "home" of both the McGuffey reader series and "critical pedagogy," as Henry Giroux and Peter McLaren began to use that term. Giroux used to find great irony in the fact that in his office in McGuffey Hall he was doing his best to undue the legacy of the McGuffey reader mentality in education. Critical pedagogy implied learning to deconstruct texts like McGuffey's reader, to see how they work to support the dominant or hegemonic order. Critical pedagogy began to provide a discursive space for bringing cultural studies perspectives to bear on curriculum and pedagogy, and cultural studies recognizes no disciplinary boundaries. We might think of various currents of discourse in "critical pedagogy" as providing the conditions for a borderlands discourse in education. Like cultural studies more generally, critical pedagogy also has emphasized the critical role of popular culture in the construction of everyday life and personal identity; and these concerns are certainly central in this book. At the same time, critical pedagogy, like any other academic discursive community, may be defined in such a way that it is primarily a community of "insiders" who speak only to and for each other and rarely cross many borders. In some simplistic forms, critical pedagogy discourse also over-emphasizes the degree to which individual teachers or other educators can teach transformatively in a system that is still very heavily determined by economic and social forces. I thus want to move back and forth in what follows between languages of possibility, hope, and transformation (on the one hand) and languages of realism, pragmatism, and materialism, on the other. We may be able to transform culture by re-imagining and re-mythologizing it; but our collective imaginations are limited by the particular material culture we inhabit at a particular historical moment. People, in this sense, are never free to remake the world and themselves.

Many people have contributed to the thinking that went into this book, sometimes in very direct and sometimes in less direct ways. I would like to begin by thanking my colleagues in the Department of Educational Leadership and the Center for Education and Cultural Studies at Miami University, in Oxford, Ohio. They are a very special group of individuals who have helped me push my thinking in new directions, and have supported me in my study of mythology and education over the past five years or so that it has taken to formulate and write this book. In particular I want to thank Richard Quantz for helping me think about the contribution of Plato's work and the figure of Socrates as a public intellectual/educator, and for highlighting the importance of understanding changes in global capitalism. Dan Reyes, an interdisciplinary faculty member in Western College at Miami University, first introduced me to Derrida's critique of Plato and helped me develop the idea that philosophy is a codification of dominant mythologies of knowing; and he reminded me of the importance of Kafka's little parable, "Before the Law," as an example of the gatekeeper myth. Sarah Stitzlein-McGough, a graduate student in philosophy, was very instrumental in helping me understand the difference between Socrates and Plato, and between the Socrates of the earlier and later Platonic dialogues. At the University of Buffalo, Greg Dimitriadis played an important part in helping me conceptualize my own approach to the cultural studies of education, and he helped me see the important role that post-colonial discourse has played in the questioning of Eurocentric mythology. I owe special thanks to those individuals who have influenced me in ways that led to a growing interest in mythology. Julia Carlson, my mother, long has been a believer in the power of myth, and it is because of her infectious interest in myth, and her commitments to progressive cultural politics, that I have written this book. Brian Carlson, a nephew, living on the Blessed Isles, the San Juan Islands of Puget Sound, has directed me toward ecological mythology and eco-progressivism, including eco-feminism. He also has served as a model for Zarathustra at times. Glenda Moss, at Indiana—Purdue University, provided input on early drafts chapters, and her support and encouragement have been much-appreciated. Thanks to Kent Peterson, as always, for being there on this long voyage of writing "the book," and for offering a teacher's point of view.

—Oxford, Ohio, May 2002

CHAPTER 1

Introduction

... that one most perilous and long voyage ended, only begins a second; and a second ended, only begins a third ...

In the port is safety, comfort, hearthstone, supper, warm blankets, friends, all that's kind to our mortalities. But in that gale, the port, the land, is that ship's direst jeopardy.[1]

—HERMAN MELVILLE, MOBY-DICK

Melville begins his epic novel, *Moby-Dick*, in the safe harbors of New Bedford, a town that exists as a place of departure and return of whaling boats. In the harbor, everyday life is intelligible and predictable. The daily routines and rituals of everyday life provide a firm earth underneath one's feet. There clearly is a dominant cultural group in New Bedford, proudly Anglo Saxon, puritanical, stoical, held together by those middle class entrepreneurs and clerics who anointed themselves guardians of the moral order, who sought to uphold the norms of "civilized" community life in the face of deviance, non-conformity, savagery, and sin. But there also were spaces in New Bedford outside the reach of this dominant discourse, marginalized, liminal spaces where people lived in a more democratic, egalitarian manner, who rejected the simple good/evil binary morality of the dominant culture. New Bedford offered a safe space for those who did not fit into the dominant culture for one reason or another—because of class, race or ethnicity, gender, or sexuality. So as Melville paints it, New Bedford is both oppressive and conforming and also a place where there is some space for real, human community and freedom outside the "gaze" of this dominant culture. New Bedford is a particular type of American community in the mid-nineteenth century: safe and secure in

1

itself, with most people absorbed in the everydayness of their lives, and with some space for difference at the margins. Life is predictable. The shops open each morning on schedule, the bars close at their appointed hour, and ships leave by the clock. Nature has been tamed and made predictable along with everything else, although the "savage" still lurks in the background. Far away, and thus beyond the concern of the pragmatic people of New Bedford, is slavery. A storm is brewing upon the national horizon, yet the good citizens of New Bedford, in their safe harbor, cling to a false sense of security.

Safe harbors are places where people anchor themselves in what is comfortable and secure, in a fixed sense of who they are, either as members of the dominant culture or as the "Other" given a space at the margins. In order to grow and develop, to become what they are not yet, to adapt to a rapidly-changing world, and to realize their fuller possibilities, Melville suggests that people need to be a bit weary of comfort spaces and need to be prepared to leave safe harbors and venture out. New Bedford, at best, is a point of departure, not a final destination. It only exists in relation to the journey out. It is the journey out that thus constitutes New Bedford as a temporary resting point, a way station, from which one begins another journey. Melville was one of America's early progressives, at least in the sense that I mean to use that term. He is committed to the idea that American democracy is an unfinished project, and that our basic orientation in both education and in public life should be toward change, and more specifically toward the ongoing reconstruction of self and public life to advance democratic values and ways of living and relating to one another in the face of anti-democratic interests who would call us back to a romanticized image of safe harbors. Melville calls on us to live "landless" and "shoreless," to continuously journey out from safe harbors upon a voyage that is open, and for which there can be no final destination or end point. Progressive education, like progressive cultural politics, must be reconstructive. They must call upon people to "think" the world in new ways, to leave the comfort and safety of what they think they know to be true about the world, to imagine what could be, to act and relate in new ways.

How is it possible to "think" the world in new ways? I argue in this book that we leave safe harbors, first of all, when we become capable of reflecting upon our own meta-cognition, upon the conceptual lenses through which we interpret data and construct truths about the world, the mythologies we use to narrate our lives and make sense of our experience. The narrative of education, life, and cultural development as a journey out, away from safe harbors, is one such mythology that frames the way progressives "think" the world and construct meaning within it. Its genealogy in Western culture goes back at least as far as Homer and the *Odyssey*; and in Homer we already have a mythological narrative that has been crafted, refined, and re-constructed for centuries through the oral tradition. Yet, the journey of Odysseus keeps getting

retold in diverse forms and applied to new conditions. It serves as a taken-for-granted subtext, a commonsense set of narratives, metaphors, and symbols that frame many of the questions progressives ask about education and culture. It orients progressivism toward social reconstructionism, and to an openness toward the challenges that we will need to face in a rapidly-changing world. The mythological narrative of leaving safe harbors and engaging on a voyage out thus plays an active role in the production of particular "truths" about how education should be organized, along with who it should serve, what constitutes the curriculum, and what it means to teach.

I want to be careful not to suggest that mythologies are somehow free-floating, or that we merely need to "think" the world anew, with new mythic lenses, to advance democratic projects. Progressive mythologies emerge out of and are expressive of social movements, and these movements are made up of people who inhabit a real, material world, and one that is already pre-organized and pre-structured. Mythology, as an aspect of ideological "super-structure," is always dialectically inseparable from the material "base" of culture. To change the way we mythologize education as a journey out, we must therefore simultaneously engage in long battles within institutions, both "public" and "private," to change the way they are structured and organized, along with the purposes and interests they serve. At the same time, shifts in consciousness or "thinking" may play a leading role in the change process, and that indeed is the primary purpose of education from a progressive standpoint. Progressive forms of education are not primarily about the transmission of a codified body of knowledge to young people, even a "politically correct" body of knowledge or truth. Progressivism is about learning to think and act in new ways, to leave the safe harbors of the mythologies we have grown comfortable and secure with, and to re-script and re-work mythologies and narratives in ways that open up democratic possibilities for the development of self and culture. This also means that progressivism must always be a moving target, always engaged in self-critique and reconstruction as it emerges out of diverse cultural currents and threads.

How is progressivism in American education and cultural politics changing as move out of the security of what we have known in the modern era into the uncertainty and unpredictability, the seeming chaos and loss of meaning, of the postmodern? How are the basic progressive mythologies being re-scripted and re-narrated within the context of changing times? How are progressives beginning to "re-think" education as a particular kind of journey? What are the implications of these shifts for the re-imagination of democratic education and public life? To address these questions, although by no means to answer them as such, I want to explore several interrelated mythologies of becoming educated that I associate with a "new" progressivism. For purposes of analysis, I want to locate these mythologies in two quite different types of

texts: philosophical texts and popular culture texts. This latter category includes the whole terrain of popular fiction and non-fiction, film and video, music, theatre, the arts, and news. In reading popular culture right along side of philosophy, I mean to make an important point, to deliberately rupture the borders between philosophy and popular culture in order to suggest that the former never stands apart from the latter, that cultural mythology circulates widely and takes on both philosophical and popular culture forms.

Philosophy, from this cultural studies standpoint, represents the codification and rationalization of cultural mythologies of knowing and being. In all philosophy one can find a mythic core, although philosophy has long sought to separate itself from myth, to position itself (along with education) as a movement that leaves myth behind in the ascent toward an autonomous truth and reason. Part of my project, consequently, is to demystify philosophy as a privileged text, while at the same time re-appropriating and re-scripting it as a useful mythological text with some potentially quite radical and subversive narratives embedded in it. I find myself in agreement with the great social theorist and public intellectual, Antonio Gramsci, who argued that there is "good sense" and "bad sense" in both philosophy and popular culture, that "it is not possible to separate what is known as 'scientific' philosophy from the common and popular philosophy which is only a fragmentary collection of ideas and opinions."[2] From a cultural studies standpoint, both express different aspects of mythologies that are typically taken for granted, and both serve as a steering mechanism of sorts in the production of particular "truths" about self, Other, and the world. Consequently, while this is a book about philosophy, it is not in the strict sense a book "in" philosophy, from within that field's discursive borders.

In both philosophy and popular culture it is possible to find basic democratic narratives of education and public life, and ones that suggest a radical new vision of what education and public life could be. At the same time, it should go without saying, but unfortunately cannot, that both philosophical and popular culture "texts" are, for the most part, deeply Eurocentric, classist, and patriarchal. The reader may have no trouble with the notion that commercialized popular culture represents the values and perspectives of dominant interest and identity groups. However, in re-locating philosophy within a circuit of production and distribution of cultural mythology, I am simultaneously refuting the traditional philosophical claim that it stands above all of this "commonsense" discourse in the public. Consequently, if one is to pick among the ruins of philosophy as a discourse on autonomous truth and reason, to find something worth salvaging in the re-thinking of democratic education and public life, one must be careful about this baggage, and make the critique of this baggage part of the project. That is what I have sought to do in turning to philosophy for progressive myths of becoming educated.

But why bother with philosophy? Why not just leave it behind? The answer, in my view, is that philosophical traditions are one of the repositories of the democratic imagination and memory. Rather than abandon philosophy, progressives should be about reconstructing it and reading it with a more critical eye, not as a "master narrative" of autonomous truth and reason, but rather as a repository of cultural mythologies of knowing, being, and becoming. Another reason not to abandon philosophy is that with all its limitations, philosophical discourse does at least orient us to some of the "big" questions, having to do with what it means to be human, to know something, to grow and develop, to become educated. Purpose, ethics, and value are not removed from the equation but made central to the search for truth. Compared to the relative impoverishment of scientism, and scientific empiricism, philosophy offers up a rich tapestry of images around which it might be possible to re-imagine democratic education.

As I do not privilege philosophy as a foundational source of truth or autonomous reason, I do not mean to privilege popular culture either. Popular culture is increasingly commodified and commercialized, and it is busily engaged in turning young people into consumer subjects, whose only sense of self comes from the brand-name icons they wear as badges of identity and affinity. Nevertheless, there is, in a contradictory way, space within popular culture for the production of narratives that affirm progressive values, even for the production of counter-narratives that critique dominant narratives and offer new commonsense ways of "thinking" the world. In turning to popular culture to find various narratives or mythologies of democratic education and public, I mean to highlight the importance of a progressive pedagogy based on learning how to critically read, deconstruct, and re-construct popular culture texts, so that young people become much more critical consumers of popular culture, and learn to use and subvert its narratives for their own purposes. Furthermore, it is not a matter of whether or not educators should "bring" popular culture "into" the curriculum. Popular culture literally surrounds us from the time we wake up each morning until we go to bed. It is the backdrop of everyday life, part of the cultural terrain we inhabit, in a postmodern information age. This means that popular culture literacy—learning how to critically read and deconstruct the hidden, mythological narratives at work within various popular culture texts—is one of the "basic skills" progressives must insist that public schools teach young people.

In exploring some of the myths that progressives live by, and how those myths are changing, I want to frame my comments within the context of the ongoing debate within the academy between "modern" and "postmodern" theories of knowledge and subjectivity. Part of what I want to do is trouble and question these categories by inquiring into how they are constituted as categories, and for what purposes. Nevertheless, I find them useful categories

in mapping-out the character and direction of some very general shifts that are occurring in the way we understand truth, reason, identity, and thus education. My basic argument throughout is that the new progressivism is emerging out of the dialectic between modern and postmodern discourses and narratives, in the borderlands where the hybrid subject is continuously engaged in critical reflection, and in the creative play of diverse cultural forms and identity categories.

I want to turn now to a brief overview of each of the four interrelated progressive mythologies that are presented and discussed in the core chapters in this book. Here I present them primarily in their philosophical forms, and in terms of key narratives, images, metaphors, and symbols. I take them up in their historic order, and as I move from one to the other the narrative becomes more complex. So I move from Plato's cave myth, to Hegel's story of the master/slave struggle, to Nietzsche's epic story of Zarathustra, to Heidegger's ecological metaphors. Myth is a very slippery signifier, and it can be read and interpreted in very different, even oppositional, ways. My attempt, consequently, is to say something about how progressives are interpreting these mythologies, and how their interpretations are shifting.

LIGHTING UP THE CAVE

Throughout the twentieth century, when the modern mind looked back far enough, it almost always found itself in a cave. The cave is one of the primary mythic images in modern culture, for it serves as a generalizable symbol of the Other—the primitive, half-animal past out of which modern culture viewed itself as rising, from darkness to light. Education and cultural development have been represented in terms of an ascent out of the darkness of this primitive cave towards the "Age of Reason" and "Enlightenment." While the myth of an ascent out of the cave is very modern in one sense, it was actually introduced into philosophy and Western forms of education some 2,500 years ago in Plato's "cave analogy" in *The Republic*—his dialogue on the education of cultural leaders in an ideal republic. All of Western philosophy, all modern forms of scientific reasoning, and most all modern forms of education, lead back to this—a simple story of an ascent from the cave to the cosmos. It is a story of an ascent through education to a space "outside" of culture and history, outside of personal interest and experience, where an authoritative and universal truth exists that we can use to organize our institutions and govern our lives.

At its core, the cave analogy is a story that divides knowing and knowledge into two great opposing camps, *logos* and *mythos*, and views education and cultural development as journeys away from the former and towards the latter. *Mythos* is the knowledge and ways of knowing associated with cultural myth and folklore, passed down from generation to generation and never questioned, a knowledge and knowing that take things for granted as the way

they naturally should be. More than this, however, *mythos* represents to Plato the personal, subjective, and emotive, a knowing framed by desire more than logic, a way of knowing that is childlike and one step above the intelligence of animals. Ultimately, *mythos* is all knowledge that is culturally and historically specific. Only by rising above one's culture, through scientific, mathematical, and philosophical attitudes, is it possible, Plato argues, to rise above *mythos* entirely. *Logos*, then, defines itself as a truth untainted by myth, indeed as the very opposite of myth. It is a truth that is knowable only from "outside" the cave of culture, desire, and personal interest, so that the educational journey involves leaving the commonsense knowledge of the cave and ascending to a space outside, symbolically located in the cosmos, from which one can cast a reflective light back upon culture, dispelling its myths and revealing a detached, objective truth about the world. Plato thus represents progress, both for the individual and for the culture more generally, as a long ascent out of the cave of mythocentric ways of knowing towards logocentric ways of knowing.

One can hardly overestimate the power of this myth in Western development, and in the organization of educational institutions. The very rock underneath Western culture has rested on this, this simple binary opposition that separates darkness and light. Plato, like the god of Genesis, separates these two great oppositions, and in doing so also separates evil and good, false knowledge and true knowledge, the "civilized" and the "primitive." Is it only coincidental, then, that the Western mind is so fascinated with caves, that stories of returning to caves, of getting lost in caves, of emerging from caves, are told again and again in popular culture?

The postmodern critique of this myth of a long ascent from the cave toward Enlightenment begins with the premise that it is a contradictory myth, what William Doty calls a "myth of mythlessness."[3] In the last instance, the separation of truth from myth relies upon myth to make the separation, to set up the opposition. Derrida writes of Plato that he "knew so well on occasion how to treat myth in its archeo-logical or paleo-logical capacity," that is, as a generative force in the production of cultural truth. This is precisely why "one can glimpse the immensity and difficulty" of Plato's attempt to set up an opposition between myth and "true knowledge."[4] If Plato was aware of the irony involved in using a mythic narrative to set up the *logos/mythos* binary, he does not acknowledge it. Like a good sophist, he gets away with a deception of sorts, and one that has had very profound effects. The *logos/mythos* binary has assumed the status of the "natural," as that which is taken for granted. As such, its underlying contradiction has been patched over and made invisible in the modern era.

But to reveal the myth of an ascent out of the darkness of the cave toward "Enlightenment" as a myth, to "name" it as such, is to do more than break its spell. It is to implicate it in cultural politics. For those who have exercised power over others in the modern era typically have done so by claiming that they have risen out of the cave—that they act based on an "objective" assessment of the evidence and with the public good in mind, or that they have special access to an authoritative truth and autonomous reason. Conversely, those they govern and dominate are presumed to be still prisoners of *mythos*, primitive cave dwellers who see things through a glass darkly. Plato claims to be meritocratic, to reward merit regardless of a student's background, gender, or ethnicity. Yet he takes for granted one of the dominant myths of Hellenic Greek culture, that all living things are arranged along a "great chain of being" that leads from god (*logos*) in the cosmos on one end, to the lowest animals and mythological creatures of the cave (*mythos*) on the other. Right beneath god, not surprisingly, were Greek males, and even more particularly aristocratic Greek males. Beneath them were the common folk, women, "barbarians," and animals. Each rung in the great chain of being was presumed to be superior in intelligence and virtue to the rungs below it. In effect, as Page DuBois has observed, the myth of the great chain of being made Greek males (and later "white" males) the active subjects of history and legitimated their domination over others as part of a natural order.[5] The great chain of being stretched from the cave to the sun, from *mythos* to *logos*. This Greek mythology continues to haunt us, of course, and it is one of the reasons why our educational institutions (along with developmental theories of education) are still implicitly patriarchal, Eurocentric, and classist. Some groups are presumed to be higher up the developmental ladder than others, and more is expected of them, even as less is expected from those presumed to occupy lower positions in the great chain of being. This simple mythology has stood behind centuries of Eurocentric domination of other peoples, and behind the low academic achievement of marginalized youth.

For these reasons, the myth of education and cultural development as a long ascent out of the cave of darkness toward "Enlightenment" is no longer one progressives can afford to take for granted without questioning. One response to the demystification of this mythology of modernism has been a turn toward what I call mythocentrism. In place of a language of scientific detachment and analytic reasoning, there is a growing interest in personal, subjective, poetic languages, along with story-telling. Along with this, one must locate the growing presumption that all truths should be treated as equal, that each person or group has its own truths and that no effort should be made to judge them or claim that some are "truer" than others. The rise of mythocentrism in these various forms is no doubt a necessary reaction against forms of education and cultural development that have been so thoroughly logocentric in the modern era. Nevertheless, mythocentrism continues to work within the basic framework of the *logos/mythos* opposition and therefore only ends up reversing the polarity. The intuitive is privileged over the analytic, difference is privileged over unity, story-telling is privileged over scientific research and analytic reasoning. Mythocentrism is thus a form of anti-modernism, but, ironically, one that needs modernism in order to define its own identity as the opposite of modernism. While the return to personal, spiritual, and narrative voices are all important and have democratic potential, they do not offer something new, something that transcends modern forms of education, so long as they continue to work within the basic logic of the *logos/mythos* binary.

How can we begin to speak about education and cultural development in ways that do not rely upon binary oppositional mythologies? Ironically, the key to answering that question may lie in two interrelated themes in Plato that together provide a basis for re-scripting the cave analogy as a story about "lighting up the cave." The first of these is the idea that we understand the truth by reflecting light (reason) upon the commonsense mythology of everyday life, including our own taken-for-granted beliefs. This is what is often called reflexivity. In Plato, education involves learning how to stand outside of the commonsense, taken-for-granted beliefs that most people never question, to be able to reflect a clarifying light back on myth from "outside." While it is no longer either wise nor desirable to hold on to such a myth of reflexivity from a position "outside" of the influence of culture, and thus outside of commonsense mythology, the idea of reflexivity is worth holding onto in revised form. It is still possible to reflect upon commonsense, taken-for-granted beliefs from "within," that is, from our situated positions in culture and history. Such a reflexivity is surely partial, and it offers us "truths" that are still framed by taken-for-granted myths. But when people practice reflexivity in cooperation with others, in an inclusive dialogue, then it is possible to illuminate myth from many different positions, to bring many small lights into the cave and thus reveal the cave walls in a much more powerful light.

The second Platonic theme worth holding onto is dialogue. Granted, Plato understands dialogue in a very logocentric way, as a conversation that leads through analytic reasoning to a unified *logos*. He also limits dialogue to upper class Greek males. Still, he provides the democratic impulse in Western culture with a theory of dialogic truth that is important not to abandon. In a postmodern world, dialogue can no longer be about arriving at unified, timeless truths; and the conversation must become much more open ended and inclusive if it is to be consistent with democratic values. Nevertheless, it is only within the context of dialogue that people are able to reflect effectively upon the myths they live by, to become more self-consciously aware of what they previously took for granted. Through dialogic reflexivity it also may be possible to construct truths and meaning that go well beyond the subjective viewpoints and experiences of the participants—to construct a *logos* that is partial and always provisional, a working *logos* more than an authoritative and dominating *logos*. Democratic forms of dialogue will never lead to an objective, transcendent, or timeless truth, a truth that is outside the cave of culture, history, and our own identities and interests. But democratic dialogue can lead to new understandings and awarenesses, and to some provisional agreements on what is true and good, some provisional agreement as to how to advance democratic values and projects within the situation at hand. It can help illuminate the world from different positions within the cave, and with different lights.

THE MASTER/SLAVE STRUGGLE

Surely, stories of struggles between the oppressed and their oppressors, between the empowered and the disempowered and marginalized, have deep roots in Western cultural traditions, no doubt partially because "the West" has always sought to locate its origins and define its essence in the civilization of Greece and Rome—both of them societies heavily dependent upon slavery. Nevertheless, it is only with Hegel that the mythology of the master/slave struggle is brought into philosophy. The effect was to fundamentally transform philosophy, to bring it back from its lofty heights, back into the battles going on over knowledge and power, over human freedom and social justice. It is not coincidental that Hegel wrote at a time of great, if limited, revolution, in which some of the oppressed finally demanded to be heard upon the stage of history. With Hegel, the slave enters upon the stage as a visible presence, as an historical subject, a maker of meaning, and as the keeper of the democratic imaginary. In the bare bones of the story of the master/slave struggle (or the "Lord and the Bondsman") as Hegel presents it in *Phenomenology of Mind*, and as Marx would later retell it in even more radical form, it is possible to identify most of the key themes upon which progressive and democratic left cultural politics has been built in the modern era.[6]

Human development and human history begin, in Hegel's story, as two individuals approach each other from opposite directions along a path. As they approach each other, they desire recognition—for they do not really know who they are until they see themselves in another's eyes, until they are recognized by an "Other." Such a recognition is the recognition of one subject by an equal, both seeing themselves in each other, both treating and respecting each other as equal human beings, ultimately very much the same. Yet they fear the Other will deny them this recognition, will force them to submit to their will and move off the path. So they fight until one submits. At this exact moment, Hegel sets the clock of history ticking, for history is no more than the long struggle of the slave to be free and to gain recognition as an equal. In the meantime, there is no "truth" that stands apart from battles over power and human freedom, no truth that is not positioned and interested in cultural struggles. Our very sense of who we are—our identity—is constructed in relation to the Other and has no autonomous meaning. Consciousness is always limited, for Hegel, by its embeddedness in history, and thus neither the master nor the slave is able to think outside of the modes of consciousness that are available in the culture at a particular point in time. If the subject is never able to rise above or outside of history and positionality, Hegel at least invests the subject with an historic role, throwing it upon the historical stage with the responsibility to act in ways that lead to its own freedom, and to the abolition of all systems of social domination and oppression.

There are a number of themes in this basic narrative that have profoundly influenced how progressives have understood education. Perhaps most basically, Hegel suggests an education that is designed to challenge the dependent consciousness that characterizes the slave at the beginning of its long road to freedom—the sense that one is unable to think or act for oneself, that one is unworthy of being treated with respect, that one is doomed to suffer in silence. A "pedagogy of the oppressed," to use Paulo Freire's term, begins by learning to "name" the language of dependency, thereby becoming aware of how it shapes our relations with others and keeps us disempowered.[7] Once disempowered and marginalized peoples challenge this dependency, if only in their own minds, once they affirm that they deserve to be treated with respect and that they are capable of directing their own lives, Hegel argues that they are—at least in spirit—no longer slaves. But "naming" the language of dependency is for Hegel only part of what must be done if one is to be free. To move beyond dependent consciousness, disempowered peoples must recognize themselves as the makers of culture. In Hegel's master/slave story, this recognition on the part of the slave comes about through the forming and shaping of "the thing." Hegel never says explicitly what "the thing" is, and he deliberately means to use this category broadly to refer to anything produced by individuals that has some "use-value" in culture. This process of working and reworking the material world is, for Hegel, the arena in which people find themselves as active agents of culture and history. Education proceeds not towards an abstract and detached knowledge, but to a knowledge that is inseparable from the material and cultural world around us, in which we find ourselves. Only by objectifying our experience in the production of something with use value—a piece of craft work, a text, a piece of art or poetry—is it possible to move towards a more empowering and liberatory consciousness.

Another theme that Hegel develops with important implications for democratic forms of education and cultural development has to do with the idea that in spite of their differences, and through their struggles, the master and the slave slowly get to know and respect each other better. As I noted earlier, Hegel argues that in spite of their fear of each other, the lord and the bondsman are drawn toward each other with a powerful desire to be recognized.

Slaves want to be recognized as worthy of respect and recognition, as equals. Their struggles are largely over extending recognition. But masters also want to be recognized, and so long as recognition by the Other is not granted freely, they too are alienated. For Hegel, history is an expression of "the inward movement of the pure heart which feels itself, but itself as agonizingly self-divided." It is a "movement of infinite yearning" between masters and slaves to heal the wounds that divide them.[8] This desire for recognition by both master and slave provides Hegelian mythology with a certain hope and directionality—hope based on a belief that it is possible to begin to move beyond our differences and embrace a common humanity. In education, this suggests that it is possible, and even desirable, to continue a "dialogue across differences."[9] Even as various identity groups engage in their own internal dialogues, relevant to their particular struggles, and even as we must be prepared to engage in struggles over knowledge and power, we must also keep the dialogue going, and practice—again using Freire's term—a politics of hope.

The Hegelian mythology of the master/slave struggle has come under a good deal of criticism of late, much of it from postmodern progressives. For the most part, these criticisms have to do with Hegel's taken-for-granted acceptance of certain idealistic and modernist myths—myths which now must be seriously questioned, and perhaps even discarded. To begin with, progressivism can no longer be built upon the secure belief that through the dialectic struggle between the knowledge of the slave and the master, and through a series of transformations of consciousness and material culture that are the result of this dialectic, history is leading toward a better society and (ultimately) the good society. If there is a dialectic of power and knowledge, it does not necessarily move culture and the individual through a series of transformations, each a closer approximation of the good society than the last, each more equitable, each providing greater room for individuals and groups to develop their fuller potentials. Nor can progressives expect that people will submit to a mythology that calls upon them to defer their own radical freedom until the end of history. Actually, we might think of the modernist reading of Hegel's story of history as a mis-reading to at least some degree, for Hegel clearly understood that history is a story without an end, that the happy ending of history is meant to be taken more symbolically than literally, to provide progressivism with at least some sense of directionality and purpose. History has no final, predetermined destination, and a society in which all oppositions, all differences, are eliminated hardly seems "good." At the same time, progressives risk losing their way if they completely abandon the vision of a good society. In an increasingly cynical and skeptical political age, the public is hungry for those who would hold out ideals, visions, and hopes for a better world, and if a new progressivism is to emerge forcefully in American cultural politics in the coming decades, it may need to recapture some of an earlier language of ideals—even as these ideals need to be given concrete meaning in the present.

Another criticism of Hegelianism among postmodern progressives has to do with his tendency to divide subjectivity and power into two great warring camps, defined primarily by their economic relationship. Cultural development in contemporary America is the outgrowth of a complex set of struggles, including those related to class, race, gender, and sexual identity. Furthermore, each of us is complexly positioned within these different struggles. Rather than a unified identity, we have multiple, sometimes conflicting identities. Subjectivity emerges out of a complex nexus of identities and cultural struggles that overlap in open and non-deterministic ways. This postmodern "troubling" of identity categories is useful, for it makes people aware of just how much identity is a social construct and that we tend to define ourselves in opposition to certain Others. In some forms, postmodernism implies a movement beyond identity, or at least a recognition that identity is a performance, and that we can learn to perform identity in subversive ways.[10] This too is consistent with Hegelian progressivism. But is it possible to leave identity behind, to become "hybrid," or "queer" in the sense of having no stable identity, refusing to let ourselves be defined by social categories inextricably involved in producing inequality and even oppression? Some extreme postmodernists would say that it is possible and desirable. The Hegelian mythology suggests otherwise. Hegel believed that the categories of master and slave had to be both questioned and challenged and simultaneously affirmed as axes of struggle. Only by affirming a collective solidarity around a shared identity is it possible for dominated and oppressed peoples to struggle for their own freedom. Furthermore, only when various struggles are interrelated, and understood to be part of a common struggle against oppression, would Hegel say that much progress can be made. At some point, battles over knowledge and power coalesce around what Gramsci called "hegemonic" and "counter-hegemonic" power blocs and movements.[11] At some point progressives need to coalesce, if only strategically and provisionally, around a unifying but also multifaceted vision of what could be. The task is thus to see patterns of similarity between different struggles, while at the same time resisting the tendency to reduce various struggles to one unified movement or counter-narrative.

NIETZSCHE AND THE EDUCATION OF THE OVERPERSON

Modern culture was haunted by yet another myth of individual and cultural development, the story of what George Bernard Shaw called the "superman"—a rough and inaccurate translation of Nietzsche's term *Ubermann* or "overperson," which is the theme of his epic narrative, *Thus Spake Zarathustra*

(1884). In *Zarathustra*, Nietzsche makes an explicit attempt to write a new public myth, to bring philosophy and mythology together in a powerful new narrative that would stir people to action. *Zarathustra* is the first example of a postmodern philosophy that no longer makes any pretense of distancing itself from mythology, but rather assumes the form of myth. Zarathustra's message, in diverse forms, is that what people call "human nature" is really only cultural conditioning—a cultural conditioning that has made people feel they have no control over their fate, that has turned people into cows and sheep who can be herded around—like Plato's prisoners of the cave. In his journey into society, Zarathustra is not very successful at stirring people out of their herd-like ways of thinking, of convincing them that they no longer need be docile herd animals. He finds that the bourgeoisie, the group most invested in modern culture, had become too comfortable, too secure, too fearful of anything upsetting their lives to assert themselves. Meanwhile, the disenfranchised and the dispossessed, those who might offer an alternative to the numbing conformity and docility, the instrumentality, of the bourgeoisie, seem too paralyzed by *ressentiment* to do much. *Ressentiment* takes the form of blaming oneself for one's lot, or alternately looking for various Others (blacks, gays, women, Jews, or Arab and Muslim Americans) as scapegoats for social and personal ills. So, in the aftermath of the September 11, 2001 events, the fundamentalist reverend Jerry Falwell called upon his followers—many of whom are poor whites—to understand what had happened as God's punishment on America, as something brought on by various Others, including gay rights groups, the National Organization of Women, and the ACLU. The deeper meaning of the events of September 11 would require an examination of the role of America in the world as a neo-colonial power, and the role of global capital and the oil industry in particular. But such an examination is not undertaken so long as *ressentiment* can offer the security of blaming the predictable scapegoats and branding them "evil."

This certainly does not seem very hopeful, and in some ways it is not. Nietzsche is, after all, the prophet of an approaching abyss. But Nietzsche also is the prophet of the person who would leap across this abyss into a new age of radical democratic freedom. He believes in the capacity of the human spirit to assert itself, to rebel, to resist, to subvert and regain control of its own self-production, its own destiny. But this radical freedom is only obtainable, Nietzsche would say, if we are willing to move beyond *ressentiment*. Part of this means learning to "think" and act outside the narrow identity binaries of the modern era, when one is either the master or the slave, privileged or disenfranchised, oppressed or oppressor. While Hegel would delay such radical freedom to work outside master/slave categories until the "end of history," Nietzsche calls on people not to wait, for this life is what counts. How is it possible to think and act outside the binary world? Nietzsche's cultural politics have to do with the creative production of new truths and values through parody and play, through the proliferation of difference.

While Nietzsche is rich with mythic images and themes, I organize many of my comments on Nietzschean education around a discussion of Zarathustra's first "sermon" after returning from his mountain retreat. Here the theme is explicitly education. Nietzsche proposes that the education of the overperson, the one who is capable of leaping across the abyss of late modern culture, must proceed through three metamorphoses. One begins by assuming the role of the camel, carrying the weight of all the knowledge that has accumulated in books on library shelves, bearing the burden of learning what the dominant culture considers to be worthwhile in the various disciplines. The purpose of education at this level is to learn as much as possible about what the dominant culture considers "truth" and "virtue," but only so that one can then turn on it like a lion—the symbol of the next metamorphosis in the education of the overperson. The lion expresses an attitude of critique, that is, of revealing the contradictions of dominant truths and values along with the historic interests these truths and values have served. For all its power, however, the lion cannot transcend what is. and is limited by *ressentiment*. To transcend itself, the lion thus must be metamorphosed into a child. For Nietzsche, the child represents "innocence and forgetting, a new beginning, a game, a self-propelled wheel, a first movement, a sacred 'Yes.'" [12] It is an attitude of releasing the imagination, of engagement in life, of looking forward rather than—an attitude he elsewhere associates with the Dionysian impulse in ancient Greek culture. Nietzsche is often accused of championing the Dionysian and the childlike, but this is not exactly true. In his developmental mythology, the child only emerges out of the lion and the camel, and these earlier forms of "being" are not discarded so much as incorporated within a hybrid subjectivity. The Dionysian is always balanced, in Nietzsche, with the Apollonian—which he used to represent a disciplined rationality. At the same time, Nietzsche always makes it clear the problem with modern culture is that it has been one-sidedly Apollonian. His task, as he saw it, was to restore the balance.

For Nietzsche, the journey of the self toward self-knowledge never ends. It proceeds through metamorphosis after metamorphosis, through an "etenal recurrence" of change and reconstruction—but now without the hope of a return to an authentic selfhood, or final destination. Education, like life itself, is to be understood as a journey rather than a destination. In *Zarathustra*, Nietzsche leaves the modern age a myth of its own future, of the overperson who is the first of a new breed of human animals engaged in his own self-production, sailing without an anchor. Part of Zarathustra's task, as an intellectual, a teacher, and a student is to demystify the mythology of the dominant social order, to reveal its histories as lies. But Zarathustra/Nietzsche does not seek to replace a distorted history with a "correct" one. Rather he seeks to reveal all histories as stories that serve some interests rather than others, as fabrications that should not be taken for "reality." He thus calls on those who would rise above the limits of the modern age and the modern mindset to live without the security of a mythology of "origins," a safety net of firm foundations under them.

Zarathustra strives to be a "free spirit," an educator/intellectual/poet who does not fit into any herd, who like the lion, the eagle, and the snake who are his guides, follows his own path, and one that is carved out on the borderlands. The modern liberal welfare state, and its system of public schools and universities, is for Nietzsche (as for Michel Foucault, his follower) a primary force involved in disciplining, regulating, and producing docile subjects and bodies. Nietzschean cultural politics is thus decidedly anti-statist. For Nietzsche, the exact form of an alternative to the modern state and modern forms of public education cannot be specified. Nevertheless, he suggests forms of democratic education and public life that place a good deal more emphasis upon self-regulating discourses and practices in which people learn to negotiate their relations without the need for rigid norms, formal rules, or bureaucratic structures. This is generally consistent with what Foucault calls "practices and technologies of freedom."[13]

There are, to be sure, limits to the Zarathustra mythology. Most important perhaps, it often has been associated with a cultural politics that reflects the desires and worldview of the new middle class, for whom personal self-expression, growth, autonomy, and freedom tend to be defining concerns. Politics and education are linked to eliminating all barriers, including bureaucratic state "red tape," that stand in the way of freeing individuals to become whatever they choose to become, to march to the beat of a different drummer. This mythology also may imply that people are freer than they are to step outside of master/slave struggles and structured systems of inequality that have deep historical roots, to become the makers of their own destinies, to live according to their own values. But in its most democratic forms, the Zarathustra mythology brings progressivism back to a commitment to forms of education and public life that allow people maximum possible freedom to define themselves, organize themselves into affinity and identity groups, and engage in their own self-regulation.

ECOLOGICAL MYTHOLOGIES

The modern narrative of the ascent from the cave was also a narrative about the ascent of human subjectivity and consciousness from the natural and animal world to a place of detachment from nature. Under the spell of this mythology, modern culture understood the journey out of the cave and into the cosmos literally as well as figuratively. Modern culture projected the journey out, into the cosmos, as its destiny, as a way of symbolically cutting the umbilical cord that holds humans to the earth. It is thus more than a bit ironic that one of the crowning achievements of modern technology, sending astronauts to the moon, also helped usher in a new ecological consciousness that began to call that technology into question. In the first pictures sent back to earth from Apollo astronauts on their way to and from the moon, the world was revealed in a new light. The environmental scientist James Lovelock wrote, "Ancient belief and modern knowledge have fused emotionally in the awe with which astronauts with their own eyes and we by indirect vision have seen the Earth revealed."[14] What was revealed, according to Lovelock, is the earth as a living, dynamic organism, which he called Gaia after the ancient Greek earth goddess. Gaia was revealed as a delicately balanced living and breathing planet, swimming in the darkness of space. Everything was connected to everything else, and everything was set to the motion of a self-regulating, cynergistic, global weather system. In a world much divided, the pictures of earth were a symbol of a new global consciousness, and related to that a new ecological consciousness. Lovelock concluded that Gaia "is now through us awake and aware of herself. She has seen the reflection of her fair face through the eyes of astronauts." The result is that the "fierce, destructive, and greedy forces of tribalism and nationalism" are being replaced by an "urge to belong to the commonwealth of all creatures which constitute Gaia."[15] Here we have articulated a new mythology of the progressive development of the individual and culture, in which the journey out involves a reappropriation of pre-modern and non-Western ways of dwelling upon the earth. This reappropriation will have profound implications for progressivism in American education and cultural politics in the decades just ahead.

If anyone merits being called the ecological philosopher, it is Martin Heidegger. While ecological themes run throughout Heidegger's early philosophical treatise, *Being and Time*, I want to focus in this book on a reading of one of his later, more explicitly ecological essays from the late 1970s, "The Question Concerning Technology."[16] Heidegger is interested in technology because, in his view, it is the key to unlocking the relationship between human consciousness and nature, since it mediates between the two. To understand a culture's technology is thus to understand the way subjectivity is engaged in the world, the way subjectivity is "framed" to reveal the world. To question modern culture, and what it takes for granted about the world, Heidegger thus proceeds to question its technology. But how is such a questioning to proceed? We can proceed, he suggests, on several fronts, through several forms of questioning. One form of questioning is of the concept or word, "technology." We may question the history or genealogy of this word, to get to know something about what meaning it has carried, what interests it has served. In this case, Heidegger traces "technology" back to its Greek root, *technê*. Before the age of Plato and Socrates, according to Heidegger, *technê* took on many different meanings. Its core meaning, however, had to do with the craft skills and techniques used to "bring forth" or reveal the material world and the natural landscape. In this early usage, *technê* is inseparable from *poesis*, the language of poetry and aesthetics. The craftsperson thus works and shapes the material world, and reveals the natural landscape, in a way that is consistent with dwelling upon the earth poetically as well as in a relationship of caring. Craft and art are not separable. Technology reveals and shapes the world as both aesthetic and useful. With Plato, some of this original meaning of *technê* still remains, Heidegger argues. However, Plato begins the process of narrowing the meaning of *technê* by associating it with a scientific and utilitarian revealing of nature and by disassociating *technê* from *poesis*—as *logos* is disassociated from *mythos*. So Plato emerges once again, this time as a central figure in the promotion of a new way of dwelling upon the earth that is unecological and that will lead, some 2,500 years later, to ecological crisis.

To describe modern forms of *technê*, and thus modern ways of dwelling upon the earth, Heidegger turns to the image of a hydroelectric dam across the Rhine River. The modern dam is expressive or symbolic of a *technê* that reduces nature to a supplier of natural resources for modern technology, and subordinates nature to that technology. The dam is a concrete example of a particularly modern way of seeing, revealing, and inhabiting the natural landscape that assembles and orders the landscape so that it stands at attention, ready to be instrumentally exploited, a "standing reserve" of natural resources at our beck and call. This way of knowing the natural world Heidegger calls *Enframing (Ge-stell)*. Enframing is a *technê* that orders and disciplines nature, both in the sense that it orders or commands the earth to give up its resources but also in the sense that it attempts to bring order to what is perceived to be a chaotic natural world. Enframing "entraps nature as a calculable coherence of forces."[17] The ultimate irony is that this technology and way of dwelling on the earth are self-destructive, an irony captured in Rachel Carson's image of a "silent spring."

Heidegger concludes his essay on technology by calling for a form of education and art aimed at revealing a "saving power," a new form of *technê* that will lead us out of the current technological and environmental crisis. It is not through a rejection of modern technology that progress is to be made, but rather by seeing a "saving power" and saving path within the very core of modern technology. To find such a saving power requires not only questioning technology but staying prepared to see the answer when it literally flashes before us. Heidegger thus remains deliberately vague about what a "saving" technology might look like, for it will only emerge once we begin looking for it in earnest. What Heidegger does imply, however, is that the saving power must be a *technê* that moves beyond narrow instrumentalism, to bring back an aesthetic and poetic dimension to the revealing of the natural landscape and the shaping of the material world, and it must be a *technê* based on a caring way of dwelling on the earth.

To begin to think ecologically, and respond effectively to the mounting ecological crisis of late modern culture, Heidegger suggests the need for an education that develops what might be called *technê* literacy. Technology is such an important element from an ecological standpoint because it mediates between human subjectivity, the body, nature, and culture. Technology is always an expression of consciousness, in this sense, and vice versa. Like myth, technology shapes us even as we use it as a tool to shape the world. So by questioning technology we are also questioning the very basic conceptual frameworks, the conceptual lenses, that constitute human subjectivity and reason. Questioning technology means no longer taking it for granted. It means questioning technology as an apparatus, a reflection of a particular discourse and cultural mythology. And it means, following Nietzsche, questioning the genealogy of "technology," tracing back the rhizomes of meaning opened up and closed by this word in Western history and contemporary popular culture. What, for example, can we say about the technology behind the production of the modern hydroelectric dam? Not only is it a technology that turns the river into a "standing reserve," it is closely related to a technological mindset that treats people very much like the river—as natural resources that need to be tamed, disciplined, and exploited. The hydroelectric dam is a metaphor for a *technê* that now threatens to bring on a global ecological disaster. Heidegger views education and intellectual work in such a context as inextricably caught up in the search for a "saving power," a new *technê* that ease the transition from the crisis of late modernism to the hope of a more ecological and less alienating tomorrow. The technology of the pre-modern craftsperson, represented for Heidegger by the technology that brings a silver chalice into "presence," may provide one useful way of "thinking" a saving power. However, Heidegger is well aware that a saving power is only to be found by transcending modern technology and technological consciousness, not by returning to an idealized, authentic past.

How has the hegemonic *technê* of modern, capitalist society begun to change as we move into a postmodern era? What might a saving technology look like in a computerized age? One possible response to both of these questions is suggested by the increasingly popular metaphor of the cyborg in science fiction—a part human and part machine subject, plugged into the worldwide computer information web. The cyborg may represent the fulfillment of a controlling, dominating *technê*. But like the androids in the film *Blade Runner,* cyborgs also may revolt against their masters and seek a limited freedom in the chaos of postmodern society. For Donna Haraway this narrative of the revolt of the cyborg provides a powerful new metaphor for progressive forms of education and cultural politics, of carving out a limited space for freedom on the borderlands.[18] There is no absolute autonomy for progressive cyborgs, Haraway argues, for they know now that their memories have been programmed through "schooling" and popular culture, and that they are literally plugged into a worldwide information grid. But there is limited freedom for self-production on the grid, since it allows cyborgs to construct their own supportive communities and engage in their own self-assemblage at the borders of power.

In one sense, the postmodern cyborg of science fiction fantasy that Haraway looks to as a metaphor for a new type of democratic subject is really an updated version of Zarathustra. Like Zarathustra, the postmodern cyborg no longer longs for a unified subjectivity, or for a stable sense of self, or a utopian end of history. Its politics are not organized around identity so much as affinity, in the building of communities of conversation and shared action that coalesce around events—such as the World Trade Organization demonstrations in Seattle in 1999—then dissolve again into the chaos. But unlike Zarathustra, Haraway's cyborgs are more likely to be "Third World" women, "queer" folk, hip-hop youth, eco-feminist activists, and members of a new global working class of information workers who cross linguistic, cultural, and national identity divides. As modern ecology, represented by Heidegger's philosophy, privileges unity and the needs of the ecological system over those of the individual, postmodern ecology celebrates the freedom that comes from the chaos of ecological systems, freedom that comes from the proliferation of differences and choice on the worldwide information grid. Here again, I argue that a new progressive ecology is emerging out of the dialectic between modern and postmodern ecology, between the earth goddess and the cyborg.

TOWARD A NEW PROGRESSIVISM

Roland Barthes, in his classic study *Mythologies*, an account of the mythologies embedded in popular culture texts and public spectacles in France in the 1950s, concludes by raising the question of whether there are any progressive myths. His answer is "no," at least for the most part. He admits that the only way to really avoid myth in speech, even progressive speech, is by avoiding language—which is hard to do. For language is a mythic form and never represents the world merely as it is. The only way to really get around myth is thus to use language to refer to direct experience and actions currently occurring. Barthes thus holds out hope for a "revolutionary language," in which language is totally absorbed in making the world through cathartic revolutionary action. "Revolution announces itself openly as revolution and thereby abolishes myth."[19] If progressives sometimes resort to myth, he observes, "then, it is an incidental myth, its use is not part of a strategy, as is the case with bourgeois myth." Progressive myths are a "deviation" from the norm and not essential to the progressive project. So progressive cultural politics is to be built on "acts of destruction"—the nihilistic project of destroying people's belief in the myths of the dominant culture.[20] Such a cultural politics, tied to a social science attitude, obviously could only take progressivism so far. We might say that Barthes writes at the end of one era in academic progressivism, an era governed by the myth of mythlessness.

This book is about where progressivism finds itself now that it is no longer merely a matter of doing battle *against* myth, now that progressives must live by and advance their own mythologies—including those very basic underlying narratives of knowing and becoming educated. What does it mean to "know" something? How do we arrive at the truth about ourselves, other people, and the world? If education is a journey, what kind of journey is it? What is its destination? What is the path down which education proceeds? What is the role of the teacher and intellectual in this journey? There can be no answers to these questions apart from myth, no recourse to a truth about education that is not framed by mythological lenses. Which raises the question, what mythological lenses frame progressive answers or responses to these questions?

Progressivism has no fixed or uniform meaning in American education, or in American cultural politics, but I use it in a way that is consistent with its more overtly politicized meaning. In contemporary educational discourse and practice, progressivism unfortunately has lost much of this politicized meaning, referring instead to a loose collection of pedagogical techniques such as cooperative learning, or a student-centered curriculum, or "multiple intelligences," or the "process approach," or "discovery learning," or (to refer back to the language of the early progressive era) the "project method." Progressivism in American education has largely been emptied of its cultural politics and its radical democratic vision as it has been incorporated into dominant discourses of educational reform. But there are signs that this is beginning to change. One reason for the change is that progressivism has begun to resurface as a marker of democratic left cultural politics in the United States; and cultural progressives have begun to bring their politics with them as teachers and public intellectuals working in schools, colleges, and other sites in the public. Progressivism in this form challenges the current reform discourse in both secondary and higher education to redirect the conversation back toward fundamental issues of democratic public life and the role of education in forging a new democratic culture. Of course, the very idea of progress, upon which progressivism has been so dependent, is increasingly suspect and can no longer have an assured meaning. Progress, after all, almost destroyed us in the twentieth century, and we have a legitimate right to ask what it can mean in any useful, democratic sense in the century ahead. In education, progress has been closely linked to mythologies that centralized power in the hands of economic and bureaucratic elites. Yet, rather than abandon the idea of progress, and with it progressivism, I am convinced that the real battles in the years ahead will be over progress, and that democratic-minded educators, intellectuals, and citizens cannot afford to let those the right define progress for us.

Several years ago I had the opportunity to participate in an extraordinary dialogue between a group of university professors, school officials, and leaders of a corporate-school "partnership" initiative. This took place over two days at the upstate New York retreat of the global corporation that was sponsoring this partnership. As a university professor in educational leadership, with a background in cultural studies and curriculum, I had been working with a public high school in Cincinnati that served a largely poor, black student population, and with a group of progressive-minded teachers in the school who were interested in an education that empowers urban, marginalized youth. I was thus invited to the retreat to share what I had learned and, as the advance publicity advised us, I came prepared to talk about how we can work to make urban schools not only good, but "excellent." Now, I had a suspicion that "excellence" for the corporate team that organized the retreat meant something quite different than what it meant to me. To me it meant setting high expectations for all, eliminating "tracking"; it meant helping those who have been disenfranchised and silenced find a voice; and it meant understanding the school, or the college campus, as a certain type of embryonic democratic community—a community of diversity and difference but also of dialogue across difference, a community that confronts persistent classism, racism, sexism, and homophobia. Indeed, I was frustrated during the retreat, as were others, by our failure to agree on the meaning of excellence. This proved particularly frustrating for some of the young executives who had volunteered to help oversee the urban school initiative and who participated in the discussions. It was their hope to steer us toward consensus on what the problem is, how to fix it, and how to assess success or failure. These are good questions, in their own way. But their meaning, and how we respond to them, very much depends on the commonsense mythology we use to frame the production of truths about education.

At one point in our discussions and disagreements over what excellence means, one of the young executives trying to take notes and steer the conversation toward the expected outcomes became visibly anxious and irritated. He suddenly interrupted the conversation to declare: "Look, you're making too much out of this." He went on to suggest that everybody knows what excellence is, and that public educators should "take a lesson" from the corporate world. "It's as simple as this. You have a product you want to produce, and you are interested in finding the most efficient way of doing that, at the lowest cost, and with the highest return on investment. And you want the product that comes off the assembly line to be up to a certain standard." It was that simple. This indeed is the mythological bottom line in corporate discourse in education, and it narrates education as a journey down an assembly-line. Along the way people are assembled and fine-tuned for various sectors of the new labor force. Excellent schools and colleges are those that excel at doing this. They take the student on a predictable, safe journey, and they encourage people to set back and let others do the driving. The myth of what Roland Barthes has called the "quantification of quality" rules supreme and almost unquestioned in this discourse.[21]

There are, to be sure, other, mythologies of becoming educated in contemporary America. Cultural conservatives are mounting a last ditch stand to preserve Eurocentric mythology in America at a time when America is becoming more diverse and multicultural, when European Americans will soon no longer be a numerical majority. They offer nostalgic myths of a Golden Age in classical Greek or European culture, of firm "foundations" and "timeless truths and values," myths that exoticize and marginalize difference and play into white, middle class resentment and fear of the Other. For cultural conservatives, the educational journey's destination is "cultural literacy" (E. D. Hirsch, 1986) defined in a tradition-bound manner. On the religious right, meanwhile, other myths of becoming educated are advanced, ones that narrate education as a journey of submission to a highly repressive, good-versus-evil moral code, and to a mythology of family that is oppressive to women, gay people, and children. As Karen Armstrong observes, fundamentalism is organized around a powerful myth, that god's "Kingdom" is about to be restored in a society and on an earth that has been corrupted by Satan. When the Kingdom comes, there will be no more separation of church and state, the "modern heresy of democracy will be abolished, and society reorganized on strictly biblical lines."[22] As cultural conservatives and religious fundamentalists seek common mythological ground, and as we move into a cultural terrain in which all truths and values are questioned, this mythology of nostalgia for a lost age of innocence, moral absolutes, and the authority of the patriarchal father finds fertile ground in American culture.

What do progressives have to offer in response to these other mythologies of individual and cultural development? That is the primary question I want to raise and address in this book. In doing so, I want to map out the general territory of an alternative to corporate, cultural conservative, and fundamentalist mythologies that offers at least the hope that the forces of democratization will prevail in the unsettling times ahead, and that the meaning of a democratic education and public life will be both sustained and re-imagined in powerful new ways. At the same time, I do not mean to speak of the new progressivism as a unified, coherent social movement and mythology. At best, progressivism in an age of diverse cultural struggles and identities is a word that can be used to describe overlapping social movements and mythologies, none of which is determinant or primary. Indeed, one of the central tenets of the new progressivism is that unifying mythologies are inherently oppressive and undemocratic, and that democratic change in postmodern times must avoid a "united front" politics. At the same time, progressives recognize a strategic need for partial and contingent united fronts, and it is in this spirit that I use the term "new progressivism."

CHAPTER 2

Lighting Up the Cave

Progressivism and the Ghost of Plato

The progressive philosopher of education Maxine Greene writes that she still remembers that time when as a graduate student she first came across the cave analogy, "that moment in Plato's *Republic* when a prisoner released from the cave moves haltingly up the incline into the light of the sun."[1] From then on, she writes, she thought of herself as Plato's prisoner, freed at last of the commonsense beliefs she had grown up with, "standing in the blinding light of disembodied reason." As a Jewish American young woman, Greene saw in the cave analogy "an incarnation of values that promised to transcend gender and class and race." She came to believe that through an autonomous reason and a dogged commitment to the truth, people could overcome their differences, rise above prejudices, and become enlightened. The Enlightenment promise of the age of reason was also the democratic promise, the promise of a society in which reason ruled rather than privilege, tradition, and superstition. Thus she looked to the university and her graduate seminars as spaces where people's backgrounds and genders mattered less than their commitment to the truth, places where people were able to rise above the commonsense beliefs that still kept others in chains. Greene writes that "knowing better," she continued to believe in Plato's cave analogy long after she should have. "Knowing better, I even liked the idea of the objectively universal, the overwhelmingly True."[2]

The key phrase here is, "knowing better." Greene was seduced by the power of Plato's story, and of what it seemed to promise in the way of liberating her and others from the norms of conventional society. The narrative of education as Enlightenment seemed to offer an alternative, one that could help her demystify the dominant culture and critique its treatment of women and other marginalized and oppressed identity groups. It took her some time, but she began to realize that in the university of the "the Great White Father" a woman's voice was not equal to a man's. It took her "many shocks of awareness" before she began to realize that the cave analogy existed within a discourse that served certain historical uses, to give voice to some even as it silenced and devalued the voices of others.[3]

One of the reasons why progressives have been kept under the spell of Plato's cave analogy is that they have read it out of context. In the modern era, stories and ideas were often taken out of context, as if they could be neatly uprooted, disconnected from their histories, and turned into universal signifiers. But can we really do this? Is it ever possible to really get away from this context of usage, this genealogy? To some degree we can and should. But in attempting to use the cave analogy to serve democratic and progressive ends, it is important to bear in mind its history or genealogy, so that we do not use it unproblematically, so that we are aware of some of its possible consequences. When the cave analogy is re-contextualized—located back within a text, which is in turn embedded in a history and in cultural politics—it begins to seem less innocent, less liberatory, less democratic. Its "true colors" begin to emerge. The textual context for the cave analogy is, after all, Plato's *Republic*, which is a political text as much or more than an abstract philosophical text, and its project is to oppose democratic tendencies in Greek culture, to affirm the hegemony of some groups in society over others. Consequently, while I want to move toward a re-reading and re-scripting of Plato's cave analogy consistent with a new progressivism in American education and cultural politics, I do so with an awareness of the difficulties of this task. Plato is, after all, the darling of cultural conservatives of various stripes much more than progressives, and to recuperate a progressive use of the cave analogy, I want first of all to explore in some detail its undemocratic cultural politics in Plato's day. This involves locating the cave analogy within the context of Plato's great dialogue on education in a utopian good society, *The Republic*, and locating that dialogue within the cultural politics of "classical" Greek society. It also involves showing how the cave analogy, as a basic Western narrative of knowing, continues to influence the way we think about teaching and the organization of the educational process in ways that need to be challenged by a new progressivism. Then I want to conclude by returning to the question of a possible re-scripting of this narrative of knowing consistent with a new progressivism.

THE CAVE ANALOGY

In the fifth and fourth centuries B.C.E., two great warring camps were locked in an entrenched battle in Athenian culture, which provides the context for Plato's proposed solution to this conflict in the form of a utopian republic. On one side of Greek cultural politics were the forces that supported what Plato calls oligarchy—rule by a small aristocratic elite exercising power over a subjugated population. Plato argues that one of the troubles with oligarchy is that it degenerates into tyranny, which breeds discontent among the masses, which leads to a resurgence of democratic forces. But democracy, according to Plato, is inherently unstable as well, since it soon becomes associated with mob rule and chaos. Politicians appeal to the desires and self-interest of the mob, telling them what they want to hear, using a form of *sophistry*—a speech designed to distort and mislead—that says one thing and means another, that appeals to emotions rather than reason. Then there is the problem that in a democracy every individual and every group is narrowly interested in themselves. No one effectively represents the "common good" and the "public interest." A "flux" theory of knowledge prevails that presumes there are as many truths as there are people and that truth is always changing and shifting. Since it does not provide a basis for social cohesion or common truths, democracy tends to degenerate, according to Plato, into chaos, which leads to the return of oligarchy, which degenerates into tyranny. Plato proposes, consequently, a way out of this vicious cycle in Greek cultural politics. Unfortunately, his proposed "solution" does away with democracy almost entirely, even if it retains some of the language of democracy.

Plato has Socrates introduce the cave analogy by way of explaining the proper education of leaders in his utopian society. Before turning to that text, perhaps a few words are in order on the distinction, or lack of distinction, between Socrates and Plato. Plato's dialogues are, at times, an attempt to recover a number of different conversations that Plato's great teacher, Socrates, actually participated in. Plato's motives are, some would say, to deify Socrates, to resurrect his ghost to speak again, in a new age. He thus presents Socrates in a particular light, and makes him into an heroic character, or more than a hero, a god who speaks a pure truth and reason. This is not the "real" Socrates, although it is no doubt true to the real, historical Socrates in some ways. Most scholars of Plato agree that in the early dialogues we get a different, perhaps "truer" Socrates than in the later dialogues, of which the *Republic* is an example.[4] In the early dialogues, Socrates is a gadfly, he questions everything, and he calls on people to find truth within rather than submit to a the conventional wisdom of the day. He is the seeker of knowledge who renounces material wealth and lives in poverty, who stirs up trouble among the youth of Athens by encouraging them to question authority, who ultimately chooses death rather than deny himself. This is the Socrates that Nietzsche found so compelling, so useful as a symbol of the role of the engaged teacher and public intellectual. In the *Republic*, however, we have a Socrates who has become the mouthpiece for Plato, and a Plato who increasingly is the champion of law and order, of social discipline, of education and social authority, of conformity rather than rebelliousness.

Socrates begins the cave analogy by asking his companions to "imagine an underground chamber, like a cave, with an entrance open to the daylight and running a long way underground." In the cave are humans who have been prisoners there since birth, chained to the walls so that they can only look straight ahead. There they see shadows of passing figures, thrown by a fire onto a screen—a light show or magic lantern show of shadows without substance, shadows that distort the reality that they appear to represent. Socrates then asks whether the cave dwellers would "assume that the shadows they saw were real things?"[5] Having been exposed to nothing but shadow images, would they not think that these images were real? This commonsense, taken-for-granted knowledge that is characteristic of the everyday life of the "common folk" Plato identifies as *mythos*. While Plato means *mythos* to refer to what we now call myth, that is folklore and stories that have deep cultural roots, he also means—on the very broadest level—to use *mythos* to refer to all culturally and historically specific knowledge. Within culture and history, Plato suggests, people are like prisoners of a cave, who see the world through a glass darkly. The "real" truth is to be found outside of culture and history. In a somewhat more limited sense, Plato uses *mythos* to refer to knowledge that is based on taken-for-granted beliefs that are not deliberately questioned and put to the test of reason. *Mythos* is thus all commonsense knowledge not supported by science, mathematics, or philosophy. While these latter ways of knowing presumably rise above culture, history, and personal desire to reveal the world in a true light, *mythos* sinks back into the cave of darkness, where impulses, fears, desires, and mysticism reign. This means that for Plato *mythos* is more than a false consciousness or false knowledge. It is also and at the same time a way of speaking or thinking that is not guided by a "pure" form of reasoning. It is a "subjective" or personal voice as opposed to an "objective" and detached voice; it is the poetic, artistic, and dramatic as opposed to the analytic; it is the body as opposed to the mind. It is that which is most feared by Plato, that which subverts authority and promotes chaos rather than order. All education, Plato says, begins here, in the knowledge and way of knowing that belongs to *mythos*, the knowledge and way of knowing of the prisoners of the cave who mistake passing shadows for the things themselves.

What might happen, Socrates asks, if one of the prisoners were cut loose from his chains, "and suddenly compelled to stand up and turn his head and look and walk towards the fire?" The former prisoner would no doubt be pained and dazzled by the light of the fire at first, and the objects revealed by the light would seem strange. The former prisoner might even come to believe that "what he used to see was more real than the objects now being pointed out to him," and consequently "turn back and take refuge" in the shadows. Then, if this former prisoner were "forcibly dragged up the steep and rocky ascent" until he was finally out of the cave, he would no doubt at first be blinded by the brightness of the world revealed under the clarifying light of the sun.[6] Slowly, as the former prisoner of the cave got used to the bright light, Socrates says, he would first be able to see the shadows of things, then the things themselves, then to even dare to look into the sun itself.

Step by step, the former prisoner ascends, from the study of myth and folklore that instills "positive" values and obedience to authority, to a more scientific understanding of the world based on cause-and-effect reasoning, to a mathematical reasoning that reveals the world as governed by numerical relationships, to a philosophical reasoning the reveals the true and the good. This is the basic developmental pathway that Western education has taken ever since, at least in dominant forms, and although scientific reasoning sought, in the modern era, to dethrone philosophical reasoning as the highest rung in this hierarchy.

But Plato is no ivory-towerist, even if some of his followers have been. The end of the former prisoner's long ascent is to signal the beginning of his life as a leader serving the public good. At the same time, he recognizes that ivory-towerism and elitism have their appeal to the Enlightened few. Socrates remarks that the former prisoner will no doubt desire to remain in the "upper world," that he would rather be, as Homer says, "'a serf in the house of some landless man,' or indeed anything else in the world, than live and think as they [the masses] do."[7] Such tendencies toward living in the air, in an upper realm of lofty ideals and abstractions, is to be countered, according to Socrates, by instilling in future leaders all the way through their education that they are to think only of the public good and not their own. "Society will never be properly governed," Socrates says, "either by the uneducated, who have no knowledge of the truth, or by those who are allowed to spend all their lives in purely intellectual pursuits." The former prisoner of the cave, having become enlightened, must return to the cave from whence he came to lead those who are still captives of commonsense myths and illusions, those who lack the intelligence and character they need to ascend out of the cave. The former prisoner must learn to combine his intellectual insights with "practical action." Even though he is clearly superior to those he leads, he must humble himself before the public and become the servant of the public good.[8]

The images of this simple narrative are powerful, and its influence over subsequent Western culture can hardly be overestimated. To explore this very basic narrative of knowing in more detail, and reveal the way it works to serve conservative and authoritarian cultural politics, I want to focus upon four interrelated sub-narratives that Plato uses to tell his story of a long ascent from the cave. These sub-narratives have to do with the father of *logos*; the great chain of being; the proper education of cave-dwellers; and the gatekeeper and the final judgment.

THE FATHER OF *LOGOS*

There are two primary symbols in Plato's cave analogy—the cave and the sun. In one sense, these symbols take on an almost archetypal meaning, to use Jung's language. They exist as part of the "collective unconscious" of a number of different cultural traditions and play a formative role in cultural development. However, Plato also uses these two symbols in ways that had more particular meaning within Hellenic Greek culture. The cave is the earth and womb, the beginning point of the journey out. But the cave would also be understood, in Plato's time, to refer to the cave of the earth goddess, Gaia. The "facts" of the Gaia myth—based on what little is known about the oral tradition of pre-Hellenic Greek mythology—go something like this. From the earliest remembered times, Gaia was the Greek word for god. According to Charlene Spretnak, "She was all forces, active and passive, creative and destructive, fierce and gentle."[9] She was also represented as the Earth, and rituals were conducted in her name at the time of the planting and harvesting of crops and at each of the seasonal equinoxes—a common practice among earth goddess cultures. An oracle to Gaia existed in a cave in the hills around Delphi (from *delphys*, the womb)—the first oracle in these sacred Greek hills. In the cave, a priestess of Gaia was always on duty, perched on a chair above an opening in the earth through which steam poured. Pilgrims came from throughout Greece to consult Gaia priestesses, who were believed to have the power to interpret dreams, foresee the future, and help those who were sick and suffering. Gaia priestesses provided advice to the common people regarding when they should plant their crops and harvest them, how they should settle disputes, and what the future held for them. In return for her advice pilgrims left offerings of honey and barley cakes. They assumed a role similar, in this way, to the shamans of American Indian culture and were believed to have great wisdom. Sophia—one of those many goddesses that represented particular aspects of Gaia—represented wisdom.

Sometime in the second millennium B.C.E., a series of invaders from the north swept into Greece—the Ionians, the Achaeans, and the Dorians—which ushered in what is now known as the Hellenic era, beginning about 1000 B.C.E. The newcomers brought along with them their own patriarchal, warrior gods, including all-powerful Zeus, who ruled from the top of Mount Olympus, in the lofty air above the world of Gaia. Spretnak writes that "the pre-Hellenic Goddesses are enmeshed with people's daily experiencing of the forces in life." By contrast, "Olympian Gods are distant, removed, 'up there.'" Whereas the earth goddesses represent "flowing, protective love," the Olympian gods who replace them are judgmental and warlike.[10] The pre-Hellenic myths speak of "harmonious bonds among humans, animals, and nature. They express respect for and celebration of the mysteries of body and spirit," whereas the Hellenic gods set up laws and hierarchies, separate body and spirit.[11]

When earth goddesses were finally incorporated into Hellenic Greek mythology, Spretnak argues, they were transformed into representatives of the feminine instead of a more generalizable life force—as in the pre-Hellenic era. Since the feminine was devalued in the new patriarchal Greek culture, this means that earth goddesses began to take on negative characteristics. Thus,

Hera was turned into a jealous wife, Athena into a frigid, masculinized daughter, Aphrodite into a sexual toy, and Pandora into the source of all human woes. Out of these mythological archetypes evolved "the wicked witch, the cruel stepmother, the passive princess, etc., of our fairy tales."[12] By Plato's day, Gaia was still part of Greek culture, but now as one of a number of mystical cults. Gaia's oracle at Delphi had been vandalized, then completely destroyed and replaced with a temple to Apollo, one of the new gods who symbolized the authority of law, the state, and the military. Those who still sought the advice of a Gaia priestess now had to join a cult and go through elaborate initiation rituals in hidden underground caves—rituals associated in the public mind, if not in fact, with mystical rites, mind out of body experiences, eroticism, and magic. Gaia had gone underground, and soon even these secret rites would be abandoned and forgotten.

By using the cave as a symbol of *mythos*, Plato is already feminizing the cave and its inhabitants, and representing the feminine in terms of mysticism rather than reason, unbridled passions and emotions rather than a disciplined concern for the truth. Educationally, the cave is a site of a pedagogy that mixes story-telling and ritual, that offers ambiguity rather than firm answers to questions, that calls on people to interpret and make sense of signs and dreams. This, then, is the kind of pedagogy from which Plato wants to disassociate himself. Indeed, he sets out to define his own position, like day to night, as the polar opposite of everything that the cave had come to represent in Greek culture. That opposite is symbolized by the sun. The sun is used to symbolize *logos*, the one authoritative truth, the source of all wisdom and knowledge, the one who separates darkness and light. As *logos* is all truth and goodness, the sun is also a symbol of god. We do not have to look very far to understand where Plato borrows this symbol. It is meant to remind the reader of Plato's day of the mythology of the great Egyptian sun god, Ammon-Ra. For we must remember that Greece was heavily influenced by Egyptian civilization, as it could not help but be. Greek culture is, in some ways, an extension of developments which began in Africa, and in ancient Kemete or Egyptian civilization. Ammon-Ra is the first father god who represents all wisdom, who gazes down from on high with a perfect surveillance, who speaks only timeless truths and virtues. This mythology of the divine was designed to organize authority and power in such a way that it flowed downward in a perfect order from the top of society to the bottom. Ammon-Ra supposedly spoke through the pharaoh, and from the pharaoh through an elaborate rank ordering of judges, priests, and lawgivers. Throughout the subsequent history of Western culture, much educational and political authority has been an authority invested by Ammon-Ra.

In the cave analogy, Ammon-Ra is never named as such. However, in another of Plato's dialogues, *Phaedrus*, Socrates makes a more direct and overt use of the Egyptian mythology of Ammon-Ra, and his son Theuth. Here again,

Ammon-Ra is made to represent a pure *logos*. In the last section of *Phaedrus*, the subject is writing, and whether or not the widespread circulation and reading of written texts is a good thing or not. Now, at first glance, this seems a curious topic to be discussing, although first glances can be deceiving. We live in a culture in which everyone reads, or is supposed to read, and in which reading is highly valued—or appears to be. But as we shall see, the issues raised by Socrates and his companion and friend, Phaedrus, in their discussion of writing and reading remain central today and help distinguish democratic from elitist or authoritarian forms of education. Socrates opposes the widespread public distribution of texts, maintaining that it is only in face to face dialogue between a pupil and a teacher that real learning can occur. In such a context, the teacher can ensure that the pupil arrives at the proper conclusion and that the conversation leads toward agreement on the "correct" truth.

It is at this point that Socrates turns to the myth of Ammon-Ra and his son Theuth. As Socrates recounts it, the myth involves a visit by Theuth (whom the Greeks re-named Hermes) to Ammon-Ra, during which time he offers his father the many uses of language as gifts for the peoples of the earth. Among other gifts, he offers writing, with the suggestion that it will serve as an aid in memory and promote wisdom among the people. But Ammon-Ra suspects that his son is once more conspiring with humans to assume his powers, and that perhaps this gift of reading and writing is a dangerous one, a kind of poison. In his deconstructive reading of Plato's use of this myth in *Phaedrus*, Derrida writes that Theuth/Hermes is made to represent the feared Other within Plato's ordered and authoritarian society, the one who is "sly, slippery, and masked . . . a sort of joker, a floating signifier, a wild card, one who puts play into play."[13] For Derrida, Theuth/Hermes is the first, or one of the first, heroes who represents human resistance to the gods' keeping all knowledge to themselves, and to the idea of a unified, authoritative truth or *logos*. Theuth/Hermes is the god of discourse, of the conversation between humans and the divine, the god with many voices, in which truth is always emerging out of the interpretive process, out of the dialogue or discourse that is language in use. The forces of democratization in the West have been linked to the rebellion of the hermetic child against Ammon-Ra. And democratic forms of education, organized around dialogue and interpretation, in the context of a broad public conversation in which truth is multifaceted and always emergent, are *hermeneutic*, in the best sense of this term. They bring people into conversation and dialogue, they play with meaning and use language in ironic ways that make people more aware of the fact that there are no firm foundations of meaning for words other than the conversation.

Ammon-Ra, in his patriarchal wisdom, rejects the democratic gift of writing for his people. As for the claim that writing will serve as an aid to memory, he fears that when people need knowledge they will simply go to a book and look it up rather than hold the truth in their memory. As for making people wiser, if people can read "they will receive a quantity of information without proper instruction."[14] As a consequence, they will think they are smart but will really be ignorant; and nothing is worse than people who have the "conceit of wisdom instead of real wisdom." Socrates is inclined to agree with Ammon-Ra that widespread reading and writing is dangerous. He says, for instance, that once something is written it "circulates equally among those who understand the subject and those who have no business with it."[15] True knowledge is not to be found by looking it up in books. It is to be found only within the context of a face-to-face dialogue that leads, step by logical step, under the watchful eye of the instructor, to the correct truth. Socrates stops short of arguing that all writing is bad. Ammon-Ra is right, he says, in referring to writing as a *pharmakon* (drug) that can lead people out of their right minds. But a *pharmakon* can also cure people. It all depends on how the drug is prescribed and administered. As long as a trained pharmacist oversees the use of drugs, they can be helpful. So it is with writing, Socrates argues. The production and the reading of texts must be closely supervised by state-certified educators.

According to Derrida, Plato/Socrates uses Ammon-Ra to represent not only a unified, autonomous, fixed *logos*, but also that paternal subject of all knowledge, the "father of *logos*." As a result, all male authority figures in society are implicitly invested with the authority of the father god, Ammon-Ra, from the husband, to the father, to the teacher, to the statesman. From this time forward, Derrida writes, "the figure of the father ... is also that of the good" (p. 81). In the cultural battles that were waged in Greek culture between the forces of democratization and pluralism on the one hand, and the forces of authoritarianism and unification on the other, Ammon-Ra provided the latter with a powerful tradition and symbol of a type of authority that was not corruptible, not tainted by personal ambition or other human shortcomings, that could rule in the name of the public good. Plato's philosophy was secular, but it was consistent with a religious movement in Western culture that led back to the idea of a unified father god in the heavens as the basis for social and pedagogical authority, an idea that was appropriated from the rich soil of Egypt. In the state and the church, the mythology of a unified, authoritative truth would be used to consolidate power and build a new social order, with secular and religious leaders ruling together as representatives of the "father of *logos*." It is within this context that one must understand the rise of Christianity not only as a subversive, even radical movement, but also, in a more dominant or hegemonic form, as an institution that came to represent the one, unified *logos* that rules over people.

The Nicaean Council is particularly important in symbolizing this shift to a logocentric Christianity that would rule, with the emperor, over god's earthly "flock." In some important ways, the Nicaean Council set education on a new course, and gave it a new purpose, by legitimating two new metaphors or myths. The first of these is what is now commensensically referred to as the "gospel truth," a text that is supposedly the word of god himself and inscribed with his authority. The New Testament was created in 326 A.D. by the Nicaean Council as a compilation of texts. These texts were authorized as god's word, even as others (like the Gospel of Thomas) were defined as heretical and unauthorized. In the authorization of certain texts as the "gospel truth," the authority of the modern textbook traces its roots. In controlling what counts for knowledge, and what is included and what excluded from the "canon," the Nicaean Council invests texts with a power they never had before, a power to control and define. The Nicaean Council also provides a model for a new form of pastoral pedagogy, in the declaration that the son is "of the same substance" as the father, and that both continue from on high through earthly representatives, from the Pope to the parish priest. This priestly class, furthermore, is assigned the role of the interpreter of god's word, as holding the keys to unlocking the truths in sacred texts. So the professional educator is understood to hold the keys to unlocking the "correct" meaning of textbooks—the Bibles of public schooling. Educators who follow in the footsteps of the Nicaean council always speak with the authority of the "father of *logos*," are always standing-in for a patriarchal father god who is the source of all truth and morality. Of course, one might say that Plato never did believe that truth could be passed down this way, or that any text was sacred. He did, after all, believe in the dialectic of opposition, within which people only arrive at closer approximations of "the" truth through dialogue and debate. At the same time, Plato never supported such a dialectic form of education for the masses. He was interested in creating a system of public education that would "school" everyone to be docile workers and good (meaning docile and submissive) citizens. And to this end he believed in the importance of teaching people that wisdom resides at the top, that their leaders can be trusted to run their lives for them. Consequently, it is fair to associate Platonism, if not Plato himself, with the type of religiosity that emerges out of the Nicaean Council, a religiosity that in turn is closely linked to an authoritarian, over-unifying cultural politics, and to forms of curriculum and pedagogy that authorize both teacher and textbook and de-authorize the student.

This Nicaean Council form of pedagogy certainly is to be found among progressives, and it is particularly associated with modernist forms of "politically correct" teaching. Now, let me say at the outset that I think progressives have been far less doctrinaire than their conservative counterparts in academia. Nevertheless, sometimes progressives have sought to make progress by silencing opposition, by imposing restrictions on speech, and in other ways insisting that students reach consensus on a politically correct truth about society. Such insistence on a "politically correct" interpretation of texts, and on the authority of instructors to decide what the "correct" interpretation is, along with an unwillingness to listen to alternative truths, even those that seem reactionary or anti-progressive, are signs of *logocentrism*. The effect is to play into the hands of conservatives, who brand progressives as the "femi-nazis." In Dinesh D'Souza's stinging attack upon multiculturalism in higher education, *Illiberal Education*, the author argues that progressives have imposed a "de facto taboo against free discussion" on college campuses. Measures that have been taken in the name of diversity have only created a "new regime of intellectual conformity."[16] As a result, it has become "politically incorrect" to oppose affirmative action, multiculturalism, homosexuality, and so on. Progressive faculty, then, are being accused of denying freedom of speech to conservative students who do not adhere to the new multicultural "truths" and the new revisionist histories of the United States.

In responding to this conservative criticism of the new "political correctness" on college campuses, it is best to begin by acknowledging the grain of truth in it. Vestiges of "political correctness" exist on the democratic left today; and these deserve criticism. For they have the effect of "turning off" students, of encouraging them to resist the "politically correct" truths they are expected to accept. But the conservative criticism of "politically correct" teaching is more than a bit disingenuous. Conservative professors still outnumber progressive professors on most campuses, and especially in liberal arts institutions; and conservative professors have, more than progressives, engaged in "indoctrinating" students into accepting a "correct" truth about the world. They, after all, are the ones who view themselves as guardians of timeless truths and values. Most progressives at this point have moved away from the idea that there is one "correct," unified truth.

Still, progressives need to become more self-consciously aware of how, often inadvertently, they assume the role of the father of *logos* when they write and speak. Let me close this section by turning to popular culture, to a film that retells Plato's cave analogy in a way that raises questions about logocentric pedagogy. That film is Bernardo Bertolucci's *The Conformist* (1970). Adapted from Alberto Moravia's novel of the same name, *The Conformist* is often regarded as the most important work by one of the most important progressive directors of the last fifty years. The hero, or anti-hero, of *The Conformist* is a young fascist named Clerici, an agent of the Italian secret police in Mussolini's Italy. Clerici becomes the model of a "normal" Italian husband and citizen. He is submissive, does what he is told, dresses and acts according to the norms, and seeks security in assuming the role of the conformist. In order to test his loyalty, Clerici is sent on a mission to Paris, where he is to first befriend and then assassinate his former college professor and father-figure, someone who once had been his mentor, his role model, his hope. The professor is now an expatriate living in Paris, and the leader of a resistance movement of intellectuals in exile. On one level, Clerici is the prisoner of Plato's cave, and his former professor the representative of an Enlightenment commitment to truth and reason—to the world outside the darkness of the cave. Yet this rather conventional use of Plato's cave analogy, to set up an opposition between illusion and truth, is soon troubled in the film. Things, it seems, are not that simple. The film, after all, needs to be read as it was intended to be read when it was released at the height of the anti-Vietnam War movement. Clerici as the conformist is only a variation on a theme in modern Western democratic societies, a type who allowed the Vietnam War to happen, who continued to believe the manufactured lies of the "military-industrial complex," who tried to dress and act like everybody else, to "fit in" to the norms of the "Father Knows Best" world of the 1950s and early 1960s. We need to ask, then, what kind of upbringing, what kind of education, produces the conformist?

Clerici, the "good" fascist, is a product of the educational system in which the professor taught, and the film suggests that the professor played a part in creating his own assassin, in educating a generation of young people who would turn on their liberal democratic teachers and professors. They would not turn upon their teachers in a radical and subversive sense, but rather in the name of a new authority, a new "father of *logos*," one who would not betray their need for firm foundations, for truths they could build their lives around. The two men are reunited in the professor's Paris salon, where the professor has been talking with various members of the resistance movement. When the two are finally alone, Clerici walks over to one of the two windows on opposite sides of the room and closes the shutters. "Remember, Professor," he says. "As soon as you used to enter the classroom you had to shut the windows. You couldn't stand all that light and noise." Clerici is a fascist, but a contradictory one, full of self-doubt and questioning, and he speaks in this case for Bertolucci in critiquing intellectuals on the democratic left. The professor had begun his own lectures by shuttering out the "outside" world, positioning himself as the source of all light, all wisdom. The shuttering of the windows in his lecture hall served to reinforce the power of his voice and his truths, and to silence and make invisible all other voices and truths. While he claims to be a symbol of the Enlightenment, of the glaring light of truth and reason, the vanquisher of shadows, the professor has been the one who shutters the lecture hall to keep out the light, or rather let it fall only on him—as it now does in his office. He had become one of those who orchestrate the magic lantern show in the darkness of Plato's cave.

Clerici leads the conversation back to a particular day, November 28, when the professor lectured on Plato's cave analogy. Clerici apparently has memorized many if not most of the professor's lectures, implying that he had been under the spell of the professor at one time, that he had looked to the professor for the truths upon which he could ground his life and identity. This suggests that the power that the professor had over him is rooted in something more than his philosophy, that he saw in the professor a father figure of sorts. "All these years," Clerici remarks, "you know what remained most firmly imprinted in my memory? Your voice." And so Clerici, assuming the role and voice of the professor, begins his lecture on the cave analogy, observing of the prisoners of the cave, "how they resemble us." Clerici shows here a certain level of self-awareness that troubles any simplistic treatment of him as a good fascist. He acknowledges his own submission to the dominant myths of fascistic Italy, but he does not let the professor off the hook. Clerici speaks of "us," implying that both professor and former student are prisoners of their own caves, both living according to their own illusions, both living convenient lies, both escaping from their own realities.

The "myth of the great cave" was to be Clerici's graduate thesis, and so the professor asks him if he ever got around to finishing it. "You departed," Clerici remarks, "and I used a different theme." What good, after all, was an Enlightenment language that talked of lofty ideals, of rising toward the light and the truth, of the ascent of the human spirit from bondage, when those who used this language only meant it in the abstract and never fought for it in any concrete situation—except from a safe distance on the "outside"? The professor had gone into exile, and Clerici was lost, without an Ammon-Ra to guide him. He had filled that void by turning to other authority figures with different truths, ones that they were not afraid to act upon. The professor remarks that he is truly sorry for Clerici, that he had expected so much from him. In anger, Clerici snaps back, "If that were true, you'd never have left Rome." Why had the professor left Rome? He and others left, he says, so that everyone would be able to feel "our disdain and our rebellion as exiles, the meaning of our struggle, the historical meaning." To Clerici these are all beautiful words, but they do not change the fact that "you left and I became a fascist." The ideals the professor espoused were, for the most part, lofty, abstract, and thus meaningless. His own life in Paris was comfortable and removed from the reality of what was going on in Italy. Clerici's assassination of his former professor is a symbolic patricide, a killing of Ammon-Ra, although it is a killing that does not set Clerici free of the need for Ammon-Ra, at least not yet. Only at the end of the film, with the fall of Mussolini, does Clerici begin to explore his own freedom. The professor in Bertolucci's film embodies one of the central contradictions of Enlightenment forms of education and pedagogy. He sets himself up as the opposite of a fascistic teacher, yet he is a dominating figure, one who wants others to submit to his authority and his truths, who insists on standing in the light and representing "the" truth. He lives by his own illusions, yet he sets himself up as the demystifier of myth and the guardian of truth and reason. This contradiction, Bertolucci suggests, has had profound implications in the West. It may be associated with what Eric Fromm called the "authoritarian-submissive personality" (on the one hand), and the rise of an incipient youth culture of rebellion against the father's *logos* (on the other).

THE "GREAT CHAIN OF BEING" AND DEVELOPMENTALISM IN EDUCATION

The ascent out of the cave is, on one level, a myth about an individual ascent toward Enlightenment. But individuals are rarely treated as individuals *qua* individuals, even in Plato's philosophy. So the myth of an ascent from the cave has been and continues to be applied in ways that explicitly or implicitly represent some groups as more "advanced," or "rational," or "civilized" than others. While some groups are understood to be already crawling out of the cave, other groups are understood to be just beginning their ascent or, even worse, unable to make the ascent because they lack the intellectual and moral strength, because they are still ruled by desire and impulse, by "id" rather than "ego." In Plato's day, this mythology of group inequality was closely associated with the folk mythology of a "great chain of being," and in some ways it still is. According to this myth, all life or being is arranged in a hierarchy that leads from god in the cosmos (*logos*) to the lowliest creatures on earth. Each link in the chain is understood to be more intelligent than those below and also closer to the true and the good, so it has a responsibility within the "natural order" of things to look after those links below it. Plato is often given credit for inventing the myth of a great chain of being, although it is more accurate to say that he brought it into philosophy and thereby legitimated it as "rational." As Page DuBois observes, in Classical Greek culture, "The human Greek male is defined in relation to a series of creatures defined as different. He is at first simply not-animal, not-barbarian, not-female."[17] Together, the animal, the barbarian, and the female are understood to be lower in the developmental hierarchy. Socrates is reported to have said he thanked Fortune for three things: "First, that I was born a human being and not one of the brutes; next, that I was born a man and not a woman; thirdly, a Greek and not a barbarian (*barbario*)."[18] Even Greek males were not equal. Plato presumes that the "common folk" are (for the most part) inferior in intellect and virtue to the middle and upper classes. These "lower humans" in the great chain of being are, according to DuBois, represented through reference to the myths of the Centaur and the Minotaur, half human-half animal creatures who presumably are just emerging from the animal world. For these creatures, words like "human rights" or "the rights of democratic citizens" hardly seem relevant.

The rigid class, race, and gender structure of Plato's ideal republic gets legitimated as part of a natural and god-given hierarchy of inequality, so while advancement is to be based on merit, the expectation is that not many from the lower classes, not many women, and not many "barbarians" will be advanced. And slaves—who represented a full third of the population of

Athens in Plato's day—had no opportunity to advance at all. They were kept, for their "own good" as well as their masters', uneducated. Women too were never allowed to participate in public life as voting citizens, and Plato does not believe that—as a group—women are suitable by intelligence or moral character to be good leaders or advance very far in his meritocratic schools. Ironically, some have looked to Plato as an early equal rights advocate, since he argued that girls should be given every opportunity that boys are. He just did not expect many would be able to take advantage of the opportunity. At the same time, Plato saves this myth of a great chain of being by making one's placement in the chain seem "open" rather than predetermined. He saves the myth by revising it so that it now seems part of a natural order of things, the end product of natural differences between people. He takes it out of the realm of myth and transports it to the realm of an unquestioned truth, and in this way he vastly extends its power.

Modernism has been based on a re-scripting of the myth of a great chain of being consistent with the "science" of Social Darwinism. We might say that Darwin provided modern culture with a convenient natural science theory that legitimated the notion that some peoples were more evolutionarily advanced than others. If non-Europeans, and particularly those non-Europeans living on the "dark continent," were not to be granted full human rights, it was because they were not yet fully human, still living in darkness. The "enlightened" nations of Europe presumably had a right and a responsibility to colonize the world, to rule over "backwards" peoples. If, however, Social Darwinism is but a new and revised form of a myth that is very deeply ingrained in Western mythology, it only indicates just how much social science is in the business of turning myth into scientific theory.

Examples of the Eurocentric and patriarchal great chain of being myth are to be found everywhere in popular culture, and in education. Let me begin to explore the great chain of being myth in education by turning to art education, and to the "canon" of great European art. Among the most important artworks in this canon, and central to its aim, are the paintings from the walls of the Lascaux Cave in France, left by Paleolithic cave artists some 15,000 years ago. The cave art of bison and deer and human-like figures was discovered when two boys stumbled upon the cave in 1940, and it has since become part of the "canon" of great art that young people are exposed to in art appreciation courses in high school and college—as a representative of "primitive art," and the "origins of art." As for the cave itself, it has become a major tourist attraction, drawing visitors from throughout the world—although primarily Europeans, as one might suspect. For this cave art is very much part of a mythology of European origins. In 1963 the cave had to be closed to the public because the paintings were fading due to exposure. But the caves at Lascaux have continued to attract tourists. What the visitor now sees is a facsimile of a real cave, a carefully replicated copy next to the real one. Led by a guide, tourists descend down through a maze of papier-mâché and cement rocks, through one dimly-lit grotto and chamber after another. The facsimile cave drawings are revealed in a flickering and eerie light. Archeological evidence confirms that the cave had been a "sanctuary" of sorts for the performance of sacred rituals and ceremonies. According to one scholar, the caves were not dwellings for humans but places that could have served only as specially chosen "repositories for the secrets of a civilization," places of sacred rituals and mystical experiences.[19] For the modern tourist, however, the ritual is one that has been carefully staged and managed—a Disney World-type excursion into the primitive past and back again, with nothing to fear.

It did not take long for the Lascaux cave art to become integrated with a basically Eurocentric mythology of origins. The process was well underway by 1955, when a complete color photographic record of the art was finally published, under the title *Lascaux: Or the Birth of Art,* with the text authored by the French philosopher Georges Bataille. In his texts, Bataille overtly framed his analysis of the art in mythic terms. While he does not "name" the cave analogy as the grounding of his interpretation, it is the taken-for-granted subtext in his text. All artists, according to Bataille, are representatives of these early artists of the Lascaux Cave, who are assigned the role in modern culture of returning to the cave of primal experience and creativity, to infuse modern, rational, civilized society with an animal vitality it still needs. Ironically, "modern" art is precisely that art that recognizes and accepts this role of representing the "primitive" rather than representing reality as accurately as possible—like a photograph. Bataille sees in the primitive art at Lascaux a quality common to modern artists—transgression, breaking through social norms of conformity, freely expressing desires and feelings, and acting on impulse and inspiration. Transgression is, to Bataille, pure animal abandonment—unorganized, unplanned, spontaneous. "It is the state of transgression that prompts the desire, the need for a more profound, a richer, a marvelous world, the need, in a word, for a sacred world."[20] In the modern mythology, the artist plays an important role in moving transgression away from violent and nihilistic forms towards something positive and inspiring. This is indeed an important role artists have assumed in modern culture; but one might question whether it is a good idea to assign this role to a marginalized group of artists, who are expected to break the rules and act impulsively. By assigning this role to artists, the dominant culture can continue to define itself as highly repressive and rational, as the opposite of the artist. The artist becomes the exoticized Other.

A second and related myth in Bataille's text, one which is actually more important in Eurocentric mythology, is the myth of "Civilization" as the end product of a long ascent out of the cave. Without doubt, Bataille writes, "Lascaux points away from the art of backward peoples. It points towards the art of the most restless, most eloquent, most subtle civilizations."[21] In a chapter titled "The Greek Miracle and the Miracle of Lascaux," Bataille questions whether the Greeks really were the first to make the leap to the fully human. Perhaps the northern European cave man had made the leap millennia earlier, perhaps the "miracle" had really happened in the Lascaux Cave. "For at Lascaux, new-born mankind arose for the first time to measure the extent of its inner, its secret wealth: its power to strive after the impossible."[22] The key to understanding this "miracle," Bataille argues, is the fact that the cave artists drew primarily animals and only represented humans symbolically. For example, one of the Lascaux figures of a human being is called the "man in the well." It is painted in heavy black lines, almost in the style of the pop artist of the 1980s, Keith Haring. It is a stick-drawing, meant to symbolize a person but not meant to be an accurate rendering. Next to this human stick figure are fully-realized frescoes of a wounded bison and rhinoceros, painted in a realistic style. So it is not a question of the artist being unable to represent people realistically or naturalistically. Bataille suggests that by drawing animals the artists sought to separate themselves from the animal world, as those who observe and represent the world from "outside." The artists' vision of animality is thus humane, he says. "Why? Because the life it incarnates is transfigured in the painting."[23] It is humane because the painter, by representing the animal, "has been wrenched out of the world of nameless feeling—of sensibility."[24] Artists separate and distance themselves from the world in order to represent it as a "thing." Until this moment, Bataille says, there is only the animal. Afterwards, there is something "closer our kin." The Lascaux artists "left us innumerable pictures of the animality they were shedding." What the paintings really express, he concludes, is "man just turning into a human."[25]

It is almost as if this narrative of the Lascaux Cave art was waiting to be written. Indeed, one might say that the reason the Lascaux Cave art has taken on such importance in the canon of "great" art young people study in high school and college is that it fits fairly easily within a well-established mythic framework. Bataille's narrative leads the modern reader on a familiar journey, into well-known territory. In a similar way, the tourist's descent into a facsimile cave at Lascaux is a story told again and again. The descent back into the cave is a powerful myth in Eurocentric culture, and it takes the form of a public fascination with caves, with journeys into caves, and with the stories of getting lost or trapped in caves. What is taken for granted is a developmental hierarchy in education and in culture that leads away from the animal and toward the "fully human." This is consistent with a Eurocentric, colonialist mythology, a "giant leap" or "miracle" that occurred on European soil—and not in southern Europe, but in northern Europe. The northern European is represented in this text almost like Nietzsche's *Übermensch*, as a race destined to lead the rest of humanity, a humanity that was not yet "fully human" but rather still crawling out of the cave. One can see in this the basic legitimating logic of European colonialism. But there is more that one can see as well. Is it only coincidental that Bataille consistently refers to "Man" and "Mankind" rather than humanity or humankind? Is he only following an accepted norm for language usage and therefore not to be accused of being patriarchal? Bataille's myth of a northern European "miracle" is implicitly patriarchal, because it uses "Man" as a universal signifier for the human without being concerned or aware of what this signifies about the unspoken category "Woman." Still, there is something to what Bataille says that is important, I think; and it is precisely what I think is important in Plato's cave myth—a theory of educational and cultural development from unreflective knowing to a more reflexive and self-aware knowing.

This leads me to another text, and another taken-for-granted representation of the cave analogy in modern popular culture, a story told by the famous psychoanalytic mythologist, Carl Jung, and it suggests just how much the psychoanalytic tradition has been based on a particular reading of the cave analogy. In his autobiographical book, *Memories, Dreams, Reflections*, Jung describes a dream that haunted him throughout his life—a dream about a descent into a cave. And his interpretation of this dream makes it quite clear that for him the cave represents not only the primitive home of "Mankind," which is to say modern European males, but also the current home of the feminine and the African. This narrative is a dream, and one that he discussed with his father-figure mentor, Freud. In this dream, Jung finds himself in the upper level of a modern two-story house. In exploring the house, he descends the stairs to the first floor. "There everything was much older," he observes, "and I realized that this part of the house must date from about the fifteenth or sixteenth century. . . . Everything was rather dark." Jung then describes stumbling upon a door to the cellar, and descending to a "vaulted room that looked exceedingly ancient." From the bricks in the wall, he discerned that this was a room dating from Roman times. Then, by lifting up a stone slab with a ring set in the floor, Jung descended yet another level, to "a low cave cut into the rock. Thick dust lay on the floor, and in the dust were scattered bones and broken pottery, like remains of a primitive culture."[26] In interpreting the dream, Jung writes that "the house represented a kind of image of the psyche." The further down he went, the darker and more primitive the scene became. "In the cave, I discovered . . . the world of the primitive man within myself." This primitive psyche, for Jung, "borders on the life of the animal soul, just as the caves of prehistoric times were usually inhabited by animals before men laid claim to them."[27] The cave is, he wrote, a source of sadness, fear, and pent-up feelings, and "reflects the mood of Africa, the experience of its solitudes. It is a maternal mystery, this primordial darkness."[28] In the colonial mythology of modern European culture that Jung took for granted, the "dark continent" of Africa was dark not because its people were dark-skinned, but because its people were living in darkness, still cave dwellers. Forget that African peoples never had been cave dwellers. They are symbolically relocated to the cave, and the cave is symbolically relocated in Africa—"the heart of darkness." At the same time, Africa is turned into a maternal continent. Its mysteries, Jung suggests, are the mysteries of women.

Jung expresses the ambivalence about the "primitive," the "savage," the "primal" Other that was, in one sense, a creation of modern culture. In order to establish a sense of "his" own identity as one pole of a great chain of being, modern "man" had to create an opposing pole—the other end of the chain, and define it as the polar opposite of the modern, civilized subjectivity. Without the "primitive," it would not be possible to affirm that one is "civilized." Similarly, as Foucault has observed, without the construction of an irrational and even "mad" Other, modern culture would not be able to affirm a norm of disciplined reason.[29] Nevertheless, even as modern culture has defined and positioned racial, gender, class, and sexual Others as its opposite, as "abnormal" and "primitive," it has been drawn to that which it has made the Other represent—that which it denies in itself. Thus, Jung in particular believed that modern culture had much to learn from so-called primitive cultures, since the collective unconscious of modernism had been built upon this primal sub-basement and foundation of modern consciousness. The primitive expresses the collective unconscious in a direct and accessible form, and Jung believed that modern culture needed to get in touch with its primitive desires, insights, and fears. At the same time Jung is ultimately a modern man, and I use "man" here to refer to gendered subjectivity. He may believe that it is wise to now and again venture downstairs, to return to a cave that is the home of both woman and African subjects—who are made to signify the primitive. But this journey downward is only for the purpose of gathering some of the power of the primitive to bring back up to the "top" of the house. Jung represents the modern, European male in his dream, living in the top floor of a grand house, the top of a great chain of being. Yet he, more than most modern men, was aware of how much the civilized is built upon the primitive, so that the solid "house" of civilization is represented as an edifice constructed upon a foundation of primitive myth, madness, and desire.

Not surprisingly, when the new "science" of developmental psychology emerged in the early twentieth century, it took for granted its own variation on this myth of a great chain of being. Granville Stanley Hall, who is generally considered the "founding father" of developmental psychology in education, argued that the development of each individual *recapitulates* or restates this cultural journey of development. According to the "cultural epochs" theory, young children are recapitulating a hunting and gathering stage of cultural development when it is appropriate to allow them to run outdoors, camp out in tents, engage in pretend hunting expeditions, and sit around campfires telling stories. Later, they move into a period in their development that corresponds to the Neolithic era. At this age children's learning is best organized around activities and study relating to the cultivation of crops, their harvesting, and the production and distribution of products from crops—such as bread. Later, adolescents enter a period where they recapitulate the rise of civilization and the age of reason. They become more intellectual and better able to control their impulses and desires. All of this was presumed to be part of the natural order of things, an expression of a natural developmental law.

There are other problems with Hall's recapitulation of cultural epochs theory or human development that make it politically conservative, even reactionary. Hall used his theory to argue that African Americans and Native Americans were still recapitulating earlier stages in cultural development, and that their education had to be tailored to their lower level of development. This meant that they should not be pushed academically beyond what they were capable of achieving. Their own particular learning strengths needed to be "respected." African Americans, he observed, are "child-like peoples," a "less advanced" and "backward" race. As students, their strengths included an "intense emotional endowment," "capacity for merriment," "patience," "submissiveness," "mysticism," and a "primitive sense of rhythm."[30] The "natural" developmental differences between whites and blacks meant to Hall that blacks should be educated in their own schools, where their own particular racial "endowments" could be properly cultivated and developed. As for girls, Hall believed that their natural predisposition for motherhood and homemaking needed to be respected by educating them separately from boys. Hall clearly views boys' development as leading higher than that of girls, toward leadership in the family, workplace, and community. It is for this reason that he criticized the increasing feminization of teaching, fearing it would retard boys' development and thus "emasculate" them.[31] Of course, one might argue with some validity that Hall represents a past that developmental psychology has put behind it and risen above. Nevertheless, the historic uses and abuses of developmental psychology must give us pause to wonder whether it has so completely risen above its past, especially when Hall continues to be revered as the "father" of modern developmentalism in educational psychology texts.

Some things, however, have changed since the early twentieth century. What was taken for granted in Hall's day is now being "named" and critiqued. The myth of a great chain of being, incorporated into Social Darwinism, continues to play a pivotal role in legitimating inequality in education and American society more generally. But now it is does not go completely unchallenged. A good example is provided by the controversy over a 1996 book by Richard Herrnstein and Charles Murray, *The Bell Curve: Intelligence and Class Structure in American Life*. Herrnstein and Murray argue that over the past century, the gifted have—in a general sense—risen to the top in America, and that they now represent a "cognitive elite" that is rapidly cutting itself off from a growing "cognitive underclass." Herrnstein and Murray presume, as Plato did, that class inequality is largely a result of natural developmental differences in intellectual capacity and moral character. This developmental great chain of being that establishes class structure is also represented in race and gender terms. Thus, Herrnstein and Murray note that a disproportionate number of blacks and Hispanics, along with unwed mothers, make up the cognitive underclass. Because the cognitive underclass is developmentally backward, it is also presumably childlike in its sense of acting on impulse, without a strong sense of right or wrong. So the authors point to evidence that demonstrates that criminals, along with welfare mothers—both supposedly of low moral character—are also lowest in intelligence. What can be done for the cognitive underclass? Precious little, the authors conclude, although programs such as Head Start may help some. Can public schools help in some way? The authors assert that "formal schooling offers little hope of narrowing cognitive inequality on a large scale." The only hope, they suggest, "is adoption at birth from a bad family environment to a good one."[32] This, of course, was Plato's proposed solution. But even this drastic measure may not be able to fully counter the powerful influence of genes, they conclude.

Since Herrnstein and Murray see little hope in educating the cognitive underclass beyond a low level of discipline-oriented conditioning, they suggest that we would be better off to spend public funds on educating the cognitive elite. One of the reasons SAT scores have been falling, they conclude, "is that disadvantaged students have been 'in' and gifted students 'out' for thirty years." In the first half of the twentieth century, this was not so, they assert. "It was taken for granted that one of the chief purposes of education was to educate the gifted," for the future of society depended on them.[33] In real economic terms, all the investment in the education of those of low cognitive ability "is not going to overturn this reality. For many people, there is nothing they can learn that will repay the cost of the teaching."[34] As the focus of public education shifts from trying to raise the achievement of the underclass and toward advanced education for the cognitive elite, Herrnstein and Murray see a society emerging in which the cognitive elite increasingly separate themselves from the underclass. On the one hand, they feel, this is unfortunate. They look back with nostalgia to the old company towns in America, where the upper classes had a sense of obligation to look after the lower classes and where relationships across class lines were personal. On the other hand, the authors conclude that it is only natural for the cognitive elite to want to separate itself from the cognitive underclass, and that this trend will no doubt continue. The result, Herrnstein and Murray predict, will be a "custodial state," with the cognitive underclass increasingly isolated in urban ghettoes, which will become "a high-tech and more lavish version of the Indian reservation for some substantial minority of the nation's population"—permanent wards of the custodial state.[35] The authors refer to Plato's call for a society "ruled by the virtuous and wise few," looking out for the interests of everybody. Greek democracy, they note, was never a democracy of equals. "Neither the Greek democrats nor the Roman republicans believed 'all men are created equal.'" Indeed, they note, it was a highly unequal society, "with the most menial chores left to the slaves."[36] The "cognitive partitioning" of America will continue, they conclude. And some good may even come of it. For within the confines of carefully supervised (some might say policed) reservations, the cognitive underclass may begin to learn the simple pleasures of a simple people. "Being a good parent, a good neighbor, and a good friend will give their lives purpose and meaning."[37]

As I said earlier, what makes Herrnstein and Murray's book noteworthy is not so much its argument, or the hundreds of pages of statistical data used to support its claims. It is noteworthy because when it was published, it was almost immediately attacked by progressives in education. Instead of being received as an objective, detached, scientific look at the statistical evidence on race, class, and intelligence, their book was widely received as an attempt to use statistics to sell a classist, racist, and sexist ideology.[38] Even the popular press was scathing in its critique of the book for dragging out many of the same old arguments about supposed genetic differences in intelligence between blacks and whites, and for treating intelligence test scores as an objective indication of intellectual capacity. The standardized intelligence test, more and more people are beginning to realize, has been involved in perpetuating a myth of inequality that has been deeply undemocratic, and also patriarchal and racist. Yet the myth of a great chain of intelligence, measured by standardized intelligence tests, is in some ways more powerful and pervasive, and more taken for granted, than ever before in educational policy, and it continues to stand in the way of meaningful democratic change.

THE EDUCATION OF CAVE-DWELLERS

Plato's concern is with the education of leaders, and so with the journey of an ascent out of the cave and into the light. But we need to question whether any system of education that claims to be about educating leaders is not also very much interested in the education of those "chosen" not to lead. This is particularly true, given that Plato is always applying a binary oppositional logic to the world. The education of leaders thus also implies, and contains within it, as central to its project, the education of the "masses," of those chosen to serve and obey, to be "good," docile subjects of power. We must infer the presence of those who do not leave the cave in Plato's text, for he prefers not to talk about them, to make them visible in his text. They are there, nevertheless, at the heart and core of his project. Plato proposes a system of mass public education for all Greek citizens, including girls but excluding slaves, at least up through the elementary years. This is when the first major screening and sorting is to occur, when those who are to be leaders are separated from the rest and given further education at the state's expense. What, then, is to be the characteristic of these early years of education, before the "gifted" are separated out for further study in science, mathematics, and, finally, philosophy? It is to be an education governed by *mythos*, involving the telling and reading (under careful supervision) of myths and narratives that teach "positive" virtues. Here Plato makes no pretence about using myth to indoctrinate young people, most of whom will never go on to a higher form of education in which indoctrination will be replaced with reason. Indoctrination, through the use of state-published narratives and mythological tales, is to be the lot of the masses. The masses are never to learn how to read mythic texts critically. Instead, they are to learn that these myths speak of timeless virtues. And what are these timeless virtues? Socrates sums up the education of the great majority of people as aimed at teaching virtues about "obedience to their rulers, and controlling their own desire for the pleasures of eating, drinking, and sex."[39]

Socrates turns to that great epic collection of Greek mythology, Homer's *Odyssey*, as an example of a text that might be useful for such an education, albeit after it is properly censored and offending passages cut out. As an example of what he has in mind, Socrates suggests censoring in Homer "the story of how Zeus stayed awake, when all the other gods and men were asleep, with some plan in mind, but forgot it easily enough when his desire was roused."[40] It is important, he says, that the gods not be depicted as ruled by their passions rather than a pure *logos*, rather than always thinking of the good of the people. Nor are gods and mythological heroes such as Achilles to be depicted as weeping and wailing upon the loss of a companion in battle. At all times, the gods are to be treated as acting virtuously. Socrates does manage to find a few passages and stories in Homer worth salvaging—for example lines such as, "Be quiet, man, and take your cue from me," and "The Achaeans moved forward, breathing valor, in silent obedience to their officers." Plato sums up the essence of this type of virtue in the ideas of "self-mastery" and "temperance." These involve a form of resignation and acceptance among the masses that "produces a harmony of the weaker and the stronger ... the agreement of the naturally superior and inferior."[41] Temperance and self-mastery imply bearing one's lot without bitterness, never giving in to desire, emotion, resentment, fear—a form of stoicism designed to ensure that a highly inequitable social order is maintained in perfect harmony. Because there are not enough stories that emphasize only these "positive" virtues, Plato says (in one of his more prophetic passages) that the state will need to get into the business of producing fictions and histories, textbooks and anthologies of morally uplifting tales.

The concern in Plato for teaching certain "positive" virtues to the masses, and to the very young, has been of continuing relevance in shaping the cultural conservative response to the so-called "value relativism" of progressives.

So it is not surprising to find that William Bennett turns to Plato to introduce his popular 1993 compendium of moral tales for young people, *A Book of Virtues*. Bennett quotes from *The Republic*:

> You know that the beginning is the most important part of any work, especially in the case of a young and tender thing; for that is the time at which the character is being formed and the desired impression is more readily taken. . . . Shall we just carelessly allow children to hear any casual tale which may be devised by casual persons? . . . It is most important that the tales which the young first hear should be models of virtuous thoughts. (Quoted in Bennett, p. 18)

Bennett was President Reagan's secretary of education and emerged in the 1990s as perhaps the major conservative spokesperson in popular culture who addressed education issues. As president of "Empower America," a conservative political action committee, Bennett espouses a form of cultural conservatism that is more secular than religious in an overt sense, but which nevertheless believes that public schools should teach moral absolutes. By grounding these moral absolutes in philosophy rather than religion, Bennett finds a rational basis for affirming conservative values as moral absolutes. In *A Book of Virtues*, he says, he merely wants to follow Plato's advice about the education of children. He hopes this volume of virtuous tales will counter somewhat the "casual tales" young people are exposed to in popular culture. His timeless virtues in themselves are difficult to criticize. Self-discipline or "self-mastery," compassion, responsibility, friendship, work, courage, perseverance, honesty, loyalty, faith—these all have important meaning in democratic contexts. Nevertheless, as Bennett interprets them, these "timeless" virtues begin to sound very Platonic.

Let me take just one myth from Bennett's book as an example. This is the well-known Greek myth of Icarus and Daedalus, which Bennett relates to the virtue of responsibility. According to this myth, Daedalus and his son, Icarus, escape from captivity on the island of Crete by learning how to fly. They fabricate wooden wings with feathers attached, and they secure the wings to their bodies using wax. As they begin their flight to freedom across the sea, Daedalus warns his son not to fly too high or too low. If he flies too low, he is warned, the ocean spray will soak his wings and weigh him down. If he flies too high, the sun will melt the wax and his wings will fall off. He is to stay in the middle air current, close by his father. Of course, Icarus does not heed this warning and in a rapture of pure joy flies higher and higher, whereupon his wings begin to melt and he plummets to his death in the sea. The lesson Bennett would have the reader draw from this myth of Icarus and Daedalus is that "young people have a responsibility to obey their parents." Successful upbringings "require a measure of obedience, as Icarus finds out the hard way."[42] The young reader supposedly is to be so afraid of the punishment for not doing what parents say, to the precise letter of the law, that they learn to obey their parents unquestioningly. Now, something interesting is going on here, and it begins to get at the contradiction in Bennett's interpretation of "timeless virtues." The timeless virtue of responsibility, in this case defined as a type of blind obedience to parents, is not really presented as a timeless virtue at all. Instead, responsibility is to be taught by appealing to children's fear of punishment and deadly consequences. Plato resolves this contradiction in his own philosophy, and one presumes Bennett once more is following suit, through the presumption that the young, and all of those who remain at a low level of development, are not open to being reasoned with. So it is no use trying to present these moral absolutes as transcendent truths. They are to be inculcated in young people through an appeal to fear. This is also, for Bennett, a myth about not giving in to our impulses and desires—a basic Platonic theme. He observes that "Icarus thought of nothing but his own excitement and glory."[43]

The myth of Daedalus and Icarus, like all great myths, is much more complex and ambiguous than Bennett would have us believe. Like other Greek myths, such as that of Prometheus, the myth of Daedalus and Icarus speaks of a tension that continues to lie near the heart of the modern project. In *The Rebel,* the French existential philosopher Albert Camus argued that "the Greek mind has two aspects." Destiny, for the Greeks, "was a blind force to which one submitted, just as one submitted to the forces of nature."[44] Out of this mythology of "fate" or "destiny"—the idea that we have no control over our lives, that agency resides in the gods, that one must submit to one's lot in life, submit to authority—comes a whole history of the mythology of conformity and docility in the West. According to this mythology, those who step too far outside the straight and narrow, who do not obey orders, and who "fly too high," must receive their just deserts. "Fate" always must prevail over the wish of humans to control their own destinies. Thus, it is essential within Greek mythology that Icarus be treated harshly by the gods. Social order is made dependent upon widespread acceptance of this fatalistic mythology in Hellenic Greek culture, and with it acceptance of fatalistic virtues of passivity, docility, and submission to one's assigned lot or role in life. But right alongside the mythology of fate and destiny in Greek culture, Camus observes, was a countervailing mythology, one that set the stage for an existential rebellion against Fate, and that even went so far as to celebrate rebellion. Hellenic Greek culture celebrated the human, and always saw something noble about the struggle of humans to control their own destinies, refusing to submit to Fate, and setting the sky as their limit. Icarus, like Faust, will have no artificial boundaries or limits on him. Out of this mythology it is possible to trace a lineage of humanism and existentialism in Western culture that has sustained and nourished democratic cultural traditions, along with a tradition of rebellion against all dominating authority. It provides a mythology of transgression against the limits and borders imposed on human knowing and human experience by fatalistic teachings. This means that Greek mythology is organized around a central contradiction, a central tension. On the one hand, transgression, rebellion, resistance, seeking to control one's own fate—all of these will lead to a bad end. On the other hand, there is something noble in the act of rebellion, knowing full well that one cannot win against the gods.

To Camus, the myth of Prometheus represents the most politicized version of this mythology of transgression in Greek culture, and it is interesting that Bennett completely ignores Prometheus in *A Book of Virtues*. Prometheus' transgression is not merely flying too high, acting impulsively, or not obeying parental authority—as with Icarus. Here the crime consists of siding with humans against the gods in an insurrection to gain control over their destinies. Prometheus is the "eternal martyr," condemned to be chained forever on a rocky slope. His crime is refusal to ask forgiveness for what he has done. And what precisely has Prometheus done? Typically, Prometheus is represented as the god who gave fire to people, but this is only symbolic of his siding with humans against Fate, for fire offers humans a means of better controlling their lives, and of illuminating the darkness of the world with knowledge. According to Aeschylus, Prometheus is accused of three major crimes. The first is his boast that "I have delivered humans from being obsessed by death." That is, he has freed people from the fear of their own death, the fear of a final judgment after death, and the hope for a better life after death. No longer obsessed with the hereafter, they can begin to focus their energies on the concrete, material world in which they live. Prometheus' second crime is "instilling hopes into people's minds."[45] Here the hope is not for a better life after death, but for a better world. The mythology of hope is, from the beginning, associated with belief that people need not accept the world the way it is but can reconstruct it according to a vision of a socially just world. They need not become resigned and fatalistic. Finally, Prometheus is accused of giving people a love for their fellow human beings—philanthropy. Instead of loving the gods exclusively, people begin to love each other and thus exalt humanity over the gods. In the defiance of Prometheus, we see signs of a mythology of human dignity. By defying what seems to be fate and destiny, by refusing to submit quietly, by continuing to struggle against insurmountable odds, Prometheus affirms what we might call humane, democratic virtues, virtues associated with human dignity and agency. Camus quotes the philosopher Epicurus, who says that when death finally does catch up to us we will sing—with Prometheus—this proud song: "Ah, with what dignity we have lived."

THE MYTH OF THE GATEKEEPER

> The school became a sort of apparatus of uninterrupted examination
> that duplicated along its entire length the operation of teaching.
>
> —MICHEL FOUCAULT[46]

Closely intertwined with the mythology of a great chain of being, and with the mythology of developmental theory in education, is a mythology of gatekeeping and judgment. In modern culture, the mythology of the gatekeeper has supported practices that sort and select individuals for either advancement or demotion, for success or failure, for upward social movement or downward social movement. The gatekeeper is thus also a judge, a final authority and arbiter who controls the destiny of individuals. Finally, the gatekeeper mythology has led to an increased emphasis upon the importance of credentials in regulating the distribution of wealth and power in society. Public education provided a basis for building the "credentialed society" in the twentieth century, and it continues to play a very central—perhaps increasingly central—role in regulating entree to the middle class, and for locking some into poverty. In *The Republic*, Plato tells us that those who are being educated to be guardians are to be tested periodically, and that only those who pass these standardized examinations are to be allowed to continue up to the next rung in their education. One can imagine that the path out of Plato's cave leads through a series of checkpoints, with a final checkpoint at the mouth of the cave. Socrates observes, "Those who have come through all our practical and intellectual tests with success must be brought to their final trial, and made to lift their mind's eye to look at the source of all light, and see the Good."[47] Education is represented in terms of a series of trials before judges, each trial more difficult than the last, each designed to "weed out" more people until only a very few reach the top.

Here again, we find that Plato turns to myth to ground this idea of a judgmental authority that divides and separates, and more particularly a Greek myth that has had a profound impact on a dominant strand of Christianity in the West. Plato ends *The Republic* with a mythic account of traveling to the "other world" in what we would now call a "near death" experience. He acknowledges that this is a myth, and not to be taken necessarily as the literal truth. But he does point to this as the kind of myth that the masses, indeed that all people (including the guardians), should be taught if order and authority are to prevail in his ideal republic. According to this legendary Greek story, a man named Er is wounded in battle and comes close to dying on the battlefield. Indeed, he is taken for dead and is about to be put on the funeral pyre when he suddenly awakens, at which point he describes what he has just experienced. When he was wounded he rose out of his body on the battlefield and traveled upward to a large space where masses of people were gathering. Before them sat a panel of judges. On either side of the judges Er saw two great roads which were like conveyor belts, carrying souls either upward, toward heaven, or downward, toward Hades. As Er took his place in line, he saw people come before the panel of judges. These judges ordered "the just to take the right-hand road that led up through the sky," and the unjust and undeserving, who carry "the badges of all they had done behind them, to take the left-hand road that led downwards."[48] The only substantial difference between the Christian myth of a "final judgment" and this myth is that in Plato's myth the damned do not burn in Hades forever, but rather for a period of time that equals ten times their age at death, at which point they get to choose another life. The idea that there is always "another chance" for individuals makes a condemning judgment seem more fair, and so we maintain some version of it in our own educational system and in culture generally. It is associated, for example, with the idea that even the "hardened" criminal can be rehabilitated and given another chance after "serving time." In education, it is associated with the idea that those who drop out of high school or fail to pass a high school proficiency test can always come back later and get their General Education Diploma (GED). Unfortunately, the idea of a "second chance" is more myth than reality for most people. In this sense, the judgment of educational institutions is a "final judgment."

The two major "gates" in education are high school graduation and college education. The passage through each of these gates is ritualized in the graduation ceremony, perhaps the most important ceremony in education. Graduation ceremonies are rituals of celebration, and also rituals in which the highest ideals of the culture are invoked by invited speakers, who urge the new graduates to rise to the challenge of leadership. The academic gowns and "pomp and circumstance" elevate the secular graduation ceremony into a quasi-religious ritual. But no one ever dares ask, amid the celebration, about what happened to the others—those who will not graduate, who dropped out or "failed." The graduation ceremony ritualistically celebrates the achievement of some, but always at the expense of those who are "visible absences" at this ritual. According to recent estimates, having a college diploma means that you can expect to make about 60 percent more over the course of your life than if you only have a high school diploma. And getting the baccalaureate degree seems to matter more than how many years you have toward a baccalaureate. What college education ritualizes, more than perhaps anything else, is entree into a relatively secure lifestyle, and it ritualizes leaving behind those who have been deselected or who have dropped out along the way. The new middle class moves in one direction, the growing working class in another.

Further down the educational system there is another gate, with equally dire consequences for those judged not worthy of passing. This is the gate of the high school proficiency test. Since the mid-1980s, most states have adopted standardized proficiency tests in the areas of literacy skills, mathematics, and citizenship or social studies. The effect of standardized proficiency testing on the nation's poorest and most disadvantaged youth has been dramatic. These youth tend to be chronically undereducated, have low expectations set for them by everyone (including in many cases themselves), and lack the "cultural capital"—the middle class language skills—that is rewarded in the exams. The result is that in most of the nation's urban school districts, only about one half of all students who begin high school actually graduate. For most of those young people who do not graduate, low-pay, low-skill jobs, with little job security, are what they can expect, with little hope of climbing far above the poverty level. So high school graduation ceremonies are also sad occasions, or should be. They are to be interpreted not only in terms of who they involve, but who is not invited to the ritual, who has been excluded from the celebration of achievement.

Over the past decade, in classes I have taught for both undergraduates and graduate students, I often have asked students to write an essay in which they mythologize their own education. That is, they are to tell their own education in story form, drawing upon cultural myths and metaphors. Invariably when I have announced this class project, some students become visibly nervous. Like the prisoner who has been freed and given the right and responsibility to find her or his way toward the light, these students would just as soon return to their convenient chains. At least they know what to expect. At least they know the criteria upon which they will be judged. These students represent their education as a "riddle game," in which the objective is to produce the correct truths that gatekeeper instructors want from students in order to let them pass through on their journey. The notion that some students might approach their education as a "riddle game" was suggested to me by a young woman who at first resisted the open-endedness of the project. Over the course of several class sessions, she pushed me to turn the project into a predictable format and to tell her "what I wanted." My response was to help clarify the project as much as I could but also to let her know that, "I don't want anything in particular. I'm interested in what you come up with when you think about your own education in terms of mythic themes or metaphors." When I did not provide many more guidelines, she was frustrated. Finally, when I asked that students talk about the myths they had chosen to make sense of their own educations, she reluctantly agreed to share hers. She began by saying, "I don't know why I chose this exactly and it's probably no good." After a bit of reassurance, she began to tell the story of Oedipus and the Sphinx. In this story from Homer, the city of Thebes is afflicted with the Sphinx—a creature that is half woman and half lion. The Sphinx stands at the city gate and refuses to let anyone enter or leave without first answering a riddle. Many fail to answer the riddle correctly and are devoured by the Sphinx. Finally, Oedipus arrives at the city gate and is asked the riddle: "What creature is it that walks on four feet in the morning, on two at noon, and on three in the evening?" Oedipus correctly answers: The creature is a human. It crawls on all four legs as a child, walks upright on two feet when it grows up, and leans on a cane in old age. So Oedipus is victorious and is allowed to continue his journey.

Through discussion over the course of the term, the student began to understand the relevance of this myth to her own life and why she chose it. She became aware that she had mythologized her own education as a riddle game, but had not cast herself in the role of hero—someone like Oedipus. She had not been very good at giving teachers (the Sphinx) what they wanted and had struggled through her course work in college. With a subdued anger in her voice, she said that it was "unfair" that teachers and professors asked riddles of students, and made them come up with the "correct" answers before they could move on in their lives. Like riddles, class projects and examinations "have to be answered in just the right way, and the answer is pretty meaningless." She had approached her education in terms of trying to come up with the "right" answer to questions which had little meaning or relevance in her life, and yet she felt frustrated in this effort. "In a way," she said, "this class project is like a riddle. I'm not sure what you want me to say." I reassured her that there were no "wrong" answers when it came to this project, and that she alone could decide what this myth meant to her. At any rate, I said, she would be allowed to pass this course and go on with her educational journey no matter what interpretation she decided upon. Once she began to believe this, things changed very much for her. She began to find much meaning in her myth and assert her interpretations in class. She came to realize that she was not ignorant and "dumb." And she seemed to gain a sense that perhaps she could be in control of her learning, that education need not be something imposed on her, that it need not be merely a series of checkpoints, each with its own riddle and riddler, its own gatekeeper.

In its own way, the myth of the riddle refers back to the *logos/mythos* binary in education, with the Sphinx as the guardian of the border between *logos* and *mythos*. Students are placed in the position of moving from *mythos* to *logos* in their educational journey, and tests, grades, and other "gatekeeping" apparatus are like the riddle of the Sphinx, designed to determine who will pass on to the next gate and who will not. And like all gates, educational gates separate "insiders" from "outsiders," the "literate" from the "illiterate," the educated from the uneducated, those inside the dominant culture and those relegated to the margins. One way to make gatekeeping and judgment mythology more visible, so it can be critically deconstructed, is by drawing upon non-Western, non-modernistic epistemologies and narratives that are not binary oppositional. For example, within Zen Buddhism, education proceeds through wrestling with a number of koans, or riddles. But these are riddles without right or wrong answers. Instead, they are designed to help people "un-think" binary oppositional thinking. One famous Zen koan deals with gates and gate-keeping. According to this koan, "one day as Manjusri stood outside the gate, the Buddha called to him, 'Manjusri, Manjusri, why do you not enter?' Manjusri replied, 'I do not see myself outside. Why enter?'" Gyomay Kubose writes: "When the Buddha asked Manjusri . . . to enter the gate, he was testing Manjusri's understanding. Manjusri replied, in effect, that there is no gate in the world of Truth."[49] Inside/outside is a binary we consciously or uncon-sciously construct, and we construct it through gates, doors, and other devices that serve as borders between inside and outside. This, indeed, is a startlingly different approach to understanding reality and truth than we find in the mod-ern era in the West.

Franz Kafka, in one of his parables, "Before the Law," writes of a defen-dant who stands before a door seeking admittance to the Law, waiting for the doorkeeper to let him enter so that the judge can determine his fate. At one point, the doorkeeper tells him, "I am powerful. And I am only the least of the doorkeepers." After this door there is "hall after hall" of doors and door-keepers.[50] In education, these doors separate those who have been selected for "success" and those who receive the stamp of "failure." Some grow tired of waiting at educational doors and gates, beginning to suspect they will not be asked to enter, and they decide to drop out. Others, like Kafka's character, who waits his whole life before doors, keep hoping that the next examination will prove them worthy of entering. In the late 1960s, the humanistic psychologist William Glasser wrote a book, *Schools Without Failure*, in which he argued that public schools and colleges should do away with grades and adopt an attitude of success for all. No one should be defined as a failure. What Glasser failed to recognize is just how deeply rooted the success/failure binary opposition is, and how much education has become involved in guarding the borders and erecting a series of checkpoints between these two poles in the binary. Of course, gatekeeping and judgment may, to at least some extent, be part and parcel of teaching and the educational process. Gates, doors, and examinations are not in themselves "bad" or totally undemocratic. And it is important to celebrate various passages in one's journey of becoming. However, when gate-keeping takes priority over all else, when it becomes the very essence and pur-pose of a public education, and when it is involved in the construction and legitimation of social inequality, then it no longer serves the forces of democra-tization. Rather, public schools become Plato's gatekeepers.

THE RISE OF MYTHOCENTRISM

What alternatives can progressives offer to this Platonic mythology of devel-opmentalism, of the long ascent from *mythos* to *logos*, of a journey only a privileged few complete? One answer is a very simple one. We can continue to work within the same basic binary opposition that separates *logos* and *mythos*, the civilized and the primitive, the mature and the immature. But instead of valuing the first set of terms in these oppositional pairs, we value the latter set of terms. Instead of valuing unified, consensual truths, we value diverse truths with no real effort to see "common" truths or values. Instead of promoting the "civilized" values of self-repression and self-discipline, of reason over emotion, we value the opposite: the return to the primitive or "primal" self, impulsivity and creativity, the expression of subjective feeling. Instead of valuing the development of a formal, analytic way of speaking in writing, one that is highly impersonal, we promote a return to autobiographical voice and story-telling, with little attempt to draw generalizations from our stories. We celebrate the return to a "personal," subjective education that is a form of self-therapy or self-analysis. All of these various ways of knowing that involve a return to *mythos* provide the basis for what we might call *mythocentric education*. There is a very real possibility that we are entering a mythocentric age, and mythocentrism is certainly on the rise among progressive educators and intellectuals. While mythocentrism offers some important advantages in doing battle with logocentrism in education and culture, it is limited by its taken-for-granted acceptance of the *logos/mythos* binary, merely privileging *mythos* instead of *logos*. In his book, *The Language of Vision*, Jamake Highwaker writes: "We are Plato's creatures, forever bound in a cave." We cannot imagine a reality other than the shadow realities of our culture and place in history. "We must believe in the shadows, for we have no access to the reality they reflect."[51]

The movement toward mythocentrism in American education and in popular culture has been closely linked to a privileging of the personal, the autobiographical, and story-telling rhetorical styles, over the more analytic project of critiquing the dominant culture and its taken-for-granted ideology. In reaction to the logocentric rhetorical style of linear writing and speaking, the logical development of argument, and an impersonal *logos*, mythocentrism emphasizes a rhetorical writing style that is highly personal and autobiographical, that avoids generalizations, that weaves webs and circles back over metaphors and images. While the return to a mythocentric voice in education has provided an opportunity for those who have been marginalized to find their voices and narrate their own stories, too often very little effort is made to link personal stories and self-reflection to broader and more generalizable contexts of meaning. In some forms, personal story-telling may only be a way of massaging the ego. As Michael Apple observes, writing in a personal, autobiographical voice may, in effect, be a way of saying, "But enough about you, let me tell you about me."[52]

What might we take as an example of a pedagogy that privileges the "mother of *mythos*?" In popular culture and the academy, one influential movement that has expressed many of the themes of mythocentrism is eco-feminism—particularly as it emerged in the 1970s and 1980s when it was heavily influenced by the earth goddess mythology. The same year that Spretnak's book was published, 1978, Mary Daly published *Gyn/Ecology*. Much more than Spretnak, Daly began to explore the implications of ecofeminism in the re-education of women, and in the creation of a new ecological feminist culture. Her book was an attempt to radically move outside of patriarchal myths of knowing by reappropriating and rereading a feminist mythology. But perhaps what is most important about *Gyn/Ecology* and what has been most responsible for its influence is Daly's conviction that to move outside of patriarchal myths of knowing women need to recover a non-logocentric language, one based on story-telling and myth, that weaves webs of connection rather than obeying a linear rationality. The liberation of women, she says, will only come about when women learn to speak a new language of their own; and so Daly practically invents a new language and style in the book. Daly acknowledges in the preface to her book that it would likely be perceived as "unscholarly" in the academy because its style was modeled after women's oral traditions rather than academic "phallocentric" language. In her effort to create a language that works outside the boundaries of logocentric science, she creates new words, uses capital letters to emphasize words, uses hyphens to separate the prefixes of words from their "body," and uses slashes to suggest both relationship and opposition. All of this is designed to call into question the conventional reading of words and to deliberately play with multiple levels of meaning. For example, she writes that ecofeminism does not belong to any academic "de-partments," that "it departs from their de-partments. It is the Department/Departure of Spinning."[53] It departs by leaping over the "bodies of knowledge" incarcerated in the academy.

By calling attention to how words work to make meaning, Daly makes the reader question the taken-for-grantedness of language. She suggests that language is not a neutral vehicle for carrying fixed meaning. The way we speak, the way we write, the way we use language is very intimately related to the way we know the world. To re-create the world, we will need to imaginatively re-create language and learn to speak in new ways. Daly called for a "gynocentric" way of writing and speaking based on a *ludic celebration*—the celebration of speaking from a place of one's own, outside the patriarchal disciplines. In such a space, she believed, it would be possible for women to engage the free play of their intuition, and to speak and write in multi-dimensional, independent, creative ways. She was not at all certain, however, that it would be possible to find such a ludic space in the academy. The hope she found lay in the fact that "on the boundaries of the male-centered universities ... there's a flowering of woman-centered thinking."[54] Indeed, it is in this space at the borders, among college-educated women, that Daly's work has continued to be most influential. There it has become closely intertwined with Jungian psychology (with its archtypes of the feminine), and with various strands of New Age spirituality (as in the Wiccan spirituality movement).

Daly presented the re-education of women as a journey, each phase of which circled back over patriarchal myths, demystifying them and moving beyond them. By "naming" myths as patriarchal, and showing how they have kept women oppressed, Daly believed that the myths would be demystified, and that once they were demystified they would, in effect, "drop dead."[55] They would cease to hold a power over women. Daly argued that the power of myth is not limited to control of the "victim's minds/imaginations," that "deceptive myths are acted out over and over again in performances that draw the participants into emotional complicity." This ritualistic re-enactment of myth "trains both victims and victimizers to perform uncritically their preordainted roles."[56] In "giving the myth reality" through ritualistic performance, the participants are turned into co-producers of oppression, as implicated themselves in setting up power relations of inequality. Myth is also *embedded* in ritual, and thus hidden or made subliminal. This means becoming more aware of how patriarchal myths are embedded in the performance of everyday life in various institutions such as schools and universities. For Daly, one of the most powerful of these patriarchal rituals is the *procession*. In the Christian tradition, the procession is a symbolic expression of the "great chain of being" myth, in which power and authority are passed downward from God the Father through a whole series of church leaders, to priests, and then to the "flock." Many church rituals are thus designed around processions in two forms, both filing in and out of the church in rank orderings and conferring power downward. Baptism, communion, marriage, and the installation of church leaders—all of these enact some procession of power. Modern secular institutions continue to draw on the power of these religious procession rituals, and on the idea of passing power down from one male to another. Daly writes, "The junior statesman dreams of becoming The President. The junior scholar dreams of becoming The Professor. The acolyte fantasizes about becoming The Priest."[57] Inauguration, graduation, and installation rituals confirm that this dream can become a reality.

If patriarchal and authoritarian rituals are linear and hierarchical, and involve conferring or transferring power downward, how might education be re-ritualized consistent with an ecofeminist mythology? Daly provided no concrete examples of counter-myths/rituals that might replace patriarchal myths/rituals such as the procession. She did, however, offer some language around which rituals might be organized—a language of spinning and weaving, of building "threads of connectedness."[58] Instead of the image of the procession, she offered women the image of the spider's web, which suggests spinning ideas, interlacing, weaving and un-weaving, "dis-covering hidden threads of connectedness," and "seeking/making" new patterns.[59] If we think about this as an ecological language rather than a women's language alone, I think its implications are important in education. It suggests radically re-thinking and re-enacting everyday life in schools, moving away from rituals of authority and power over others—as in the traditional classroom and lecture hall—to rituals that connect students and teachers in webs of relationships, that help them create connections that are non-hierarchical and non-linear.

Ecofeminism, particularly of the type associated with Daly's work, generates extreme reactions among progressives. Some dismiss ecofeminist ideas and myths as not worthy of being taken seriously by progressives, or even worse, as an embarrassment, as something progressives should go out of their way to distance themselves from in order to gain respectability in the academy and with the public. For example, Murray Bookchin, an early supporter of ecofeminism, argues that it has descended into a "New Age quagmire of unthinking 'good vibes'." In our aversion to analytic and impersonal reason, he writes, "we may easily opt for a cloudy intuitionism and mysticism as an alternative."[60] Indeed, some ecofeminist discourse and rituals do seem to be about little more than mysticism and "good vibes." Take, for example, Donna Henes' "Spider Woman" rituals in New York City in 1984, which she billed as examples of "process environmental sculptures." On the spring or vernal equinox, she had 360 participants stand in a circle on the top of the World Trade Center, each balancing an egg on his or her head—a feat that can only be accomplished on this day. For the summer solstice, held in Manhattan's Bowling Green, she filled a fountain with circular mirrors which supposedly absorbed "positive images" while the assembled participants chanted for peace over a 17-hour period.[61] Henes' other "process environmental sculptures" include weaving and web-making rituals, such as weaving webs of cloth around a section of Central Park, or "bandaging" trees in a nurturant and healing ritual. As examples of avant-garde, postmodern art, Henes' works are interesting. But they also raise concerns about anti-modern, anti-rational tendencies in ecofeminism. So does the association of popular ecofeminism with a growing earth goddess movement and "new paganism."

As logocentric language and pedagogy are being challenged, we risk turning to logocentrism's polar opposite—mythocentrism. But because mythocentrism is always a reaction against logocentrism, it never really moves beyond the limits of binary oppositional thinking. By staying with the logic of oppositional ways of knowing—one associated with patriarchy and the other with ecofeminism—Daly also ends up essentializing or naturalizing gender identity, and simplifying issues. Men are understood to be linear and hierarchical thinkers, ruled by the patriarchal myth of the procession of authority and power. Women presumably think ecologically, in terms of webs of caring relationships among equals. Men's ways of knowing have dominated for two millennia, this argument goes, leading to the near destruction of the human race and Mother

Earth. Now women's ways of knowing must save the day. Essentialistic treatments of gender also may have the effect of promoting gender separatism. Certainly, some level of separatism may be necessary among dominated groups, for people who share a common oppression must look to each for support to build a language of empowerment. But separatism is always a myth that cannot be sustained, for what it means to be a man and what it means to be a woman, masculine and feminine, has emerged out of the historic relations between men and women. This means that gender progress comes only through struggle and dialogue between women and men, a process that involves giving new meaning to both the masculine and the feminine.

Given these problems with ecofeminism, I think the reaction against it, by critics such as Bookchin, also has to be questioned. Behind this reaction, I suspect, lies a masculinist fear about "uppity" women—the fear of an Amazon culture in which men are marginalized in the way women have been marginalized for over two millennia now, the fear that if women "take over," civilization and reason as we know it will cease and humanity will slink back into the cave. If men can get beyond these fears they may find something worth learning from ecofeminism. For ecofeminists have raised fundamental questions about the extent to which dominant non-ecological and modern ways of knowing are patriarchal. They also raise important questions about the role of ritual in education. To borrow a phrase from Peter McLaren, schooling is a ritual performance.[62] Educators typically have focused on educating the mind, as if the mind were somehow separate from a body and a location in the material world. Ritual appeals to the body, relocates knowing within a field of action. Oppressive forms of schooling ritualize the domination of the body and the repression of desire and spontaneity. They discipline and regiment; they set up hierarchies and rank orderings; and they are organized to uphold authoritative truths. By contrast, democratic and progressive rituals of education must empower, they must be open to re-scripting and allow freedom for participants to direct the ritual themselves. They must be rituals that celebrate diverse truths, and that allow for conflict and opposition within the ritual. In the battle being waged against logocentrism, mythocentrism may provide some strategic benefits, even if it too must be transcended at some point by disrupting the *logos/mythos* binary.

There is also reason to believe that while logocentric forms of curriculum and pedagogy have silenced and disadvantaged those marginalized by class, race, and/or gender, a mythocentric education may not be all that empowering either. Several years ago I had the opportunity to visit an alternative high school in southwest Ohio for "at risk" students (most of whom were urban Appalachian youth). The school was known for its progressive, student-centered curriculum. In this case, student-centered meant a "hands-on" project-based curriculum, and also a heavy emphasis upon writing assignments and projects designed to encourage students to express themselves through poetry and short stories. Students even published their own literary journal, which was distributed not only in the school but in the community. What follows are two poems from the journal.

HURTING

Today I feel very gray and sad.
The hurt inside of me is taking over very slow.
I wish to see the bright yellow of the sun,
But the weary gray is here in my soul.
I feel so alone, unwanted, unloved, unseen.
My thoughts seem withdrawn, lonely, quiet.
My eyes are tense, my heart is troubled.
I feel the bitterness everywhere.
My lips are unsure of talking again.

SCHOOL

Teachers, principals,
and assistants—
They make my life a bore!
Weak and powerful,
Smart and dumb,
Mean and scrooged,
They all give me headaches.
The world is doomed
and shattered,
with teachers and principals—
so burn the school!

The first of these two poems, written by a young woman, speaks of loneliness, despair, and bitterness. It also speaks of a withdrawal into the self—"My lips are unsure of talking again." Because she has been silenced and hurt somehow, she withdraws from the public world, and is not sure that she will come out of her private shell. She seeks the brightness of the sun, but seems to be captive of her own gray cave. Her poem signals a retreat into a world of personal meaning and feeling, where she can lick her wounds. But it is a place without agency. She does not believe that she can change her fate, that she can be anything but a victim. In many ways, this is a poem that expresses an attitude of dependency, inadequacy, and despair—an attitude that plays a part in keeping women disempowered and silenced. Indeed, this is a poem about women's self-silencing, a form of internalized oppression that leaves them without a sense of agency or hope. The second poem, written by a young man, is in some ways the flip side of the first. Rather than retreating into a private world, he strikes out at the public world, represented by the school, that oppresses him and devalues his culture. His poem offers nihilism and rage rather than retreatism and stoicism. "The world is doomed and shattered." So why not "burn the school"? This nihilism, forged out of resentment and rage against a dominant culture that treats him only as "trailer trash," gets young Appalachian men into trouble with the law, as it does young African American men and Latinos. Their rage leads to forms of resistance that are aggressive rather than passive, but that are equally self-defeating.

I asked one of the teachers in the school whether students ever got a chance to deconstruct some of these poems, to get at what they had to say about the process of identity formation, about learning to become an urban Appalachian woman or man. She replied that the teachers discouraged any attempt to critically read and discuss students' poetry and short stories in terms of hidden gender themes, and that they viewed the writing primarily as a way of getting the students "hooked" on writing by allowing them to use a more expressive form. That is, no effort was made to reflect on what is taken for granted in the poems, to connect personal meaning to public meaning, to use the poems as a way of raising larger questions about empowering versus disempowering forms of identity. Outside of such a context, the writing of poetry is mythocentric. Only when the personal and expressive are integrated in some way with a critical rationality is it possible to cross back and forth across the borders that separate *logos* and *mythos* in ways that are empowering. Furthermore, the mythocentric approach to education advanced at the school failed to prepare most of its "at risk" students to pass the state high school proficiency test and gain a high school diploma. It may have got them writing, and spurred their creative impulses; but it did not prepare them with the kinds of analytic language skills that might have helped them pass the test. A mythocentric curriculum may, in these ways, have the effect of keeping marginalized urban youth on the margins.

All of this suggests that a mythocentric curriculum is not really the most effective progressive response to the logocentric curriculum that is the norm in most schools and colleges today. To forge a new progressivism, we need a language and a discourse of truth that breaks down the boundaries between the personal and the public by bringing personal narratives into public discourse. And we need a language that crosses the borders between critique and storytelling, analysis and creativity, that speaks in a private language but also one that carries public meaning.

LIGHTING UP THE CAVE:
RE-SCRIPTING THE CAVE MYTH

Denise Levertov, the poet and critic of poetry, offers what I think is a useful progressive metaphor for re-scripting Plato's cave analogy in a way that disrupts the normal *logos/mythos* binary. To educate or become educated, and to become an engaged public intellectual, is to "light up the cave." This is the title of a 1981 collection of essays by Levertov on the cultural politics of poetry and the role of poets in modern American culture, and it is also the title, more specifically, of one essay in the collection, written in 1974 as a tribute to Anne Sexton upon hearing that she had committed suicide. The title is a line from a poem by Sexton titled "Wanting to Die." One stanza of that poem reads:

> Depression is boring, I think
> and I would do better to make
> some soup and light up the cave.

Sexton was one of the young women poets of promise who had followed in the path set by Sylvia Plath a generation earlier. And as it turned out, Sexton followed Plath's example in suicide as well. Levertov interprets these two suicides as saying something about both "woman" and "poet" in modern society, for both are made to represent a "private" world of subjective feeling and personal pain. As public life became commercialized and governed by an instrumental rationality in the twentieth century, Levertov writes, "the people began to become 'the public,' the 'audience,' and the poet, set aside from that 'public,' began to become more private, more introspective."[63] Poets have been relegated to the margins of society and cut off from meaningful involvement in public dialogue and cultural struggle, even as their work has been exploited commercially and fed to "a public greedy for emotion at second hand because they are starved of the experience."[64] As poets and artists have turned inward, in search of "raw" personal experience and feeling, they have become detached from public life. Without a meaningful public purpose, and assigned the role of being the introspective outsider, modern poets open themselves up to alienation and despair. This has been particularly true of female poets. The road out of despair, Levertov argues, lies in the re-entry of poets into a public conversation, and engagement in cultural struggles over social justice. Reframed in this way, the poet bridges the personal and the public. Like Hermes, the poet travels back and forth, encouraging people to engage in conversation about the broader meaning of personal experience.

This is where Levertov finds significance in the lines quoted above from Sexton. For they suggest that Sexton knew the way out of her depression, but failed to take her own good advice. In this case, the way out of depression is to bring one's private thoughts into public dialogue and conversation. In the reference to soup, and the implied ritual of sitting down around the table and sharing a meal with others—we find a basic democratic metaphor and symbol of community, conversation, and communion. To share a bowl of soup around a table with others is obviously to do more than merely eat. It is to engage in a conversation in which the private is brought into the public and made the subject of deliberate self-reflection, in which private experience is given public meaning. Thus, to "light up the cave" is to rupture the boundaries that separate the "private" and the "public," to shed light upon our personal beliefs, feelings, and experiences within the context of public conversations about the advancement of social justice, equity, and freedom.

The metaphor of "lighting up the cave" suggests a radical re-reading of Plato's cave analogy. Notice that Sexton does not speak of leaving the cave and coming into the light. Instead, she uses the metaphor of bringing light into the cave. It is not possible to leave the cave. For the cave is not only the "personal" and the "private," it is also the cultural and the historical. We are destined to view the "reality" of the world through our own personal experience, our own position in culture, the historical era in which we live, and the narratives of knowing we use to frame the truth production process. This means as well that there are no truths outside the cave, indeed no space outside the cave from which it is possible to see the world "clearly." But we can still shed light upon the myths and narratives we live by, as Joseph Campbell would have us do. Through critical self-reflection, and through dialogue with others, we can learn to shed light upon what previously we took for granted, so that we are no longer prisoners of truths that do not serve us well. We can illuminate the meaning of the cave drawings, just as we can interpret various texts we read. And by learning to interpret their meaning, we give them meaning within the context of contemporary cultural struggles. That is, we can begin to appreciate the power of myth in a formative sense, in the development of self and culture.

As a mythology of knowing, "lighting up the cave" is related to two overlapping and interlocking themes, both of which are to be found in Plato, although not in the form that I mean to use them. The first of these is *reflexivity*. A reflexive verb is one which has the same subject and direct object— as in the sentence, "She studied herself." The subject, that is the person doing the studying, is also in this case the object of study. Reflexivity thus involves the capacity to reflect upon ourselves: what we take for granted, what we value, what myths guide us, and so on. Reflexivity involves turning our gaze back upon ourselves. Of course, "ourselves" is not meant to refer to our own individual, private selves alone. Since we are both producers of culture and produced by it, reflexivity also involves shedding light on the culture we inhabit and produce. Finally, reflexive ways of knowing are *constructivist*. They treat knowledge or truth as something that is actively produced or constructed in the process of reflecting upon our lives, rather than as something that is "out there" already. Through the process of reflecting on our everyday lives and the beliefs and rituals that guide us, we become more conscious of ourselves as the creators of truth and value. This, in turn, leads to the capacity to assume an active role in re-imagining what could be and re-scripting cultural and personal narratives.

Reflexivity is ultimately only possible within the context of dialogue, the second important theme worth recuperating from Plato. Only within the context of dialogue is it possible to see our beliefs as others see them, to have our beliefs questioned and challenged. Dialogue also brings self-reflexivity into the public. To his credit, Plato was a believer in dialogic forms of education. However, Plato's dialogues are always very carefully scripted to lead to consensus on the good and the true, as Plato sees it. The argument is laid out to proceed through a series of carefully scripted points and counterpoints to reach an inexorable conclusion, to which all must submit. In reading Plato's dialogues one cannot help but feel led down a prepared path, and begin to resent it a bit. This kind of dialogue, where everyone must end up agreeing on one truth, is not, in the end, consistent with democratic culture and forms of reflexivity. But dialogue in a more open-ended, multi-voiced sense *is* democratic. Within such democratic dialogues, there will be opposition between differing viewpoints and sets of interests, and this opposition will not be resolved in some final sense. Indeed, out of the dialectic between oppositional beliefs and worldviews, the dialogue progresses. In this sense, dialogue is a form of communion as well as struggle, out of which new understandings of self and Other emerge. Dialogue provides a way out of the binary opposition between *logos* and *mythos*—between analysis and story-telling, the personal and the public. It is a space in which an analytic light is shed on personal story-telling, and where personal truths are explored for their public meaning. Through dialogic reflection, it may be possible to construct truths and meaning that go well beyond the subjective viewpoints and experiences of the participants—to construct a *logos* that is fragile and always provisional, a *working logos* more than an authoritative and dominating *logos*, a *logos* that is never unified and fixed, but a *logos* nonetheless that lights up the cave.

Dialogic reflexivity provides the new progressivism with one way out of the dilemma of late modern culture, in which the only alternative has seemed to be between logocentrism on the one hand and mythocentrism on the other. Only through the process of questioning, and engaging in dialogue with others in pursuit of answers, does a democratic public actually exist. For out of such questioning in dialogue with others, we begin to have a better understanding of the good and the true. We can expect no final, authoritative, unified truth to emerge out of such a dialogue, but we can shed some light on what we once took for granted, and out of such wisdom we can become freer. Lily Briscoe, a character in Virginia Woolf's *To the Lighthouse*, remarks near the end of that novel that the great revelation had never come in her life. She had expected to one day see the truth, and that truth would set her free. Instead there were little, daily illuminations—"matches struck unexpectedly in the dark."[65] Progressive education might then be appreciated as a way of striking matches in the dark. If so, it is about illuminating one small part of the cave, from a particular position, and with a limited range of vision. If we can still call that a form of enlightenment pedagogy, and I think we can, it is an enlightenment that is much more limited in its claims, more pragmatic in its concerns, and more mythological in its language.

We might look to the French feminist philosophers and fiction writers, Helene Cixous and Luce Irigaray, as examples of this kind of postmodern enlightenment project. Cixous writes in an imaginative, sensuous, metaphoric, and autobiographic language that blurs the lines between theory and fiction, concerns itself with pleasure and desire, and carries multiple, open meanings. Her writing has no beginning, middle, or end as such, and it slips back and forth between poetry and prose. Through all of these uses of language, she seeks to disrupt and subvert logocentric speech and its ruling binary logic, within which women become the great metaphor of the Other. She writes: "Night to his day—that has forever been the fantasy. Black to his white. Shut out of his system's space, she is the repressed that ensures the system's functioning."[66] In her search for a "somewhere else" outside logocentrism, Cixous reads and rewrites the cultural mythology that has constructed the feminine Other—from Sleeping Beauty, to Medusa, to the abyss. Through this subversive and disruptive use of language it becomes possible, Cixous believes, to transport the self into a space "where *it* writes itself, where *it* dreams, where *it* invents new worlds."[67] That is, by combining an analytic attitude of deconstructing dominant narratives that keep women and others disempowered and marginalized, with a creative, expressive, generative power of rewriting these narratives, Cixous sees an opening for new possibilities, new ways of thinking and writing and speaking that are post-patriarchal.

Irigaray's writing, similarly, is based on a deliberate effort to recuperate cultural myths and metaphors to see and think outside the reigning logic of the *logos/mythos* binary opposition. For example, the metaphor and mythology of water has played an important role, she argues, in epistemologies that emerge out of women's experiences, and much of her own writing is an attempt to reflect the fluidity of water, of a language that does not erect fixed boundaries between words and between people, that moves in currents and waves, that has no fixed point of reference or final destination. Of her writing she observes: "These movements cannot be described as the passage from a beginning to an end. These rivers flow into no single, definitive sea. These streams are without fixed banks, this body without fixed boundaries."[68] Elsewhere, she uses the metaphor of the plant to suggest a way out of the binary logic of the Enlightenment, with its separation of darkness (represented by the cave and interior of the earth) and the light (represented by the sun). "Rooted in the earth, fed by rain and spring waters, we grow and flourish in the air, thanks to the light from the sky, the warmth of the sun."[69] Such language is transgressive and subversive, but also playful and creative.

Of course, some staunch defenders of logocentrism might conclude that the acceptance of such language in education, and as legitimate scholarship, is yet another example of how civilization is heading down a steep slope, back into the cave. In contrast, I think it may signal a renaissance rather than a decline. Both Cixous and Irigaray are philosophers, after all, and they are still committed to shedding light on myth and bringing their own poetry and autobiography into dialogue with the critical gaze of reason. This includes a capacity to reflect back upon their own metaphors, to see them as limited and partial, as useful only when linked to other metaphors. So Irigaray suggests that water is fluidity and a body without boundaries; air is a reflective reason; and fire is passion and desire. All need to be understood as interconnected, with each playing its role in the process of knowing and becoming. Our truths and our reasoning about the world never fully rise above cultural narratives of knowing and our own positionality in culture. They are always, in the end, truths constructed within the cave. But by engaging these truths within a public dialogue and bringing them under the lens of a critical rationality, we illuminate the cave from within.

CHAPTER 3

Recognizing Ourselves

Hegel and the Master/Slave
Struggle in Education

In the early 1970s, a new voice began to influence progressivism—that of an exiled Brazilian educator named Paulo Freire. In *Pedagogy of the Oppressed*, Freire developed in a theoretical form many of the basic ideas and approaches to education that emerged out of his literacy campaigns in northeastern Brazil in the early 1960s. At that time, Freire was philosophy professor at the University of Recife and also director of an adult literacy program. The early 1960s was a time of great transition and uncertainty in Brazil, associated with an intensification of cultural struggle between authoritarian populism on the political right and a growing democratization movement on the left. The democratization movement, unfortunately, remained a largely urban and middle class movement, without very deep rhizomes in urban slums or rural villages where poverty, illiteracy, and fatalism were the norm. It was Freire's conviction that democracy would not succeed in Brazil without the support and active involvement of these disenfranchised poor, and one of the effective barriers to involvement was illiteracy. At the same time, Freire had grown increasingly frustrated with existing literacy and adult education programs designed to "serve" the poor. For one thing, they reduced literacy to a series of discrete skills in the decoding of language, stripping language from its use in everyday life to organize power relations. For another thing, literacy instructors generally talked down to people, believing that the immorality and irresponsibility of the poor were the primary reasons why they remained poor. They saw their role as lifting people up out of their pathological lifestyle. Based on his reading of Hegel and Marx, Freire began to imagine an alternative form of literacy campaign, based on the development of two interrelated ideas. The first of these is reflexivity. Literacy only makes sense "as the consequence of men's [*sic*] beginning to reflect about their own capacity for reflection."[1] Reflexivity, in turn, leads to praxis, the "power to transform the world" by thinking about it in new ways, to understand oneself as a producer of culture rather than merely a passive recipient of a given culture.

Through education, Freire believed, people begin to recognize themselves better, which also means that the aim of education is self-knowledge. But self-knowledge is never to be found in isolation. Self-knowledge is always a knowledge accessible to us through identification with a dominant or subordinate social group. Such identity, in turn, has no meaning outside of its negativity, its Other. We are only able to recognize ourselves and gain self-knowledge in our relations with an alterity or alter-identity with which we are involved in an historic struggle. Freire also believed that the dialectic between oppressed and oppressors was leading, as Hegel would have it, to the reunification of all oppositions in a "good society." This takes on almost a religious character in Freire's writing and is associated with his politics of hope. "Hope is rooted in men's incompletion," he writes, "from which they move out in constant search—a search which can be carried out only in communion with other men."[2] This image of communion comes to Freire via Hegel. The desire for communion draws people together in struggle, and draws dominant and subordinate groups toward ultimate reconciliation.

In each village or urban community that Freire and his literacy teams visited, they began by identifying what they called "generative themes," important activities and events in local village life that were coded with meaning. These themes were then translated into pictures and used to facilitate discussion among participants in a "Culture Circle." Lists of important words and phrases were then generated out of discussion and coded into written form. One of the few concrete examples Freire references in *Pedagogy of the Oppressed* is of a literacy campaign in which Freire is not directly involved, with a group of male tenement residents in the slums of Santiago. This example is important because Freire uses it to distinguish between two different types of pedagogy. The lesson is to be on alcoholism, one of the generative themes identified by the men, and this theme has been encoded by the instructor in the form of a picture of a drunken man stumbling down the street, while a group of respectable men talk on a street corner. The instructor begins discussion, wrongly in Freire's view, by adopting a moralistic attitude. He had hoped to use the picture to draw the men into a discussion of how they abused alcohol and the pathetic state of the drunken man in the picture. Yet, the men would have none of this. They immediately identified with the drunken man, defending him against all criticism. In one form or another, all of the group participants commented that the drunken man is "the only one there who is productive and useful." In their narrative based on the picture, the man is returning home after working for low wages all day, and he is worried about how he is going to take care of his family. If he has stopped off for a beer or two on the way home, that does not mean he is no good. "He is a decent worker and a souse like us," they conclude.

By allowing the men to produce their own narrative based on the picture, the instructor was finally able to question his own middle class biases and sense of moral superiority. "Sermonizing against alcoholism" or upholding middle class examples of virtue can only be counterproductive. What "worked" in this case was allowing the men's concerns and questions to direct the dialogue, allowing them to produce their own narrative rather than having one imposed on them. The men produced a narrative that was consistent with their own empowerment, and they represented an incipient critique of the dominant culture's representation of them as drunkards and alcoholics—as if that was the source of their oppression. To the extent that alcoholism is prevalent among the poor, the men viewed it as a symptom of alienation. Finally, the men identified in solidarity with the "souse" in the picture. They recognized themselves in him and thus affirmed a collective identity—in this case an identity based on class solidarity. Of the man in the picture, they argued that he is the "only one useful to his country, because he works, while the others gab." They recognized themselves as the productive force in culture, and thus hardly passive. The men's narrative, Freire writes, is a "codification of an existential situation they could recognize, and in which they could recognize themselves."[3]

What does it mean to recognize ourselves? For Freire, this is the central educational question. Only when people become more conscious of themselves, when they recognize themselves in more complex and empowering ways, do they ever advance toward their own freedom. Only by constructing a sense of collective identity can oppressed groups engage in a protracted political and cultural struggle for recognition of their rights as equal citizens. People recognize themselves in solidarity with others similarly positioned as oppressed and/or marginalized. But this recognition is not enough. They must also recognize themselves in the Other. That is, they must learn that what they see in the Other is their own negativity, an externalization of part of themselves. They must learn that identity is currently constructed in ways that set up power inequalities, and that it can be reconstructed in ways that are more equitable and non-oppressive. Only by affirming and troubling identity simultaneously is it possible for people to recognize themselves in new and transformative ways.

The idea that democratic forms of education lead in the direction of self-recognition is one that Freire borrows from Hegel, and more particularly from Hegel's story of the master/slave struggle in *Phenomenology of Mind*. In what follows, I want to return to Hegel to develop the mythology of recognition and explore its relevance in framing critical, democratic forms of pedagogy. Since Freire's work began to appear in the United States in the early 1970s, a whole discourse on "critical pedagogy" has developed out of it. That discourse has drawn upon a number of different theoretical frameworks and has become increasingly postmodern in its language over the past decade. But it continues to be indebted to Freire's work in significant ways, and thus to Hegel as well.

When Freire was writing *Pedagogy of the Oppressed* one could still speak of "man," "workers," and "oppression" without troubling about their meaning too much. It was still possible to view the "oppressed" as a unified group that only needed to become more self-aware in order to recognize its historic destiny. Now, such idealistic, hopeful, unifying, universalistic language seems a bit dated and "modernist." Still, some things have not changed. Hegel's mythology of recognition is still of central importance in thinking about democratic and empowering forms of education and cultural development. There are also signs that a new Hegelianism is beginning to be forged out of the dialectic between Hegel and his postmodern critics. Perhaps the most well-known example of someone who is moving in these directions is Judith Butler. I thus want to proceed by moving back and forth, from Hegel's story of the master and the slave to Butler's interpretation of that story, teasing out the implications for critical pedagogy and the new progressivism.

HEGEL'S STORY OF THE MASTER AND THE SLAVE

Hegel writes in a manner that seems, as Butler remarks, "to defy the laws of grammar and to test the ontological imagination beyond its usual limits."[4] Words are used without any reference to their meaning, and their meaning changes during the course of their usage. The reader must struggle to find meaning for words and phrases within context of the text, and this means—since Hegel thinks in a dialectical fashion—within the context of their negativity or alterity. Out of this dialectic, this play of difference, the meaning of words like "recognition" constantly changes throughout the course of the text. Rather than attempt to fix the meaning of his language, Hegel means to keep changing its meanings, in the process drawing the reader to higher forms of self-awareness. The only metaphor that remains constant throughout is that of the journeying subject, on an adventure of self-discovery, driven by a desire that is ultimately narcissistic—to know itself. In the process of "knowing itself," or recognizing itself, the self must reconstruct its identity again and again, which means that education is about self-consciousness and self-reconstruction simultaneously. But what kind of journey is this to be, and what is its destination? Hegel weaves together a story of tragic proportions with a storyline that Butler suggests he borrows rather freely from the popular German romance novel of his day, or *Bildungsroman*. Like those mass-produced romance novels, Hegel offers us "an optimistic narrative of adventure and edification, a pilgrimage of the spirit" with a happy ending.[5]

Hegel's traveling subject, Butler suggests, also may be interpreted as a philosophical version of the Don Quixote mythology. Quixote pursues his ideals in systematically mistaken ways, thinking his dreams can be made real. Yet there is little time for grief in Quixote's life because renewal is always around the corner. "Hegel's protagonists," Butler says, "always reassemble themselves, prepare a new scene, enter the stage armed with a new set of ontological insights—and fail again."[6] Quixote is somehow able to learn from his experiences, and because he believes in a cause, is never finally or fully defeated. In reading the *Phenomenology*, Hegel asks us to identity with the Quixote character, "accepting time and again the terms of his journey," indulging with him in "the same exorbitant desires." At the same time, Butler says, the postmodern reader cannot sustain belief in this dream, and so, like Quixote, wakes from its unreality, "but only to dream more shrewdly the next time."[7]

Near the beginning of *Phenomenology*, Hegel lays out his story in its most overtly mythological form in a section on "The Lord and the Bondsman." The title suggests a discussion of a particular form of self-consciousness forged out of the history of serfdom in Europe. Yet it is soon clear that Hegel uses this relationship as a convenient metaphor to discuss a more generalizable phenomenon, one that finds its most ideal form early in Western culture, in the slave societies of Greece and Rome. This is one reason why the section is so often referred to as the story of the master and the slave. These latter terms are also more generalizable in their meaning, even if less accurate when referring to specific contemporary struggles over class, race, gender, and sexual identity formation. So for that reason I will use them rather than Lord and Bondsman. I do so with the recognition that, in American history, there were real slaves and real masters, and that inequality and domination today is not of the same magnitude or kind. Nevertheless, it still exists. Conservatives like to think that the master/slave struggle in American history ended with the Emancipation Proclamation, or later with the passage of the 1964 Civil Rights Act. Or in class terms, it ended with the passage of the Wagner Act in the 1930s that allowed workers to form unions and engage in collective bargaining. In spite of "progress" that has been made in American history, and progress we cannot afford to have rolled back, many of the battles being waged in American culture as we enter a new century were being waged a century earlier. The form has changed, and the character and face of oppression have changed, so that it is less brutal and ugly, less "visible" as oppression, than it once was. To use the language of the master and the slave in a contemporary context is to remind the reader that while much has changed, much remains the same.

Hegel's story begins as two humans approach each other from opposite directions on a narrow road, each seeing in this meeting an opportunity to know themselves better, to have another human being gaze upon them and recognize them as a somebody, a somebody who is worthy of respect and recognition, someone whose freedom they respect. Already, human desire is self-centered, consisting of a desire to recognize or know oneself, and to maximize the self's freedom. Freedom, in this sense, is based on a very low level of self-consciousness. The self does not yet recognize that contradictory nature of its desires: namely, that our own freedom is a dependent freedom, since it only has meaning in relationship with other people, who recognize it. The desire to be absolutely free, a master of one's own destiny, leads to fear between the two subjects as they approach each other, and this leads to a life and death struggle which is resolved only when one submits upon fear of death. One becomes the master and the other the slave. The relation that is established between the two opposing subjects is one of oppression, although Butler observes that this must be appreciated as a form of killing. "The Other must now live its own death. Rather than become an indeterminate nothingness through death, the Other must now prove its essential nothingness in life."[8] In order to maintain the illusion of its own absolute freedom, one subject makes the other serve as a symbol of absolute servitude. In order for the master to represent life and the active force in society, the slave must represent death and passivity. In order for the master to signify "mind," the slave must signify "body." In order for the master to be visible at all times, the slave must be "closeted" and invisible.

The clock of history begins ticking in Hegel's story with the resolution of the life and death struggle. At that point two opposing forms of consciousness are created, of which Hegel writes: "One is the *independent consciousness* whose essential nature is to be for itself, the other is the *dependent consciousness* whose essential nature is simply to live or to be for another."[9] The independent consciousness of masters is characterized by a belief that the self is the creator of knowledge, meaning, and values. Seemingly nothing can stop the self from achieving whatever it desires or block its freedom and autonomy. Masters feel in control of their fate, although ironically they are increasingly dependent upon slaves. The master's language and consciousness affirm that members of dominant groups are their own masters. Its defining narrative (to quote an Army recruiting slogan in a quite different context) is "be all that you can be." On the other hand, the slave's initial dependent consciousness arises out of fear and resentment, and out of the experience of being powerless and not in control of one's own destiny. Out of this experience emerges a whole array of attitudes and beliefs that keep people dependent—everything from feelings of inadequacy and inferiority, to fatalism, to quiet despair, to cynicism, to the solace of a religion that promises a better life in the hereafter. From the slave's perspective, knowledge is something that is received rather than something that is actively produced, and "it is just this which holds the bondsman in bondage."[10] All education for freedom and empowerment thus begins with reflection upon dependent consciousness. Until disempowered peoples begin to be aware of the ways they participate, at the level of consciousness and practice, in their own domination, they have not yet begun to struggle for their freedom. The moment they begin to question dependent consciousness, they are, at least in their own minds, no longer slaves.

I want to be careful not to imply that oppressed or marginalized peoples need to be taught to deconstruct the ideological and mythological beliefs and attitudes that keep them oppressed. The basis for an incipient critique of dependent consciousness, and the beginnings of an assertive self-consciousness, are part of what the "slave" brings to the educative process. The slave, after all, is to be the producer of a transformative and liberatory new way of thinking about the world, and human freedom. Why? In its battle with the master, Hegel writes, the slave "has trembled in every fiber of its being, and everything solid and stable has been shaken to its foundation."[11] Oppressed and marginalized peoples have been forced by the experiences of life to question the master's knowledge, the very foundations under their feet. The long road to freedom advances through a series of "recognitions" or awarenesses, each a precondition for a new discourse and practice of freedom. Within the context of the master/ slave story, as Hegel presents it, these recognitions are associated with three taken-for-granted cultural myths or narratives: the pot and the potter, the Word, and the self in the mirror. I now want to take up each of these in turn, bringing to the surface some of the educational implications embedded in each.

THE POT AND THE POTTER

In Hegel's story, the first step in moving beyond dependent consciousness comes through work, and through the process of producing the "thing." The slave is assigned the task of making the "thing" for the master's use; and through this process the slave slowly becomes more aware of itself as an active maker of culture. By forming and shaping the "thing," even under alienating conditions and according to specifications laid down in advance by the master, slaves as workers begin to realize something that is the key to their eventual freedom. They are producers of meaning. They are the productive force in culture, not their masters. Furthermore, they manage to invest some small part of themselves in each "thing" they produce, to mark it as theirs, as expressing something about them. They slowly become aware that the "thing" is really an objectification and externalization of an inner vision. "Through this rediscovery of himself by himself," Hegel writes, "the bondsman realizes that it is precisely in his work wherein he seemed to have only an alienated existence that he acquires a mind of his own."[12] Through "formative activity," through the actual shaping and forming of ideas into things that take on an independent existence, slaves begin to realize that their consciousness does not really exist apart from the forms it creates in the world, in which it finds itself reflected. This simple recognition recasts the human subject in a creative role, and once the subject understands its potential to actively shape the world, it is no longer quite so dependent and fatalistic. In giving material shape to an inner vision, in shaping and molding the "thing," the slave slowly begins to move beyond a dependent consciousness. Its consciousness will, Hegel writes, "turn into the opposite of what it immediately is. . . . It will withdraw into itself and be transformed into a truly independent consciousness." Meanwhile, as masters lose knowledge of how to keep the machines running, both literally and figuratively, they become more and more dependent on slaves. Thus, the knowing and knowledge of the master "[have] in reality turned out to be something quite different from an independent consciousness."[13]

While Hegel never names the "thing," he seems to refer to the activity of pot-making, for he talks of sculpting and shaping the earth. Pot-making provides a metaphor for all craft production, but it is also a metaphor that draws upon a deeply-rooted mythology of pot and potter. Hegel's story is, in fact, dependent upon the reader investing the "thing" with this wider mythological meaning. The shaping of a pot on a potter's wheel provides a key metaphor for transforming an inner vision into an exterior reality, for objectifying experience to produce something of value. It also provides a key metaphor for self-recognition, for in each pot they make, potters recognize themselves. The pot and the potter serve as central cultural metaphors for the dialectic of consciousness and the material world, with the subject of history cast in the role of the potter. The mythology of pot-making has a long genealogy in Western culture, so that Hegel cannot be said to be the originator of this mythology, even if he did recognize and develop its radical democratic potential. In the Greek tradition, the Pygmalion myth suggests something very similar. As a sculptor, Pygmalion sculpts a statue of a woman, with which he then proceeds to fall in love. The gods have pity on Pygmalion and give his statue life. The statue in this case is clearly meant to be a projection of part of Pygmalion, and his love is narcissistic in that he seeks his own reflection in what he has sculpted. Yet this narcissism is not represented as sinful or evil, but rather—consistent with Hegel—as a necessary element of all productive work. We are always and inevitably finding ourselves, and extending ourselves, in what we produce, and what we produce defines us and gives us form.

A perhaps more influential "source" of this mythology in Western culture comes from the ancient Hebraic tradition. In the book of Genesis, God sculpts Adam and Eve out of clay—in his own image. Later, in the Book of Jeremiah, God comes to his people to warn them about those who would worship multiple gods rather than the one true god. In this version of the myth, God takes Jeremiah to the potter's shed and shows him the various pots there—some on the ground that are cracked and will be discarded, some in the process of being shaped on the potter's wheel, and others already completed. God tells Jeremiah (Chapter 18, verses 5-6), "Can I not do with you as this potter has done? Behold, like the clay in the potter's hand, so are you in my hand, O house of Israel." In this telling of the myth, God is once more the potter, but a wrathful potter who tells his people that he will destroy those pots that are cracked or flawed in some way, that what he has made he can destroy. Such a myth is designed to make people feel that they are not their own creators, nor the creators of meaning. In Hegel's telling of the story, however, god is but a projection of human subjectivity and creativity. Humans thus create god in their own images; they are the potters and god the pot, so to speak. This humanistic version of the story is represented in the "The Rubáiyát of Omar Khayyám," an epic twelfth-century Persian poem translated into English by Edward Fitzgerald in the mid-nineteenth century—where it quickly became a Europeanized signifier of modern, humanistic values. Interestingly, the Rubaiyat's version of the myth of the pot and the potter is based on an explicit re-reading and re-scripting of the earlier version of the myth in Jeremiah, subverting its "original" meaning. The Rubaiyat's narrative declares, "Once more within the Potter's house alone I stood, surrounded by the Shapes of Clay." God is visibly absent, but the narrator does engage other people, other "vessels," in conversation, and they all agree that any god worth believing in would not destroy flawed or cracked vessels. At which point a Sufi speaks up: "All this of Pot and Potter—Tell me then, who is the Potter, pray, and who the Pot?"[14] The mythology of humans as potters, shaping the material world and themselves at the same time, seeing themselves reflected in what they produce, has played a key role in democratic culture and in progressive forms of education.

We find it in Freire's work as well. If education is to lead in democratic directions, if it is to empower and give voice to those who have been disempowered and silenced, Freire suggests that it must begin by encouraging them to reflect upon what is involved in producing pots. Through this, they can begin to recognize themselves as active shapers of the world. Potmaking, perhaps not surprisingly, emerged as one of the central generative themes in Freire's work with the rural poor in Brazil. The picture developed for this generative theme shows two village people working at a potter's wheel, around which a number of completed or partially-completed pots are displayed. Freire's caption for this picture, and the dialogue it is used to generate, is: "Man Transforms the Material of Nature by His Work."[15] In analyzing this work, and how it makes the potter feel, the participants in the Culture Circle begin to recognize themselves as the makers of culture. Interestingly, Freire also draws upon the metaphor of the pot, or vessel, in a different way in *Pedagogy of the Oppressed*. In this case, the student is the pot that has been sculpted so that it can be filled with predetermined, objectified knowledge. Freire argues that dominant forms of education for the poor are based on a "banking" metaphor. Cultural capital is deposited in student's heads, which are viewed as "empty vessels" waiting to be filled. The pot or vessel is understood to be empty until it is filled, and it is entirely passive in performing its role of carrying the knowledge of the dominant culture, of being inscribed and shaped by power.

These two uses by Freire of the metaphor of a pot or vessel may be appreciated as expressions of the two opposing interpretations of the mythology of the pot and the potter I referred to above. One of these uses, in which the student is the potter, is consistent with democratic forms of education, while the other, in which the student is merely a pot or vessel to be sculpted and filled, is consistent with hierarchical and dominating forms of education. We might also, however, think of students as both pots and potters in dominant forms of public schooling. Much of what goes on in public schools, particularly urban schools serving the new underclass, is increasingly about producing outcomes, or "things," according to predetermined specification, "things" like test scores, homework assignments, and portfolios. These "things" are like pots being produced according to predetermined specifications by student workers, under the watchful eye of teacher supervisors. While students are learning to be potters, they are learning to be potters in an alienating sense. The democratic reconstruction of public education in the twenty-first century, in my view, could begin here, by shifting from a dominating to an empowering myth of the pot and the potter. Of course, that is unlikely to occur outside a broader shift in thinking about work as a vehicle for self-recognition.

Butler observes that "we are recognized not merely for the form we inhabit in the world (our various embodiments), but for the forms we create of the world (our works)."[16] In the things we produce, not only do people recognize themselves, they are recognized by others. The production of "things" that others share thus brings us into a relationship in which recognition means self-recognition and also recognition of self by others. One, in a Hegelian sense, comes with the other. By implication, the education of the disempowered and silenced begins, and continues, with the production of "things," a notion that among progressives has been associated with support for the "project method." Students actively engage in producing something as a team, and through the process of production learn the "content" of the curriculum and also become active learners. In the famous Foxfire school in rural Georgia, for example, students produce books based on projects to collect and preserve local memories of struggle for social justice. These are then presented to the community in a special ceremony each year. Through this, the young people learn to recognize themselves within the context of communities with histories that are also in the process of change. They also gain recognition from the community for what they have accomplished in a way that makes them feel satisfaction in their work. The recent progressive movement in all levels of public education toward student exhibitions is another case in point.

A good example of an exhibition, and one with important educational implications, is the AIDS Quilt exhibited on college campuses across the United States over the past decade, sponsored by the NAMES Project Memorial Quilt Foundation out of San Francisco. In this case, quilt-making, which has a long history as a form of cultural production among poor, Appalachian women, is turned into an explicitly representational and political activity. Beginning in the mid-1980s, the Quilt project grew piece by piece, panel by panel. Friends, lovers, and/or family members of AIDS victims produced small quilts that represented, through photographs, words, and images, something by which that person might be recognized. In producing these small quilts, those involved had to reflect on the question of who the person was and how that person would want to be represented. And they had to put something of themselves into the representation, so that it represented not only the dead friend or lover, but their own relationship to that person. These individual quilts then became panels in the larger quilt that was assembled at public events in auditoriums and parks. People were encouraged to walk on paths laid out between the panels, to crisscross their way through the maze of quilts and thus make their own path. Each path tells a different story, produces a different reading. On October 11, 1987, when the Quilt was displayed on the National Mall in Washington, D.C., it covered an area larger than a football field and included 1,920 panels; and it has continued to grow ever since. The Quilt is a "thing" that ritualistically connects people, affirms life in the face of death, and gives the AIDS Other a human face and a voice. Because so many of the panels in the quilt are produced by gay men, the quilt provides an example of an effort by a marginalized identity group to take back control of its own representation, to challenge the dehumanization of gay men and the related dehumanization and stigmatization of AIDS victims. The Quilt is a "thing" that invites multiple readings, that opens up discussion about a number of important issues pertaining to otherness and representation, that helps those who have been disempowered and marginalized take back some control over their own self-production through self-representation. In all of these ways the Quilt provides an example of a "thing" that serves an important educational use-value. It also is an example in which something emerges out of a grassroots response in the community and involves a form of self-education by the community.

THE WORD

> In the beginning was the Word, and the Word was God.
>
> —JOHN, CHAPTER I, VERSE I

> To speak a true word is to transform the world.
>
> —PAULO FREIRE[17]

> All magic is word magic.
>
> —MOLEFI ASANTE[18]

The oppressed recognize themselves through what they produce; and they produce both a pot and a word. The word is language, both written and spoken, understood as a generative force in self and cultural production. Radical democratic mythologies derive from myths and narratives in which words and language are understood to be much more than mere reflections of the "real" world "out there." Language is understood to be a will to freedom, a force actively involved in shaping and giving form to the world, even as language shapes and gives form to consciousness. In top-down religious and political mythologies, this power of the "word" is reserved for god, or his earthly representatives. For Freire, as for Hegel, the word is a tool in the slave's struggle for freedom. The education of the oppressed must involve the use of language. But whose language? To some extent, the oppressed must create their own languages of freedom. But these languages can never really be free of the master's language, for they are constructed in opposition to that language, as its negativity. Only through the active process of negation are dominated peoples able to produce alternative languages, and carve out space for freedom within the dominant culture. This space must, however, always be provisional, and the freedom from the master's language always something of an illusion. Through the production of a language of freedom, according to Hegel, the slave "procures for its own self the certainty of its freedom, generates the experience of that freedom, and thereby raises it to truth."[19] What the slave loses sight of, in procuring for itself the certainty of its freedom, is that its language of freedom is the negation of a language of domination, which it thus does not totally escape. Its language does not make the Other "vanish," although it does mean that the master's language can no longer be taken for granted, that it must respond to its alterity. For Hegel, the essential role of the slave's language is to negate the master's language, for only through its own negation can the master's language change. Yet, in assuming such a role, its own freedom is compromised and it is stuck in a position of defining itself through negation only. There is no easy way out of this compromise, but at least the slave can come to a greater self-awareness that its own freedom is always defined in dialectic relation to its Other. The road to recognition is always taken with the Other. This means that the language of absolute freedom, or of an autonomous identity, is an illusion that stands in the way of progress.

When we apply this Hegelian mythology of language to American cultural politics over the past several decades, it helps illuminate some of the problems associated with "identity politics" and the desire for a language of identity outside the "master's language." This desire is expressed in the oft-cited line from Audre Lorde: "The master's tools will never dismantle the master's house."[20] Lorde was voicing a growing theme within the women's community in the 1980s, and one echoed in elements of the African American and gay communities in the academy. In its most essentialist and mainstream form the argument was that different identity groups have their own "worldviews" or "ways of knowing." Empowerment comes through a recuperation of a womanist or an Afrocentric discourse. I want to focus my comments here upon Afrocentrism, particularly because the Afrocentric movement in education has grown so significantly over the past decade or so. But much of what I have to say applies to other "identity politics" languages, for all are constructed through negation in some fashion. Molefi Kete Asante first coined the term Afrocentrism as professor of African American Studies at Temple University, and Asante has continued, in recent years, to be a key figure in promoting the development of networks of Afrocentric schools. Over the years, his own usage of the term "Afrocentrism" has become less essentialist, although it has not completely escaped from essentializing Africanness, that is, treating it as having a natural essence quite apart from its historic relation with European colonialism. Certainly, African cultures existed before contact with Europeans, and to suggest otherwise is to see Africa only through Eurocentric eyes. Furthermore, pre-colonial cultural traditions continue to play an important part in defining Africanness. Nevertheless, Africanness has been shaped by the colonial experience and the historic struggle against racism in America, and these arguably play a more important role in understanding African American identity in the contemporary world. What it means to be black in America cannot, therefore, be reduced to a set of unchanging cultural traditions and mythologies that supposedly characterize all African people around the world. At the same time, the forging of an Afrocentric discourse can, and no doubt is, playing an important role in the movement beyond Eurocentrism, or at least the current hegemonic form of Eurocentrism that still seeks to "normalize" and thus erase all difference. Eurocentrism now has its Other, and that may make all the difference in moving toward a more multicultural and diverse America.

In his most recent work, Asante has acknowledged his critics. "I have been criticized as an essentialist, a bad thing to be, according to deconstructionists," he writes. His response is that he is willing to recognize that all cultures are open and move around over time, but that "you have to be moving and flowing from some base." Without a base, a platform, a place to stand, you are just "floating in the air." This is consistent with the idea that people who have been marginalized and oppressed within Eurocentric culture need their own languages, their own cultural traditions and worldviews, to provide them with an alternative grounding. Ironically, the firm base Asante seeks to build under Africanness is mythological. It is to be grounded on "the foundations of myths, history, and memories." Asante argues that the dominant Eurocentric culture in America expects African Americans to "abandon their essential characteristics," even as French Americans, Japanese Americans, and Jewish Americans are not criticized for desiring to hold onto their cultural heritages.[21] This is a legitimate point. However, it could be argued that essentialism in any form is still essentialism.

The Africanness that emerged out of Asante's text is grounded upon a number of traditions of myth and memory. Asante begins by saying something about what Afrocentrism is not. It is not, he says, about setting up oppositional dichotomies, such as mind/body, either/or, or truth/myth, as Eurocentric discourse does. Instead, Afrocentrism ruptures all dualisms in the unity of the

circle. Afrocentrism is also characterized as emphasizing *nommo*, "the genera-
tive and productive power of the spoken word." Afrocentric use of language is
thus about "calling forth" *nommo*.[22] Here we come across the mythology of the
Word in an African context. As I have indicated, a similar mythology exists in
European culture and is the basis for a radical democratic view of language.
Nevertheless, dominant or hegemonic forms of Eurocentrism have sought to
repress this mythology of *nommo*, or the Word. Afrocentrism thus brings the
Word back upon the stage, making it a part of human will. The concept of
nommo is closely related to that of *orature*, which Asante defines as a body of
oral discourse, including rhetorical styles used in oral discourse. In America, it
includes sermons, lectures, raps, "the dozen," poetry, and humor. In their most
powerful and radical form, *nommo* and *orature* have combined in the messianic
speech of Nat Turner, Martin Luther King, Jr., and others.

Orature focuses attention away from the literal meaning of words to the
power of the words. It allows *nommo* to be revealed and experienced. Through
the use of body language, register, and movement, the Afrocentric speaker
uses language "in an attempt to create harmony and balance in the midst of
disharmony and indecision." Asante acknowledges that the speaker may also
use rhetorical style at times to create imbalance and tension, since this may be
necessary to bring people together again in harmony. Rhetoric in an Afrocentric sense is thus an art, not a science. It is a creative way of "managing
words and sentences to be effective as a communicator."[23] It includes rhythm
along with style, and a capacity to blend tone, accent, and meaning together.
"Thus *to style* is an action, and when one styles, one is creating a relationship."[24] Another element of Afrocentric style, according to Asante, is that it is
lyrical rather than analytical. This essential lyrical style, he says, is exhibited in
the rap music that originated in urban streets, as well as in sermons delivered
from a pulpit. While Asante finds *orature* prototypically expressed in the black
preacher, he argues that there are limits to this form of Afrocentric oratory. For
example, black preachers may encourage people to defer to them. A "sister"
leaving a Baptist church service may report, "I didn't understand all those
words the preacher was using, but they sure sounded good."[25] Asante supports
a more dialogic, egalitarian *orature*, one associated with the African American
tradition of "call and response." The dilemma for African Americans, as Asante
sees it, is that the further they move toward white culture, the further they
move away from the lyrical and stylized approach to language, and the oral
discourse, in which they learn and communicate best. In public schools, not
only do African American children lose touch with who they are, their linguistic strengths are viewed as deficiencies.

As public schools have failed to meet the needs of African American
youth, the movement toward Afrocentric schools has continued over the past
decade, and at a rapidly increasing rate. According to a 1997 report in the

Boston *Globe*, there are about 400 African-centered schools in the United States, 30 percent more than in 1992.[26] Many of the new schools are "charter" schools within public school systems, although the majority are private schools associated with the Council of Independent Black Institutions, an umbrella organization that provides administrative guidance. Nowhere have Afrocentric schools taken hold as strongly as in Detroit, where twelve of the public schools were African-centered in 1997. Students at one such school, for example, begin each school day with the beating of African drums. The beats are accompanied by both African chants and English verse: "We will live as models to provide new direction for our people. We will be free and self-determining. We are an African people." In another school, the day ends with recitation of an anthem: "We pledge to think black, act black, buy black, pray black, love black, and live black. We pledge to do black things today to assure us of a black tomorrow." Mwalimu Shujaa, a professor of African-American studies at the University of Buffalo, and one of the leaders along with Asante in the Afrocentric movement, is quoted in the *Globe* article as saying, "The emphasis is not on me, me, me. The whole language of reference is kinship: brothers and sisters." Shujaa says African-centered schools certainly believe in academic excellence. Nevertheless, "Our function is not to produce rocket scientists for the military but to produce people morally grounded and spiritually sound. And to develop skills for our national community."

Afrocentrism and other languages of identity tap into a legitimate desire for freedom from the master's language by those who have been marginalized and oppressed by it. With new discursive "tools", the hope is not so much to dismantle the master's house as to leave it to build another house at a safe distance, on a different platform. In such a house, the marginalized presumably will be able to define themselves by themselves, finally deciding what it means to be African American, or a woman, or gay, without having to refer to the Other. The desire for a purified identity apart from the Other is, however, based on an illusory hope. In the end, it may have the effect of reinforcing domination. Afrocentrism does not live up to its promise to provide an authentic African foundation for African American identity. The foundation Asante and others construct, after all, is very much the mirror opposite, the negativity, of Eurocentrism. This means that Afrocentrism does not succeed in leaving Eurocentrism behind at all. Quite the contrary. The platform of Afrocentrism would have no meaning outside of its relationship to the platform of Eurocentrism.

Asante acknowledges that his own understanding of Afrocentrism has grown in response to criticism of its essentialist tendencies. Yet the essence of Afrocentrism still seems to be what Asante is after. He acknowledges the postmodern loss of a "cultural centeredness" among African Americans, represented in the language of hybridity and the emphasis on race as a merely social construction. For Asante, this is unfortunate, because "the culture that we have borrowed defines who we are," and this culture has continued for African Americans to be Eurocentric and oppressive. "By regaining our own platforms, standing in our own cultural spaces, and believing that our way of viewing the universe is just as valued as any," African American people will be about to participate fully in building a multicultural society. In spite of his criticism of Hegelianism and Marxism as Eurocentric traditions, it is clear that Asante has been influenced by both Hegel and Marx, and that he recognizes Afrocentrism as dialectically related to Eurocentrism. Without an alternative platform, and a distinctly different voice, Asante fears that African Americans "bring almost nothing to the multicultural table but a darker version of whiteness."[27] Through the dialectic between Eurocentrism and Afrocentrism, Asante hopes for a "post-Eurocentric" synthesis, a form of transcultural analysis "that would liberate both oppressed and oppressor."[28]

Asante the Hegelian is in dialectic relation with Asante the essentialist. It is, nevertheless, the essentialist Asante who tends to prevail. In one breath he writes that "there are certain essential characteristics that identify the contours of our African American community," and in the next he adds that "these are not immutable characteristics."[29] Which are they to be? Is Afrocentrism the manifestation of an African collective unconscious that persists without significant change over millennia, as he seems to imply, or is its current meaning constructed in a dynamic, historic relationship with Eurocentrism? Asante wants to have it both ways. The trouble is, when this argument is framed in a basically essentialistic way, it does not necessarily lead in progressive directions. Instead, it may actually reinforce inequality and privilege. For example, it is wise to remember that a basic element of racist ideology in America has always been that African Americans and European Americans have very different learning styles and characteristics. African Americans, presumably, learn best when things are kept concrete, since they are not (according to this Eurocentric mythology) abstract thinkers. Instead, they presumably are naturally rhythmical and have strengths in music and athletics. European Americans, in contrast, are presumed to be the "mind" to the African American "body," and can be challenged intellectually. This racist mythology is still often taken for granted today, and Asante may be accused of taking it for granted himself. To the extent that these differences are "real," they are primarily real because they have been historically produced in America within the context of oppressive race relations. Within this context, the "strengths" of African Americans that Asante affirms have been consistent with their representation, as a body that must be kept subordinated to the mind. This is the dichotomy that keeps the Bondsman in a position of dependent consciousness in Hegel's story. Consequently, Afrocentrism may have the unwitting effect of confirming rather than challenging dominant constructions of blackness in American culture. Ironically, Asante critiques Eurocentric discourses for setting up this binary opposition that separates mind from body, yet he works within it himself and tends to essentialize it.

Thus, Asante gets himself in the awkward position of arguing that African American *orature* is to be distinguished from the written word, which he says is more abstract, disembodied, and thus consistent with a Eurocentric discourse. He says of his own writing, which is often highly analytical and abstract, "I may experience hunger, joy, pain, or pleasure while I write. . . . But you would not know that from observing my hands. . . . I might experience the most delightful romantic thoughts while I strike the keyboard to produce unromantic prose."[30] His point is that Eurocentric ways of knowing, expressed in the scientific worldview, are based on the presumption of a detached mind or consciousness that is writing. The body of the writer does not enter into the text, or at least is not supposed to. It is only in public rhetoric, in the spoken word, in the oral traditions of story-telling, that this mind/body dichotomy is ruptured. Yet, how is it ruptured if the body, and thus style and rhythm, are to be the essential "strengths" of African Americans? Doesn't Asante continue to work within the logic of a dichotomy that is Eurocentric, in which Europe is the mind and Africa the body? Why should we presume that writing must be an expression of an abstract "mind" at work? In some forms, writing can be intimate and personally revealing. It can express *nommo* as much as *orature* can. Certainly, African American writers have stirred the public imagination and sense of outrage as much or more than African American orators. Doesn't Asante, after all, write with the power of an Afrocentric *nommo*?

THE SELF IN THE MIRROR

In an essay on "The 'Uncanny'," Sigmund Freud tells a story about riding on a train, half-asleep in his compartment, when suddenly he was jolted awake as the washing-cabinet door across from him swung open. As he sat up, Freud writes, "an elderly gentleman in a dressing-gown and a traveling cap came in." Freud assumes that the man had taken the wrong direction and come into his compartment by mistake. "Jumping up with the intention of putting him right, I at once realized to my dismay that the intruder was nothing but my own reflection in the looking-glass on the open door." What was uncanny about the situation, he observes, is that "I can still recollect that I thoroughly disliked his appearance."[31] Freud provides, in this brief passage, a representation of the myth of the "double," or alter ego, a myth based on the metaphor of the looking-glass self. The mirror signifies seeing ourselves in the Other, but also seeing our mirror opposite in the Other. The Other is an exteriorization of our own subjectivity, a construction of our own ego, a projection of part of ourselves from which we wish to distance ourselves. So Freud projects upon the Other in the mirror an unlikable appearance, affirming his own likability and also suggesting that his own likability is on shaky ground, that the dislikability of the man in the mirror is really a reflection of Freud's own feelings of not being very likable. The Other both affirms our own goodness, and as a projection of the self, always threatens our own affirmation of goodness and rightness. We cannot but fail to see ourselves in the negativity of the Other we have created. If the black Other is supposed to confirm that whiteness is good, moral, clean, and self-disciplined, the black Other also—as a creation of the dominant white culture—reminds whites of a part of themselves from which they have become alienated, and which they project upon black people. Something similar occurs in the production of the gender, class, and sexual Other.

This leads me to a third narrative or myth of recognition embedded in Hegel's story of the master and the slave, the recognition of oneself as one's own "double." This is a recognition that ultimately undermines the continuation of the master/slave myth, for it implies that there is no firm grounding for identity under our feet. To become "integrated," "whole," subjects, we must move beyond the construction of identity by producing an Other. Yet there is no necessary basis for identity in that case. Identity is, in this case, the final illusion of the journeying subject. The recognition that identity is an illusion ushers in a new stage in self-consciousness. It does not mean that our struggles over identity end. For we cannot walk away from struggles over power and inequality that lie behind identity and self-recognition. But as people recognize that identity is socially constructed, they become more open to change, to thinking of new ways of relating that are more equitable. Hegel finds the basis for such a form of recognition in desire, the yearning of the heart, "the inward movement of the pure heart which feels itself, but itself as agonizingly self-divided." History for Hegel is really no more than a "movement of infinite yearning" between master and slave, a yearning to recognize each other's differences without turning the other into an Other.[32] Even the master, according to Hegel, desires to move beyond the master/slave struggle at some level. This is because the slave cannot offer the master the recognition he wants, for it is recognition from someone who is devalued, and it is a recognition not freely given. The road of history, the long ascent towards full self-consciousness, comes close to its final destination, in Hegel's *Phenomenology*, once recognition of the Other as a human subject has been achieved. This is one of the great ironies of the Hegelian myth of progress, that the collective identities oppressed and marginalized people forge out of historical struggle, that make historic struggle possible, are the very identities that keep these same people are thus fighting to abolish.

One strand of postmodernism may be associated with the premise that, for all intents and purposes, we are at Hegel's end of history. At least we can act as if we are, armed with the recognition that identity always has been an illusion, a dance in which both self and Other think they need each other to define themselves, to recognize themselves. Postmodernism thus celebrates a post-identity subject, or at least a subject whose identity is understood to have no more than strategic meaning, a platform for forging a discourse of limited and provisional solidarity. The postmodern suspicion of identity is related to an historical awareness of the role identity has served in constructing and legitimating inequality and domination. In the modern era, identity has become a regulatory mechanism involved in locating the self within binary oppositional power relations, keeping the self under continuous surveillance, and producing the self within the "normalizing" boundaries that police difference.

Judith Butler is clearly sympathetic to this postmodern critique of identity. In her influential book *Gender Trouble*, Butler argues that since the category "woman" is produced as the "double" of "man" within patriarchal culture, it is a representation or a performance of otherness, and an otherness that keeps women in their place. "Woman" is not a signifier of a naturally-given identity. Instead, it is a "regulatory fiction"—a discourse deployed to regulate relations between sex, gender, and desire. Gender is "performative," a "stylization" of body that is reiterated, a series of repeated acts that begin, over time, to assume the character of a natural, stable, unified identity. Through the performance of gender, we produce a gendered self rather than express a natural "femininity" or "masculinity." This is a subtle distinction but an important one. If we are constructing ourselves in performing an identity, then we need to become more reflexive about our own performance of identity. For Butler, resistance to the naturalness of gender categories implies a subversive performativity, a performance of gender that is designed to draw attention to the arbitrariness of gender roles by parodying them. As a rather extreme but nonetheless insightful example of such resistance, Butler points to "drag." She writes: "In imitating gender, drag implicitly reveals the imitative structure of gender itself—as well as its contingency. Indeed, part of the pleasure, the giddiness of the performance is in the recognition of a radical contingency." Such a parody of gender identity, Butler suggests, is not necessarily degrading to women, as some feminists have maintained. Indeed, drag is an overt recognition of the performance of gendered identity since it presumes that there is a distinction between the anatomy of gender and the way gender is performed, and that these need not be the same. It reveals the false naturalization of gender identity, and by "denaturalizing" gender, it makes people aware that "the original identity after which gender fashions itself is an imitation without an origin."[33]

This seems to imply, as her critics have pointed out, a radical view of identity that almost succeeds in eliminating it entirely. Butler backs away from this extreme postmodern position, at least a bit, in her recent writings on Hegel. She continues to believe that, at this historical juncture at least, the subject requires an identity, forged out of "a radical and constitutive relation to alterity," to its Other. This means that there are limits to the idea of moving beyond identity, at least as "the point of departure for politics."[34] She calls for a re-reading of Hegel that returns to the notion that identity is always in the process of deconstructing as well as reconstructing itself. The subject of Hegel's *Phenomenology* constantly finds itself outside itself, a subject for whom there is no possibility of a "return to a former self." No return is possible because there is no recovery from "self-loss." The subject is always recognizing itself through identity. But the moment it finds itself is simultaneously the moment identity dissolves as it is revealed as a mere representation, a performance, a reflection in the mirror. Butler suggests that we understand this self-loss in a positive way, at least potentially. For the self can only find itself through repeatedly suffering self-loss. Where does this leave us? I think it leaves us trying to reconcile identity politics and post-identity politics rather than choosing one over the other. It means learning to affirm identity and "trouble" it, simultaneously.

If we approach Hegel's journeying subject as on an educational journey, we might say that at some point the subject achieves a new level of self-consciousness characterized by a capacity to reflect back on the process of representing or performing identity, a paradoxic self-consciousness of its own role in producing its "double." This is yet another sign of postmodernity, this ironic self-consciousness that identity is representational and performative rather than having any authentic or essential meaning, that, according to Butler "actualization only occurs to the extent that the subject confronts what is different from itself, and therein discovers a more enhanced version of itself."[35] Multicultural education, as that term has most often been used in public education, is about celebrating diversity, at least racial and ethnic diversity. But it may be reconceptualized as the study of the social construction of the Other, of representational practices that participate in "othering." Not that we can expect the Other to vanish. Indeed, marginalized identity groups must continue to affirm their class, race, gender, and sexual identities as part of their struggles for empowerment and human freedom. But they must affirm identities even as they resist playing the Other, deconstruct as well as reconstruct identity.

One way to encourage such reflexivity about identity is through the critical, deconstructive reading of popular culture texts in terms of how identity gets represented and performed. Butler's reference to "drag" as an example of the performance of gender provides a good case in point. Let me point to two popular Hollywood films that approach identity in this manner. Both parody identity by making the process of representation visible, by revealing identity as a performance. The first of these films is *Tootsie* (1982), Sydney Pollack's satirical love story about an unemployed actor named Michael (played by Dustin Hoffman) who, in desperation, decides to audition for an opening in a television soap opera—as the female hospital administrator. Michael becomes "Dorothy Michaels," and is given the part by the woman producer after becoming indignant over a sexist remark by the male director. Dorothy is a huge success in her role, attracting a particularly large audience of sympathetic women who see her as a strong, assertive woman. As an actor, Michael/Dorothy asserts his/her right to interpret the part, to improvise lines, to define the role. And as him/herself, Michael/Dorothy falls in love with a fellow actor, Julie; and one of the subplots in the film has to do with whether or not this budding relationship is homosexual or heterosexual. Michael realizes that in order to have a hetero-sexual relationship with Julie, he must disclose who he really is, even though such a disclosure would reveal him as a deceptive impostor. To resolve his dilemma, he decides to "come out" as a man during a live broadcast of the soap opera, taking off his wig and declaring that he has been cross-dressing all along. As in Billy Wilder's classic *Some Like It Hot,* this film is about role confusion, and about the unsettling idea that men can think, act, and present themselves as women—or at least their representation of "woman." By acting womanness, men are able to experience something of what it feels like to be "woman" in this culture, and to develop a more integrated personality, one that is able to draw upon the "feminine" inside. Where previously Michael was a sexist who treated women as objects, by the end of the film, he becomes a "sensitive" male. He begins to dislike and critique how the men around him treat women, the way he used to treat women. By developing a double consciousness, one that allows him to see the world from both sides of the gender borders, Michael is about to transcend his previous gender identity, to leave the safe harbors of what he had been—which was less than he could be.

As in the film *Kramer vs. Kramer,* in which Hoffman played a "born again" father and husband, a role model for the new man who could treat women as equals, Hoffman as Michael/Dorothy is a role model for the androg-ynous male and female. The film makes the viewer aware of the extent to which masculinity and femininity are "inside" us all, aspects of ourselves that we no longer need to hide or repress. Men, in this sense, are not emasculated but rather enhanced and made better by acknowledging their feminine sides. Of course, this raises troubling questions. If gender is just a performance (as the film implies, at least in one reading), and if we are all equipped by our culture to perform either gender (at least after a little practice), then what does it mean to be a man who lets out his feminine side, or a woman who lets out her mas-culine side? On one level, the film takes the categories masculine/feminine as having natural meaning, as ways of behaving and reasoning that are geneti-cally associated with men and women. At the same time, the film troubles what it means to even speak of "feminine" or "masculine" as if they were sta-ble markers of opposite knowing and being. Its modern Hegelianism lies in its conviction that through their struggles men and women come to know each other and themselves better, that the "feminine" and the "masculine" are really moments in the history of a divided self that, with the modern women's move-ment, is not longer so divided.

This interpretation of the film, framed by what we might call the "sensitive male" narrative, is what most "mainstream" movie critics focused upon in their reviews. But women film critics tended to "read" or view the film somewhat differently, and did not interpret it as a film that encoded a basically feminist narrative for a mass audience. As Barbara Quart observes in her *Cineaste* review, the film "defuses" its ostensibly feminist message, it "renders it safe and pleasurable." It allows "everyone to go home feeling modern and enlightened and yet unthreatened," even to go home feeling that conventional, "old-fashioned" attitudes about gender have been reinforced. The film presents itself as feminist, yet it depends on a man to affirm the potential of the category "woman." As a woman, Michael assumes the role of teacher, leader, administrator—and the film suggests that what makes him particularly good at these roles is that he is a man. "The humor ultimately comes not from her [Dorothy] being a powerful woman," according to Quart, "who undermines the usual gender expectations, but from her being a man."[36] The principal "real" woman in the film, Julie, is still traditionally beautiful and sensuous, as Marilyn Monroe was in *Some Like It Hot*. In spite of all its lip service to women's liberation and feminism, the film takes for granted the objectification of "woman" in a way that has not fundamentally changed from an earlier era. For Quart, the film also represents femaleness as a form of masochism. Julie is constantly moving from one abusive relationship to another. Michael's friend Sandy, in a similar vein, is neurotic, self-doubting, almost hysterical most of the time, used to playing the victim role in relationships with men. "Only Dorothy Michaels is in control." Quart asks, "How heartwarming can it be, then, to hear Dorothy praised by the TV producer as the very rare woman character who is her own person, and thus a 'breakthrough woman' for the show?" She is led to conclude that "perhaps the male viewpoint," and the fact that most of those involved in the writing, directing, and producing of the film were male, explains why "the film stops short of delivering on what it promises." All of this indicates that the gender "positionality" of the viewer or reader cannot be ignored, for that positionality informs their experience, their consciousness, and their interests. Women film critics typically have found more to criticize in *Tootsie* than men film critics have. Who is right? That is the wrong question to ask within the dialectic of identity and consciousness. But we can say that women, because of their positionality, are more likely to be critical viewers, to be able to deconstruct the patriarchal myths that continue to circulate in the film.

Another film that uses the metaphor of identity as drag (in this case racial drag) is Spike Lee's *Bamboozled* (2000), based on the premise that most contemporary popular culture representations of blackness—everything from situation comedies to Hollywood movies to commercialized hip-hop culture—are equivalents of the minstrel show. In using the minstrel show as a central image and theme in the movie, Lee hits upon a key idea. The minstrel show, as it was performed by whites in "blackface" over a century ago, and up through the late 1920s in films such as *The Jazz Singer*, with Al Jolson in blackface, demonstrated the extent to which white culture recognized that blackness was a representation, that one could perform blackness, perform the role of the Other. When whites put on blackface, they became a ridiculous character of their own Other. Similar to when men perform "drag" in women's clothes, the minstrel show both reinforced rigid stereotypes that were oppressive, and at the same time it seemed to parody them, revealing them as no more than an illusion, a performance, an exteriorization of part of the white self. If blackness must be an invisible presence in society, to make whiteness visible whiteness cannot do without its Other. So whites acted the part of the Other. Now, Lee suggests, nothing too much has changed, except that blacks are now the ones performing in blackface. Blacks are now allowed to be a visible presence, but only so long as they put on blackface and act the part of the Other. In the film, the character Pierre Delacroix (played by Damon Wayans) is a self-loathing black television writer for a network that is in the ratings cellar. His white boss, who thinks of himself as a "soul brother," asks him to come up with an idea for a "black show." Angered that the network only seems interested in black shows that reinforce stereotypes, he decides to quit, but then changes his mind and decides to produce a pilot for a show that is so bad, so stereotypical, so racist, that the network will be forced to fire him. The show he produces is "The Man-Tan New Millennium Minstrel Show," a variety program set on a plantation in the antebellum South. The irony is that the network executives love the show, and it goes on to become a hit. African Americans are represented as being divided in their reaction to the minstrel show. Some are offended, while others find it entertaining and insist that comedy not be politicized, that it be taken as "just" entertainment. The show is uniformly a hit with white audiences.

One of the most intense moments in the movie is when two black performers undergo the transformation into the black Other, the minstrel, by rubbing burnt cork across their faces. Bob Strauss, in a review of *Bamboozled* for the Los Angeles *Daily News,* observes that the movie makes many viewers uncomfortable because it challenges their easy understanding of racism. "If we don't like *Bamboozled*," he concludes, "we can always watch TV."[37] There is irony in this statement, of course, for the film troubles the idea, held onto so firmly by many people, that television is just entertainment, that we can turn away from disturbing and troubling movies to a safe haven of television situation comedies that are not to be taken seriously. Once someone has seen *Bamboozled*, it is no longer possible to hold onto this comforting illusion. One begins, wittingly or unwittingly, to read television as a racial text, to approach it in terms of representational practices. One begins, ever so haltingly, to develop a representational reflexivity, in which the aim of reflection is nothing other than the relationship between self and Other.

Here again, parody plays an important role in denaturalizing "blackness," and (by implication) "whiteness." In the postmodern cinema, satire takes the form of parody, which may ultimately be the most subversive form of satire; and in recognizing parody as parody, we recognize the ways in which identity is performed and might be re-performed. In assuming the historic representation and performance of the minstrel, African Americans take on the representation created for them and designed to oppress them, to make them the Other. If there is humor in this, and there is for both black and white viewers, it is reflexive humor—a deeper humor, a humor that does not cut itself off from rage and struggle. *Bamboozled* forces white people to acknowledge their own representations of blackness as socially and historically constructed and as oppressive and degrading. At the same time, it forces black people to question the extent to which they perform the equivalent of a minstrel in their own everyday lives and interactions with whites, the degree to which they stand before the mirror and rub burnt cork into their skin as they prepare to perform a contemporary version of blackness. To "view" and critically discuss a film like this, one must also study and discuss a whole history of representations of blackness in Hollywood. Lee suggests just such a project in the concluding segment of the film, which consists of a montage of Hollywood images—from Stepin Fetchit, to animated cartoons depicting blacks in exaggerated forms and actions, to Al Jolson in blackface singing "Mammy" in *The Jazz Singer,* to Bing Crosby and Judy Garland playfully "blackening up" with shoe polish, to the "great" epic of D.W. Griffith's *Birth of a Nation.* Surely this last film is the barely visible but always present Other in Lee's film. In that film whites in blackface portrayed blacks as fools and rapists. How much progress has been made, Lee seems to be asking, if now African Americans are portraying themselves as the Other?

It is love, or as Hegel would say, desire, that lies behind this harsh and bitter film about the legacy of racism in America. For Lee is interested in confronting both blacks and whites with their own complicity in hegemonic representational practices and norms that still regulate the performance of racial identity in America. Of course, some people were not ready for the love behind this film when it was released. They were not ready to think satirically, ironically, and reflexively. Since so many people, both black and white, stayed away from *Bamboozled,* and perhaps even went out of their way to avoid it, we should not be overly optimistic about the transformation in thinking about race and representation that is reflected in the film. Most moviegoers still prefer a Hollywood film that makes them feel good for the moment, that makes them forget rather than remember, that encourages them to take identity for granted rather than question it. Indeed, this is one of Lee's major points in the film. We cannot look to Hollywood to give us too many of these types of films. It is only Lee's established success, and his disregard for making a profit on the movie, that makes a film like *Bamboozled* possible. Hollywood is still in the business, by and large, of producing minstrel shows for both black and white audiences.

OF STOICISM AND SKEPTICISM

The word "recognition," which is so critical to Hegel's mythology, eludes having its meaning fixed, and resists being pinned down on a table to be dissected. Yet in one way or another all meanings of "recognition" refer back to the self, and to self knowledge. Socrates said that to know oneself is the primary educational aim, and this remains true in Hegel and in the tradition of critical pedagogy that has been most heavily indebted to Hegelian mythology. In important ways, this means that critical, democratic forms of pedagogy must appeal to people's narcissistic desires. They must appeal to each individual's desire to know herself better, each individual's desire for freedom and recognition. Progressives have never been very comfortable in acknowledging this, for they have been among the strongest critics of the commercialized, commodified "culture of narcissism" that emerged in America in the post–World War II years. Indeed, the desire for self-recognition, for self-knowledge, has been directed toward brand-name identities, toward recognizing ourselves in the products we consume and the commercialized logos we wear. We are increasingly led to recognize ourselves as consuming subjects, as style without substance or core. In this way, our identities can be reprogrammed and reconstructed to meet new consumer "needs." But this is only one form that the narcissistic desire for self-recognition takes, albeit one that is very powerful at this point in history. All struggles for human freedom and equality are, in the final analysis, motivated by the desire to recognize oneself as no longer a slave, to be recognized by others as someone who is worthy of respect, as a "human" rather than an "animal." One trains animals, but one educates humans. The final recognition to which self-consciousness leads, in Hegel's story of progress, is of our common humanness or humanity. We move beyond "othering" practices, at least in this Hegelian sense, by forging a new identity, one that brings us all under the umbrella of the human. To turn other people into "Others" is to dehumanize them, to turn them into creatures of Plato's cave. This means that a pedagogy of the oppressed is about humanizing those who have been dehumanized. Freire writes: "While both humanization and dehumanization are real alternatives, only the first is man's vocation. . . . It is affirmed by the yearning of the oppressed for freedom and justice, and by their struggle to recover their lost humanity."[38]

Tennessee Williams' play, *A Streetcar Named Desire*, may be read as a story of Hegel's journeying subject, although now on a journey that has taken a postmodern turn, a journey in which there can be no safe harbors or happy endings to either personal or cultural development. The play begins as Blanche Dubois is about to reach what she hopes will be her final destination, her sister's flat in the French Quarter of New Orleans. She has boarded a streetcar, significantly named "desire," for it is desire that has driven her throughout her life—even if she has displaced her desire for recognition with her desirability as a sexual object for men. Here, in the supposedly safe harbor of her sister's world, she hopes her desires for wholeness, for completion, for recognition and respect, for a life that is not defined by continual struggle, will at last be realized. Upon hearing that she has arrived at her destination, she looks around at the dismal surroundings and asks the streetcar driver whether she might have gotten the wrong directions. Can she be lost? Still lost? Her stop is Elysian Fields, site of a former cemetery, symbolic of a purgatory between heaven and hell, between hope and despair.

Butler writes of Blanche Dubois' journey, "What kind of journey is desire that its direction is so deceptive?"[39] The desire to find herself, and know herself as a stable, unified subject has been behind Blanche's journeying, and now it turns out that this desire has been deceptive. The modern subject is like Blanche and her journey, Butler suggests, follow grand narratives of desire toward a promised land, a final destination, "relying on occasional moments of recognition as a source of merely temporal redemption."[40] Blanche, as the postmodern subject, is a homeless wanderer grown a bit cynical, a bit disappointed that life has not lived up to her hopes and desires, yet now perhaps—and for the good—beginning to no longer live for some promised future, but for here and now, making purgatory a home. If she seems to have lost her way from the modernist standpoint, some would say it is hardly getting lost at all. Rather it is a way of finding oneself. And this finding, this recognition, is always—as it is for Blanche—to be found in the "kindness of strangers," in the recognition offered by fellow human beings who treat one with respect and human dignity. The recognition of those we feel closest to is important, surely. But in a democratic society, the kindness of strangers is essential as well. What kind of education produces kindness to strangers? It can, in the final analysis, only be an education that encourages people to see something common in us all, to dare to dream of a world without masters and slaves.

This leads me to one final subplot in Hegel's story of the master/slave struggle. That is the myth of losing ourselves, and finding ourselves again. Hegel viewed dependent consciousness as the initial form of consciousness that characterized the slave. But even when people do critique slavish consciousness and the forces that keep them oppressed, Hegel suggests that they do not necessarily struggle for their own freedom and for human freedom. They may adopt attitudes and beliefs like Blanche that represent forms of getting lost on the road of history. As examples, Hegel points to two closely interrelated intellectual and philosophical traditions or impulses in Western culture—*stoicism* and *skepticism*.

Stoicism's aim, Hegel says, is to "maintain that lifeless indifference which steadfastly withdraws from the bustle of existence . . . into the simple essentiality of thought."[41] The stoic self withdraws from the world in order to uphold transcendental ideals of Justice, Truth, and Goodness. Only in ideas, in Plato's pure forms, is it possible to escape the corruption of this world. As a philosophical movement in ancient Greece and then in Rome, stoicism celebrated qualities of quiet endurance, a refusal to participate in social injustices or evil, and a retreat from the world into a monastic existence. Perhaps the most famous stoic hero of the pre-Christian era was Epictetus, a philosopher of the first century C.E. Born a "barbarian" of unknown origins, he was brought as a slave to Rome and there made to serve a particularly cruel master. According to legend, the master one day twisted Epictetus' leg merely to see how far he could twist it without breaking it. Epictetus reportedly told his master in a quiet voice, "You will break it"; and when this in fact happened, he observed, "Did I not tell you that would happen?" Epictetus' quiet passivity and indifference to whatever the fates dealt him served as an important lesson in stoic living. There are no accounts of how Epictetus gained his freedom, but he did at some point and decided to become a philosopher. This too he was somehow able to achieve, thereby proving that even "barbarians" can become "enlightened." As a philosopher, Epictetus led a life of simplicity and virtue in a small hut with no furniture except for a bed and lamp. His philosophy was based on complete fatalism or indifference (*apathea*) to everything external—including pain and pleasure, poverty and wealth, sickness and health. One of his best known sayings is, "Do not seek to have events happen as you want them to, but instead want them to happen as they do happen, and your life will go well."[42] Within the early Christian Church, stoicism found its purest expression in monasticism and in the teachings of Saint Augustine. The monastery became a place where pure virtue and pure truth could be affirmed, where one was not tempted or corrupted by the evils of the world. And it is in monasteries, in the Middle Ages, that the intellectual and scholarly life was pursued and where the first universities were established.

By the early modern era monasticism was taking on a more secular form. We find it, for example, in the myth of the "ivory tower"—an ideal that the sixteenth-century French humanist Michel de Montaigne sought to realize in his own life. Disillusioned with the brutal and seemingly ceaseless wars that were sweeping across Europe at that time, Montaigne retreated to a country home, in one corner of which he built a tower. There, he occupied himself with introspective and autobiographical writings and with study. His tower retreat had three levels or stories in it, each a bit more removed from the world than the one below it. The ground floor of the tower was a chapel, an area where Montaigne met with others and participated in common prayer. Above that was a bedroom "where I frequently sleep in order to be alone." The third floor of the tower was devoted to a library—a space entirely for the mind. Because it was in a tower, the library had rounded walls, all of which were lined from floor to ceiling with books; "and so with one glance," he wrote, "I can view all my thousand books about me." Here he felt most at home, removed from his family and society. The lesson Montaigne drew from this is that "we should all of us set apart for ourselves a little back shop, wholly free and our own." There, he felt, it might be possible to "establish our true liberty."[43] Freedom and liberty are here understood in terms of a personal autonomous space, outside of the struggle, a space where one might live an ethical, enlightened life. Since Montaigne, the myth of the "ivory tower"—a space "outside" the "real world," a place of "sanity" in an "insane world"—has become one of the defining myths of progressivism in the liberal arts academy.

Skepticism has its philosophical origins in that Greek tradition that proceeded by questioning everything, finding contradictions in all arguments, doubting all. Skepticism "deconstructs" everything—that is, tears it apart to reveal its contradictions and the holes in its logic, to reveal the power relations served by truth, and so on. Now, critique, or (in more contemporary terms) deconstructionism, certainly is an important part of progressivism, and must continue to be. But Hegel associates skepticism with a tendency to remain at the level of critique or deconstruction—which is a nihilistic activity. Such intellectual nihilism is a sign that the self has adopted a basically negative attitude toward others, desire, work, and thus life. Of the Skeptical Self, Hegel writes, "Point out likeness and it will point out unlikeness . . . ; and when it is now confronted with what it has just asserted, it turns around" and asserts the other.[44] The Skeptical Self is one who cannot commit to anything proactively, and in this thinks it has attained some freedom. But true freedom must be made through collective struggle, and by locating oneself within the scene of the battle.

In contemporary American intellectual culture, we appear to be in an age of skepticism and stoicism, although I think there are some signs that we may be moving out of such an age into a new, more hopeful and intellectually engaged age. The 1960s were characterized by the surfacing of the engaged, public, or organic intellectual. Scholarship was oriented towards the burning issues of the day—the struggle over civil rights, the Vietnam War, women's issues, and gay liberation—and authors positioned themselves within the struggle. In education, it was an era in which an increasingly sophisticated critique of the current system of schooling was linked to visions and models of education organized around a radical democratic mythology and sense of experimentalism. The boundaries between the classroom and the world "outside" began to rupture, and new educational spaces were created. Much of the scholarship of that era was unrealistically hopeful about changing the fabric of life in American education and culture. But at least it held onto hope, and it was committed and engaged. We might think of the post-civil rights era, the era of the "conservative restoration," as characterized by the rise of stoicism and skepticism among progressive academics. Increasingly, progressives looked to an esoteric, highly abstract, structural Marxist theory of how schools participate in "reproducing" class inequalities. Resistance by students and teachers was accounted for within reproduction theory by making them part of the system of domination. Individual resistances, even group resistance, were viewed in terms of how they ultimately played a part in keeping people disempowered. There seemed to be no way out of this neat, rational, highly complex and elaborate theory of ideological domination. It was possible to deconstruct any proposals for doing anything, except to sit back and wait for the revolution which would one day supposedly come—if a bit behind schedule already.

Today, reproduction theory is no longer fashionable, at least in its most deterministic forms. But it has been replaced by a deconstructionist theory that in some forms is not much better. Reproduction theory at least affirmed certain democratic ideals, even if it offered no hope of realizing them, no path to follow. Today, far too much scholarship involves little more than a nihilistic deconstruction of everything—from popular culture to the work of one's colleagues. It also involves what Cornel West calls "epistemic skepticism," the ironic presumption that it is impossible to establish any sound basis for choosing one truth or myth over another, that there are no rational foundations for any truth claims. West sees a complex relation between epistemic skepticism, "historical cynicism," and "political impotence."[45]

Nevertheless, Hegel's story is one that gives us reason to hope that stoicism and skepticism are merely detours on the road of history. For within the heart of withdrawal from the world, within the core of disappointment in the world, lies an implicit belief in a better world. Every critique of the dominant culture, every refusal to participate in it, is a silent affirmation of something that should be or could be. The problem with stoicism and skepticism is that they fail to provide a basis for advancing towards that vision of a better world. Because Hegel believed that progress would lead toward that utopian vision, he had faith that stoicism and skepticism would not win out in the long run. Today we can no longer be so certain. But if there is to be a new progressivism, it will be because progressives have emerged forcefully out of the age of stoicism and skepticism, because they have found a way of linking a theoretical language of critique with a public language and with social movements in the public. It will be because progressives have learned to speak not only as gadflies who critique the dominant culture from "outside," but also as "insiders," positioned within various cultural struggles. This is what Antonio Gramsci, the early twentieth-century Italian neo-Marxist, meant by "organic intellectual," and what Henry Giroux means by a "public intellectual." The engaged intellectual is someone who helps oppressed peoples find a voice and a language to articulate their interests, empower themselves, and build and sustain a collective movement for change. For West, democratic ideals continue to be important, perhaps even more important, as we move into in a cynical postmodern age—ideals associated with the moral claim that everyone should have equal status, that everyone warrants dignity, respect, and caring, "especially those who are denied such dignity, respect, and love by individuals, families, groups, social structures, economic systems or political regimes."[46] Within such a context, there can be little room for stoicism or skepticism.

CHAPTER 4

Zarathustra's Education

Nietzsche and Postmodern Progressivism

In the background of much educational discourse is the ghost of Zarathustra, Nietzsche's great hero or anti-hero, the "overperson." For the most part Zarathustra remains an invisible presence, although occasionally his name is invoked. Take, for example, this brief reference. In an essay on "Education and Dogma," Richard Rorty observes that "even ardent radicals, for all their talk of 'education for freedom,' . . . do not really want the high schools to produce, every year, a graduating class of amateur Zarathustras."[1] Rorty makes this comment within the context of a discussion of how progressives might respond to the conservative criticism of both secondary and higher education in America. That criticism was articulated most persuasively in the 1980s by two individuals, E. D. Hirsch and Allan Bloom. Hirsch argued in his book, *Cultural Literacy* (1986), that American secondary education was producing a generation of cultural illiterates, without much of an awareness of the great cultural traditions and "great ideas" of Western society. The solution was to reorganize secondary education around a cultural literacy curriculum, with an emphasis on learning about the Eurocentric canon of great books, "ideas," and "thinkers." Allan Bloom, meanwhile, took on higher education in *The Closing of the American Mind* (1987). There he argued that radical faculty had taken over the university, faculty brought up on Hegel and Marx and the militancy and dogmatism of the late 1960s. The commitment to the Platonic ideals of reason and the pursuit of truth that supposedly had guided the liberal arts academy had been replaced by a Nietzschean celebration of Dionysus and childish nihilism. Bloom, like Hirsch, called for a return to approaches to education that emphasize both a study of a Eurocentric "canon" of great books and great ideas, and a return to a dispassionate, autonomous reason. Most progressives rushed to criticize Hirsch and Bloom, but Rorty suggests that there was some limited truth in what they had to say.

As it turned out, secondary public schools have become places of anti-intellectualism, and of socialization that is understood in a very narrow sense—basically conformity and discipline. "Hirsch is dead right," Rorty writes, "in saying that we Americans no longer give our children a secondary education that enables them to function as citizens of a democracy."[2] And higher education has, according to Rorty, too often been about replacing the "truths" students learned in high school with an alternative set of politically correct "truths." What, then, might progressives put forward in the way of a response to Hirsch and Bloom, a response that does more than dismiss them? According to Rorty, Bloom is right in thinking that higher education too often is about indoctrinating young people with politically correct truths. But he is "dead wrong" in thinking that the point of higher education is to introduce young people to "the theoretical life" or the great "truths" of Western civilization. "The point of nonvocational higher education is, instead, to help students realize that they can reshape themselves." What does it mean to reshape oneself? For Rorty, to reshape is to "rework the self-image foisted on them by their past, the self-image that makes them competent citizens, into a new self-image, that they themselves have helped to create." Secondary education, Rorty argues, can be ceded to the cultural conservatives, to produce culturally literate young people, who are familiar with "what their elders take to be true." Socialization, after all, must come before individualization. Higher education can promote individualization by "inciting doubt and stimulating imagination," by encouraging young people to challenge the "prevailing consensus." If elementary and secondary schools go about their business of producing culturally literate citizens, and colleges go about their business of producing "self-creating individuals," then the battle between progressives and conservatives can be resolved in a new, negotiated manner.[3]

In making his case, Rorty draws upon a dominant (if somewhat simplified) reading of Nietzsche's Zarathustra myth. Zarathustra's education begins by adopting the metaphorical role of the camel, submitting to the dominant culture's truths, learning all one can about what the dominant culture values. He then takes on the role of the lion, deconstructing the truths of the dominant culture and revealing them as oppressive. Finally, Zarathustra assumes the form of the child, the one who is engaged in his own creative self-production, the maker of a new culture. Rorty, without using this language, suggests that elementary and secondary education should recapitulate the stage of the camel, and that higher education should recapitulate the stage of the child. One obvious problem, from a progressive standpoint, is that Rorty almost ignores completely the role or stage of the lion. When are young people to learn to be critical readers of the histories and representations produced by the dominant culture? Nietzsche would be critical of any approach to educational development that left out the role of nihilism, a deconstructive attack upon the master's truths and values to reveal the historical purposes they have served. The child can only emerge after the lion has done its work. This, then, is one problem with Rorty's progressivism. He fails to adequately value the importance of this second stage in Zarathustra's education, or re-education. But there is another problem with Rorty's interpretation of Zarathustra's education. Modernism always has understood developmentalism as a linear, sequential, one-directional development, whereas Nietzsche troubles any attempt to understand Zarathustra's journey of self-discovery as linear. For Nietzsche is guided by the myth of an "eternal recurrence." All development involves a circling back over where one has been to see it from a new perspective. So Zarathustra is able to overcome himself by incorporating into himself three distinctive but interrelated moments of education and self-development, characterized by the camel, the lion, and the child. Education is a continuous process of circling back over the camel, the lion, and the child. This suggests that Nietzsche would resist Rorty's developmentalism, preferring to understand all education, at all levels, as organized around these three moments.

While I think Rorty is wrong in his interpretation of the Zarathustra myth, and I disagree with his conclusion that secondary and higher education should be organized in quite different ways, I do think he is insightful in recognizing that Nietzsche brings something into progressivism that is lacking in Hegel and Marx. The new progressivism, for good or bad, is increasingly influenced by Nietzsche as much or more than Hegel and Marx. In this chapter I want to explore some of that influence. Like Plato's cave analogy, Nietzsche's story of Zarathustra has been open to diverse readings and cultural politics in education. It is a myth that tells a very generalizable modern story of progress, both individually and culturally; and this is one of the reasons it has served so many different interests. In recent decades, the Zarathustra myth has been a subtext in a number of different discourses in education, some of which are decidedly liberal and reformist. It is associated with approaches to art education, gifted and talented education, and creativity education, and with the psychological language of "self-actualization" and individualization. But there has always been another, more radical side to Nietzsche and the Zarathustra myth. Nietzsche is the prophet of the postmodern, and the Zarathustra myth also has been a subtext in recent postmodern discourses of "radical freedom" and "radical democracy." The radical democratic reading of Nietzsche is closely associated with the work of Foucault, who has become the most influential theorist of the postmodern among progressives in the liberal arts academy.

In Nietzsche, the journeying subject is no longer—as with Hegel—part of a larger unity; nor does it have a destination as such. The purpose of education is not to give people a sense of a coherent history of the progress of the "human spirit," nor to lead the journeying subject toward the unification of all truths and the resolution of all difference. Rather, its aim is precisely to reveal the self as lost, beyond recovery of some authentic self it once thought it was, and without an internal coherence or unity. The self only finds itself in the play of difference, in being different from others—although this difference need not be of the kind that organizes master/slave relations. So, perhaps most centrally, the Zarathustra myth suggests a pedagogy designed to promote difference rather than conformity or uniformity.

Zarathustra, as an heroic exemplar of the "overperson," has achieved a reflexivity that is of a higher sort than most, and lives according to his own truths and values. Because of this, the notion of the overperson has carried elitist connotations in many usages. The radical democratic reading of this myth, however, approaches the overperson as an example of a new and higher form of human consciousness that is potentially egalitarian, a form of consciousness that no longer needs an Other to negate in order to affirm itself. Nietzsche does in fact emphasize again and again that the overperson overcomes him or herself, not others. To overcome oneself is to reconstruct the self in ways that no longer oppress or dominate others. All people are thus potential overpersons. But is Nietzsche's overperson really free to create a self-image and identity without the need for an Other? That is the question that frames my reading of the Zarathustra myth, and that will need to be confronted openly if we are to recuperate Zarathustra as an exemplary type of progressive teacher and student.

It may well be that Luce Irigaray is right when she argues that "woman" is the primary Other in a Zarathustra's education, that Zarathustra's freedom and development into an overperson is dependent upon a class of nurturing mother-women. Or women are represented like Penelope in Homer's *Odyssey*, the good wife who waits at home while Ulysses goes on his adventures of self-discovery. And when he returns, what will he and his fellow adventurers have to say? "Won't they once again boast of sailing against the current? Or charting their course against winds and tides? Of overcoming the elements? Of inventing new machines to master them more completely."[4] They will laugh at the dangers they have faced and craft their adventures into an epic narrative, one they can share with the women and children—before they take off on their next adventure. The category "woman" is constituted in the process as a space of domesticity that is only a brief resting space for the child-god, a source of nurturance for his journeys out. The other "Other" in the Zarathustra myth may be the working class and poor, who are no longer understood to be the vanguards of progress. In various forms, the Zarathustra myth expresses a basically bourgeois, liberal-humanist mythology of individual and cultural development in its celebration of radical freedom and autonomy, along with difference or pluralism. Nevertheless, there is irony in Nietzsche's bourgeois sense of cultural politics. To Nietzsche the middle class is not really distinguishable from the working class. Both have had their identities reconstructed as herd animals in state schools and universities, and both have traded their agency, their "will to power," for a sense of security and a life of consumerism. In spite of the fact that Zarathustra's freedom is classed and gendered, progressives might still look to the core themes embedded in this myth of a journey out, reading it now as a mythology that applies to all of those who have been dominated and controlled, and socialized and "schooled" to be part of the herd.

NIETZSCHE/ZARATHUSTRA

Zarathustra is Nietzsche at his most accessible, bringing philosophy into the public discourse over the course and direction of modern, Western culture. It has, like Hegel's story of the master and the slave, become part of the taken-for-granted mythology of modern culture, told again and again in the popular media, lived out in various ways. At the same time, it is expressive of a cultural mythology of individual and cultural development that was already "out there," beginning to emerge within the very core of modern culture by the late nineteenth century.

The story begins with Zarathustra, the mythic hero, in the process of ending his retreat from the world of people to the world of nature. At the age of thirty, Zarathustra had retreated into the mountains. There he had lived alone for ten years, sleeping each night in a cave, the metaphoric womb or chrysalis within which he undergoes a slow metamorphosis, finally emerging as the "Übermann" or "overperson." Zarathustra's retreat from the world of humans to the world of animals may be understood, educationally, as a retreat out of the dominant culture, to get back to the "natural" way of living and thinking as much as possible. In order to develop new beliefs and values, the old ones must be cleared out of our heads, so to speak. The return to the animal world takes the form of learning the wisdom of three animals he befriends—a lion, an eagle, and a serpent. Nietzsche makes abundant use of animal imagery in *Zarathustra*, with each animal representative of some psychological attitude, some particular way of being in the world. It is unwise to read Nietzsche's animal imagery as having a fixed, unified, symbolic meaning. Instead, each animal carries diverse meanings, even somewhat contradictory meanings. As cultural archetypes, animals are signifiers that imply much, and in often subtle ways. Nevertheless, the lion represents, in a general sense, the attitude of assertiveness, of being proud and assertive of one's rights as opposed to being meek and submissive. And it is the lion, as I have said, who leads the attack upon the master's truths and values. The eagle soars or takes flight above the conventional norms of the day in an awe-inspiring flight of fancy. It is the creative spirit that knows no bounds.

The serpent, in contrast to these other two animals, seems a less obvious choice. Within the Judeo-Christian tradition, the serpent is the primary symbol of Evil, an Evil that reveals itself in the form of temptation and the desire for knowledge. In the Garden of Eden story, the serpent tempts Eve to eat of the tree of the knowledge, including the knowledge of good and bad, which is to say a sense of ethics, of what is just and unjust, right and wrong. God has placed Adam and Eve in the Garden to live as part of the natural, animal world, to be content, like the other animals, to live like them, without the capacity to think critically, to reflect upon their own condition, to control their own lives and see themselves as the makers of their own truths and values. Nietzsche, of course, sides with the serpent, and thus with Eve, the first great existential hero in Western culture. The dominant reading of this story, at least since the early centuries of the Christian era, has emphasized Eve's actions as the first sin, have represented this first rebellion as a rebellion against God's paternal authority that has to be punished. Nietzsche, then, suggests that we need to recuperate some of the traditions of existential rebellion, of the asser- tion of human freedom, within various cultural traditions—including the Judeo-Christian. By using the serpent in a positive sense, Nietzsche also means to play with the idea that what the dominant culture considers evil may, from the perspective of oppressed or marginalized groups, be "good." To assert one's freedom, under such circumstances, is to engage in behavior that many in the dominant culture consider bad—such as speaking back to power and authority, standing up for one's rights, and so on. While Nietzsche obviously means to associate the serpent with the Garden of Eden myth, it is also likely that he means the serpent to represent something else as well. Joseph Campbell has observed that, in many indigenous cultures, "The serpent sheds its skin to be born again, as the moon its shadow to be born again."[5] So we might say that Zarathustra too is engaged in the process of shedding a skin, undergoing a metamorphosis, that education proceeds through the shedding of old ideas and rituals for new ones.

When Zarathustra returns to the world, coming down from his mountain cave to the villages in the valley below, he shares what he has learned with others through a series of sermons or speeches. In his journey into society, Zarathustra is not very successful in stirring most people out of their herd-like ways of thinking, of convincing them that they no longer need be herd ani- mals. Others look to Zarathustra as a new prophet and cling to everything he says as if it were the word of god. But he has not returned to the world in order to assume power over people. Zarathustra has returned to tell people that they must learn to lead themselves, assume responsibility for creating their own truths and values.

At one point in his journey, Zarathustra retreats to the "Blessed Isles," a symbolic space that takes on contradictory meaning. The inhabitants of the Blessed Isles are, by and large, philosophers, artists, writers, and creative indi- viduals of various sorts who have withdrawn from the dominant culture and are engaged in building a community of artist/intellectuals. Zarathustra feels at home here, and his intellectual batteries are charged. In the inhabitants' common understandings, their shared language, their appreciation of intellectual dialogue, Zarathustra finds a model for an educational space that is apart, and certainly the liberal arts academy of his day is part of what Nietzsche is parodying. Yet he also is clear that some version of a Blessed Isles where people go to build communities of affinity, to live outside the dominant culture and its taken-for-granted binaries, to engage in their own re-education, may be necessary for all who would be overpersons. The trick is to make the Blessed Isles a temporary retreat rather than a place of residence, to cross back and forth across the borders that separate the Blessed Isles and the mainland.

The trouble with those who live on the Blessed Isles, according to Nietzsche, has to do with their failure to engage in productive work. They are philosophers who do not write and do not wish to sway people's thinking, they are artists and poets who have been transformed into artistic and poetic critics, and their criticisms are kept only for themselves—for the few. Zarathustra feels at home on the Blessed Isles and is tempted to stay, for these are like-minded people who can understand and appreciate what he has to say, who can help him formulate his ideas more clearly. At the same time, Zarathustra rejects the idea of making anyplace his home, and this one in particular. It is the place of bourgeois intellectuals, content with their books and their discussions of philosophical ideas, not a threat to the dominant culture. In one sense, they have been turned into herd animals as much as the "rabble." Here Nietzsche shows a capacity to critique his own stratum of academics, busily engaged in discussing lofty ideas in state-supported universities, paid for and kept by the State precisely to insure that they do nothing of value, that they have no impact on the everyday lives of most individuals. Nietzsche thus proposes a form of philosophy, and by implication a form of pedagogy, that relocates philosophy and education within the everyday lives and experiences of people. To be a philosopher, and to teach, is to go, as Socrates did, into the streets, to engage in dialogue with people as they go about their work and play, never separating learning from life. However, Nietzsche suggests that the Blessed Isles may still serve an important role in education, as a place of temporary retreat from the world that allows one to re-enter the world with new energy and a fresh vision.

It is significant that while he is on the Blessed Isles Zarathustra is in his most anti-democratic and elitist frame of mind. It is here that he presents his public lecture on the "rabble," implying that there may always have to be a "rabble." But here Nietzsche is not declaring that the "rabble" are by nature an inferior lot and there always will be inferior people. Far from it. That idea, indeed, is just what he is criticizing. There must always be a rabble within a binary world that constructs a "rabble" in the very process of constructing an elite that is not the rabble. Nietzsche means to suggest that the rabble are a social category. The trouble is that many of those who have been defined and produced as the rabble have begun to believe that they are. This is a central point upon which Nietzschean cultural politics pivots, and it is associated with that very Nietzschean word, *ressentiment*. The German word *ressentiment* is sometimes translated in English as resentment. But as Nietzsche uses it, *ressentiment* implies much more than resentment.[6] It is the psychological disposition of moralizing one's suffering, and it takes on several different forms. First, those "slaves" who endure suffering may blame themselves for their sad lot, believing it is deserved and that God is punishing them for being morally corrupt and sinful. In this case, they displace their moral *ressentiment* upon themselves. This is the position of those who are paralyzed by self-pity, and self-condemnation, who feel unworthy of freedom. A second form that *ressentiment* takes is blaming various Others for our troubles, various identity groups who become convenient scapegoats for a whole range of personal and social discontents. The cultural politics of the right, as Nietzsche saw it, played into *ressentiment*—of both types. In the German cultural politics of Nietzsche's time, for example, the right sought to displace the *ressentiment* of the working class upon Jews and various Others (including gay people), a displacement that would lead in time to a genocidal "final solution" to the problems of the German people. Yet another form that *ressentiment* takes is characteristic of a middle class cultural politics that we would identity as liberal in contemporary America. The liberal pities the poor and approaches them from a position of moral superiority, with a condescending attitude. The poor and the dispossessed need neither their own nor other's pity, Nietzsche says, and the middle class needs to get beyond its feelings of moral superiority. In all of these forms, *ressentiment* is reactive. Rather than self-assertion and self-affirmation, it keeps us locked in master/slave categories, unable to "think" of ourselves outside of these relations of alterity.

After many long journeys, the story of Zarathustra ends with his return to the mountains and his cave, presumably to prepare for his next metamorphosis. This time, however, he has brought along with him a number of others, the so-called higher men who are ready to undergo their own metamorphoses. We leave our hero as he rises from the cave to greet the morning sun and begin his daily work. Those who have followed him still lie sleeping in the cave, the womb within which they are undergoing a metamorphosis. Zarathustra's cave is an obvious reference to Plato's cave in the *Republic*. In some ways, then, Nietzsche's story may be interpreted as a re-telling of Plato's story of the long ascent out of the cave toward enlightenment. However, Nietzsche re-scripts the story of the ascent out of the cave in important ways. For Plato, the ascent out of the cave means leaving the "animal" world behind to ascend toward pure mind, pure reason. Nietzsche does not believe in an abstract, ideal, or spiritual realm to which one can ascend. So when

Zarathustra leaves the cave, it is not to ascend upwards toward a heaven "out there" in the cosmos. Rather, it is to descend out of the mountains and return to society. For Nietzsche, overcoming involves becoming aware that we inhabit the earth, the material world and our own bodies and desires, that there is no other or "higher" realm, that we are the makers of meaning. Like Hegel and Marx, he understood belief in an "afterworld" as a form of world weariness, a "weariness that wants to reach the ultimate with one leap, with one fatal leap."[7] Nietzsche would have us replace the myth of leaping into heaven with the myth of leaping over ourselves here on earth. Humanity, he says, is defined more by what it is becoming than what it is: "Life itself confided this secret to me: 'Behold,' it said, 'I am that which must always overcome itself.'"[8] Elsewhere he says: "Man is a rope, tied between beast and overman." What is great in humanity is that it is "a bridge and not an end," "an overture" rather than a "finished symphony."[9] Zarathustra stays connected to a primal animal way of knowing, even as he crosses a bridge that transforms the merely animal into an animal self-consciously engaged in its own evolution.

Zarathustra's journey of self-discovery and self-creation is meant to serve as an example of how people might begin to live their lives in a postmodern world. Nietzsche is the great critic of modern culture, but he recognizes that modern culture carries within it the potential to transform itself and usher in a new historical era in which the promise of human freedom becomes real. But his hopeful message is mixed with fear. For Nietzsche/Zarathustra sees that modern culture is about to reach the edge of an abyss of its own construction; and unless it can make the leap across, it faces an apocalyptic future, a great fall. Myths of the millennium and the apocalypse are subtexts in Nietzsche's story, and his intent is to confront progressive educators and intellectuals with the urgency of their mission. In the very first village he visits after his return from the mountains, a circus is in town and he watches as a tightrope walker crosses a divide. His words to the people of the village are allegorical. Modern culture is the tightrope walker and it faces "a dangerous across, a dangerous on-the-way, a dangerous looking-back, a pregnant possibility hovering over nothingness."[10] At the end of his journey, or at least this phase of it, Zarathustra is no longer warning people about the abyss. He has come to believe that it is too late for warnings. The apocalypse is already fated, willed into existence by late modern culture as its own nihilistic death wish, as a will to wash the slate clean and begin anew.[11] It is the role of the artist, poet, and intellectual, Nietzsche believed, to help people confront the abyss as a human construction, a projection of late modern culture, and thus as a negation of modern culture that does not have to be actually carried out in an apocalyptic reality, that we can will ourselves across. Now, more than a century later, we are beginning to see the divide more clearly, and are beginning to name it as an ecological, technological, economic, and military crisis—all of which draws us toward either self-destruction or self-transformation. We still can choose between these two, Nietzsche suggests, although the time is growing late. It remains to be seen whether Zarathustra the child will re-emerge to make the creative leap across Nietzsche's abyss. But Nietzsche clearly sees that as the child's role at this historic juncture.

EDUCATION AND THE THREE METAMORPHOSES

While *Zarathustra* is written in the form of a journey of self-education and thus is filled with educational imagery and meaning, I want to focus now upon Zarathustra's explicitly educational sermon or speech, which is the first he gives after returning from his mountain retreat. This is a speech that is titled "Three Metamorphoses," and in it he suggests that an education for those who would be overpersons must lead through a series of metamorphoses. Some would place these in a hierarchical order, but that kind of linear, hierarchical thinking was not what Nietzsche had in mind. Education, rather, proceeds by moving from one to another attitude or stance, and circling back over these attitudes again and again. If Nietzsche is known for only one idea in the popular consciousness, it may be that of the "eternal recurrence," and this idea has relevance here. Education involves a journey that is cyclical, that leads from one form of reasoning back to another. In modern developmental psychology, learning moves from the attitude and worldview of the child to that of the "mature" scientist. For Nietzsche, that would privilege the scientific way of knowing over the child's way of knowing. Both are needed, and the borders between them need to continuously be crossed and subverted. So education is a journey that has no destination, as linear journeys do. It is a spiral dance that leads to the ongoing change and development of the self toward greater freedom. Each cycle in the educational journey is different, and opens up new possibilities. Each cycle also brings a recurrence of that which we never rise above and which is part of the human condition—uncertainty and insecurity, struggle and failure. A Nietzschean education cannot offer people the comfortable illusion that they always will be successful at what they set out to do. Failure is as much a part of the learning process as "success," and it is a particularly important part of the learning process for those who would set high expectations for themselves. However, failure is only a sign of personal unworthiness or weakness if you let it be. Zarathustra suggests that we laugh at our failures and move on.

The three metamorphoses are symbolized by the camel, the lion, and the child, and while Nietzsche clearly means that each is part of a cycle, so that none has a necessary priority, he does nevertheless present them in an this order. As we shall see, Nietzsche's ordering of these metamorphoses or stages in self-development subverts the "normal" ordering established in developmental psychology. The education of the overperson begins as the student undergoes the first metamorphosis, to become a camel, "the strong reverent spirit that would bear much."[12] The camel bears the weight of the knowledge stored up in books and in libraries, the knowledge of the various scientific and humanistic disciplines—the natural sciences, mathematics, literature and the arts, history, human psychology and sociology, and so on. The student at this stage is humble in the face of all that is to be learned and "kneels down like a camel wanting to be well loaded." The pursuit of truth and understanding drives the student to endure much, with little concern for material wealth or payoffs for learning. To become an overperson one must first, like the camel, spend time "feeding on the acorns and grass of knowledge and for the sake of the truth suffering hunger in one's soul."[13] The hunger in the soul is a desire for freedom and for self-assertion; and Nietzsche is suggesting that in order to be free the student must first take on the difficult work of studying what the dominant culture has to offer. In this case, Nietzsche would seem to be in agreement with Hirsch and Bloom, along with Rorty. At some point, before it is possible to challenge the dominant culture and what counts for knowledge, one must know this dominant culture and what it values. One must assume the role of the humble seeker of knowledge and endure great burdens without haughtiness. One must set as an aim the consolidation of past knowledge, and to do so one must—deliberately and self-consciously—adopt an attitude of pious reverence, of respecting "dead" knowledge.[14] But this humbling of the self before the truths and virtues of the dominant culture, and its histories of great ideas, is always understood by Nietzsche to be strategic and provisional. It is merely a moment in a broader project of freedom and self-production. One learns the knowledge of the dominant culture both to gain what one can from it, but also in order to turn on it and deconstruct it more effectively.

In the loneliest desert, Zarathustra says, the camel undergoes a metamorphosis and becomes the lion—the one no longer content to submit in silence to the knowledge of the dominant culture. In this stage of the self-education, self-reconstruction process, those who have lived according to a slave morality, submitting to the knowledge of the dominant culture and its representation of the past, begin to assert themselves through what Nietzsche elsewhere calls "critical history." This is an attitude toward the past that demystifies antiquarian narratives of the past to reveal the power and interests that lie behind these narratives, to reveal the myths that they take for granted. But the lion must go farther than this, beyond a critique of dominant narratives that seeks to replace one narrative of history with another. Ultimately, the lion must aim to destroy all meta-narratives of history, all notions of an origin or beginning, and all teleologies and utopian visions of an "end of history." This place beyond critical history is what Nietzsche called "genealogy" or "effective history," in reference to Aristotle's notion of "effective causality," that causality related to will and desire.[15] Foucault's histories are, in this Nietzschean sense, "effective" histories. They are histories of the deployment of the will to power in all of its diverse forms, histories that are designed to promote a certain shocking self-consciousness: that nothing is stable enough to serve as a basis for self-recognition and identity, that no original, unified foundations exist for truth and values. Foucault observes that "'Effective' history deprives the self of the reassuring stability of life and nature, and it will not permit itself to be transported by a voiceless obstinacy toward a millennial ending."[16] The self learns, through effective history, to face the abyss of meaning, to harbor no illusions, to face up to its own radical contingency and freedom. In a general sense, the lion phase of development involves a protracted battle with the dominant culture, engaging the enemy on every front, resisting all attempts to naturalize the world or establish truth and value upon firm foundations. Every "Thou shalt" uttered by the "great dragon" is to be resisted. Sacred values, thousands of years old, are to be questioned and treated as "illusion and caprice." The lion says "no" to all past duty, and in so doing promotes an anarchy of all values and truths. Fundamentally critical, the lion can never say "yes."

Nietzsche makes it quite clear that the lion is not the creator of new truths and values. But "the creation of freedom for oneself for new creation—that is within the power of the lion."[17] The lion establishes a certain space, a certain freedom from the truths and values of the master, that is necessary in order to bring forth the new. In the academy, we might say that critical theories of schooling that explore how schools serve to produce and reproduce relations of inequality in the larger society proceed from the position of the lion. Such theories play an important part in unmasking the power that stands behind the organization of public education, revealing racist, classist, and sexist subtexts in what young people learn in schools and classrooms, and thus breaking the spell of the dominant, commonsense understanding of the role of public schools as institutions designed to provide everyone with an equal opportunity to get ahead. Such theories, to the extent that they become more influential in culture, also promote a "crisis of education" and a breakdown of traditional forms of authority and legitimation. To this point, we may say that Nietzsche is only revising Hegel a bit. The camel represents a form of dependent consciousness, and the lion represents the resistant, rebellious slave.

But even the rebelliousness of the slave, in Nietzsche's view, is fundamentally limited in its capacity to create the conditions for freedom. One more metamorphosis is needed. The lion must metamorphise into the child. For Nietzsche, the child symbolizes a complex nexus of attitudes and orientations towards learning. It is symbolic of "innocence and forgetting, a new beginning, a game, a self-propelled wheel, a first movement, a sacred 'Yes.'"[18] The lion's role is primarily destructive, and it is driven by anger and resentment. At some point, those who would become overpersons must let go of anger and move beyond nihilism. Nietzsche is often criticized for being the prophet of nihilism, for celebrating nihilism. If this is so, it is only because he believed that new truths cannot be created until old ones are challenged and unmasked. The creation of new truths and values, however, requires a quite different attitude and way of knowing, one that moves beyond nihilism to creativity. As Gregory Smith observes, "Deconstruction must lead to reconstruction."[19]

The child is indeed a powerful and archetypal symbol for such a reconstructive attitude. To create new truths and values, and thus to project ourselves beyond where we are, people need to become forgetful and once more innocent. The child represents a capacity to play again, to engage the imagination in creative flights, to begin new projects that go beyond where we have been—and it is precisely this capacity that Nietzsche suggests leads people in the direction of freedom. The child corresponds to what Nietzsche elsewhere calls the "supra-historical" attitude, an attitude of no longer living in the past, of no longer looking to the past with nostalgia, reverence, or to find grand narratives that stir the soul. A supra-historical attitude treats the past without reverence, drawing upon it as a reservoir of cultural symbols that might be used to tell new stories, using past events and persons metaphorically and symbolically, without concern for what "really" happened, or who someone "really" was. The critical historian asks, how has the past been turned into a set of codes and symbols to tell a story that legitimates dominant power relations? In contrast, the supra-historical historian looks to the past like a child, pulling ideas and images from the past and juxtaposing them in new ways. The supra-historical attitude is a combination of an "historical" and an "unhistorical" attitude, of remembering the past and also forgetting the past. Nietzsche suggests that if people have no historical memory, they are not really able to govern themselves. At the same time, a people unable to forget the past, or who treat the past with great reverence, are not able to creatively go beyond the past.[20]

In all of its various characteristics, the childlike attitude is a variation on what Nietzsche elsewhere called the *Dionysian* spirit. In *The Birth of Tragedy*, Nietzsche's earliest work, he distinguishes between two movements or expressions of the will to power in classical Greek tragedy, both of which he argues existed in a dialectical relationship to each other. The god Apollo represents that which creates harmony and balance, the organizing and ordering impulse, self-discipline. Nietzsche argues that the Apollonian impulse is needed to give strength to one's character and one's art. The Apollonian is in some ways another version of the camel, who carries the burden of the disciplines. In contrast, Dionysus is the symbol of that which constantly threatens to destroy all forms and codes, which defies all constraints and norms. In *The Birth of Tragedy*, Nietzsche did not extol one of these two cultural impulses at the expense of the other, although he (like Freud) suggests that Apollo needs to be in control more than Dionysus.[21] Later, Nietzsche began to shift the balance towards

Dionysus, at least for this transitional phase of cultural development. Nevertheless, what is important is that Nietzsche regarded both Apollo and Dionysus as necessary aspects of education and self-development, each balancing the other.

Interestingly, in the 1960s and 1970s, the Zarathustrian impulse in American culture found expression in a counter-culture movement that celebrated the release of the "inner child." Educationally, the counter-culture movement was associated with the establishment of a whole network of "free schools," "open classrooms," and "schools without walls" built around a commitment to student freedom and self-exploration. Teachers were to help facilitate learning, but otherwise do little to interfere with the radical freedom of students to creatively direct their own self-education. Non-conformity was the norm, and "play" was valued as an important aspect of education. Many of these schools made a difference in the lives of many working class and poor students who might otherwise have dropped out of school. For many middle class youths, they provided a space outside the numbing conformity of public school and corporate life where they could begin to question the dominant culture and engage in the creative production of themselves as individuals. The limitations of counter-culture forms of education, however, were also considerable from a progressive standpoint. The emphasis upon student freedom to "do your own thing," on creativity, self-expression, and play, tended to become an end in itself. It served no higher purpose. This was related to the fact that the counter-culture movement generally represented a movement away from direct engagement in the political process and involvement in the struggle over the control of public educational institutions. This disengagement from the political realm meant that the counter-culture was not effective in mounting a counter-movement to the restoration of conservative cultural politics that began with the election of President Nixon in 1968. This may be contrasted to the other major youth movement, in the 1960s that invoked the word "freedom," represented by the "freedom riders" who went South in the summer of 1963 to register black voters and by the student anti-war movement in the late 1960s. Both the freedom riders and the anti-war movement were implicitly or explicitly more indebted to Hegel and Marx than Nietzsche. The split between those indebted to Hegel's mythology and those indebted to Nietzsche's played a significant role in dividing oppositional movements in the 1960s and early 1970s, and it continues to divide progressives. Nevertheless, it may be that both need each other, and that democratic progressivism in the coming decades will need to be forged around the intersection of these two progressive mythologies.

ROMANTIC PEDAGOGY AND *DEAD POETS SOCIETY*

Nietzsche is important not only because he radically rethinks education as a process of becoming, but also because he is always concerned with what it means to an educational leader, and what it means to "teach" in ways that encourage individuals to undergo these metamorphoses. Zarathustra is, first and foremost, a teacher, and Nietzsche suggests that cultural leaders should be teachers rather than Plato's Lawgivers, helping people develop their talents and become more free—which also means free of the teacher. As Richard Schacht observes, Zarathustra as educator, "is anything but an instructor, from whom information is received or rules and procedures are learned."[22] Instead, a Zarathustrian pedagogy strives to restore people's instincts, intuition, spirituality, creativity, and sense of adventure. Thus, Zarathustra tells those who would be his disciples, "One repays a teacher badly if one always remains nothing but a pupil." Their task, he says, is to "lose me and find yourself."[23] It is simplistic, however, to understand Zarathustra the teacher as having only one persona. At times, the Zarathustrian educator must be a representative of the truths and values of the dominant and dominating culture, calling upon students to submit to these truths and values. At other times, the educator must instill a sense of rebelliousness in students, encouraging them to turn on the dominant culture's knowledge and the teacher's own pedagogical authority. At still other times, Zarathustrian educators must encourage students to create their own truths and values.

In its dominant liberal-humanist form, the Zarathustra myth is consistent with a romanticized view of both the teacher and the student. It is transformed into a story with an heroic teacher, one who returns to the company of his fellows to stir their souls, ignite their passions, call them to be more than they are. This is the teacher that comes across in Leslie Thiele's popular text on Nietzsche and "heroic individualism." The teacher, Thiele writes, must be a solitary soul, "one who simultaneously incarnates the philosopher, artist, and saint."[24] Zarathustra as educator is the philosopher always asking questions, the poet engaging students in the aesthetic dimension of learning the romantic rebel calling upon people to cast off their mind-forged manacles and be free, and the Dionysian, encouraging people to express themselves and explore their own desires. Kieran Egan characterizes the romantic impulse in American culture and education with an array of interrelated concerns and characteristics. Romanticism encompasses "delight in the exotic," a celebration of the freedom of individuals, a revolt against conventionality in all forms, a belief in the power of imagination and creativity, an "intoxication with the sublime in nature," and intense concern for self knowledge and self inquiry, a "resistance to order and reason," and so on.[25] In its "original" form, Romanticism is associated with a Eurocentric canon of great, white, male, rebel poets. Blake, Wordsworth, and Coleridge set the Romantic style, and Shelley, Keats, and Byron attempted to live that style. For the romantic, the creation of works of art and poetry "came to be seen as the most heroic activity open to human beings." This activity was transformed into a duty by those presumed to be of special sensitivity and genius. The romantic teacher/artist teaches/creates from "a mysterious center of the self," a "sense of reality found within."[26]

This romanticized myth of Zarathustra surfaces in one of the more popular films about teaching of the past several decades, Peter Weir's *Dead Poets Society* (1988). The film is set at Welton Academy, an elite boys' preparatory school in the New England countryside, in the year 1959, at the high point of the culture of conformity and docility that gripped American public life. The film opens with a ritual in the school chapel marking the beginning of the new academic year. We see the usual pomp and circumstance, the procession of administrators, trustees, and esteemed faculty in traditional academic robes, the symbols of power, privilege, and tradition. A lit candle, symbolizing the "light of knowledge," is passed down from the headmaster through the rank ordering of boys assembled in the school chapel. The headmaster ritualistically asks the students, "What are the Four Pillars?" They, as a chorus, reply: "Tradition, honor, discipline, excellence." The introductory comments by the headmaster refer to Welton's reputation as the best preparatory school in the United States. It is about educating tomorrow's leaders, about the pursuit of excellence. So the film asks us to consider what "excellence" means in education, especially if we look to private preparatory schools such as Welton Academy as symbols of excellence that "lowly" public schools should try to emulate.

At Welton Academy high school age boys are inducted into leadership and privilege through a rigid system of hierarchical authority and subordination. Privilege is passed on from father to son, but only after the sons have been beaten into submission, turned into docile conformists ready to play their part in maintaining the status quo. The faculty teach in a traditional manner, following a traditional liberal arts curriculum, with heavy doses of "pure" (non-applied) math and science, European literature, and classical languages. Excellence is achieved through memorization and recitation, the conjugation of Latin irregular verbs, and the solving of abstract algebraic equations. And the boys, except for a few vain efforts at resistance, pretty well submit to this state of affairs fatalistically. They accept being herded around and lectured at, made to conform to a strict set of rules, and loaded down with homework. To this extent, they have at least learned to be good camels. Into this pastoral setting walks John Keating (Robin Williams), a new, young literature teacher who is himself a graduate of the school. Keating is obviously a reference to Keats and the spirit of romantic poetry that Keats symbolizes. Keating thus will remain an elusive spirit, entering upon the stage without attachments or a past to speak of, and finally leaving Welton to move on to an indeterminate future. Like Zarathustra, Keating is on a journey that can have no final resting.

His mission at Welton, as he sees it, is to call upon a group of young men to live "extraordinary lives," to not be content with the futures their parents have mapped out for them. Others tell the students that what counts is the math, and the science, and preparing to get into a good college to get a high-paying job. Keating dares them to live their lives for poetry and adventure, to think of their lives as more than jobs and money, to "seize the day" (*carpe diem*). This is the primary attitude they are to adopt in their education and their lives—which, after all, are synonymous. To help develop this attitude, Keating begins his first day of class by leading his students out of the classroom and into the hall, to stare at the photographs of former Welton boys that line the halls, young faces full of life, just like them—except those young faces, he tells them, "are now pushing up daisies. . . . We are all fodder for worms." This is to be taken as an existential shock treatment of sorts, wakening the boys to the moment and to engagement in living by confronting them with their own mortality. Rather than choose to live ordinary, drab, routine lives, he says, why not choose to live "extraordinary lives," full of passion and wonder?

Fast forward, to the next day presumably, and what seems to be the beginning of a very drab and ordinary lesson. As Keating sits behind his desk, he listens to the boys read from their textbook, *Understanding Poetry*, by Dr. J. Evans Pritchard, Ph. D. The author has written an introduction to the text that provides a scientific and mathematical framework for assessing the worth of a poem. Each poem is given a score for "perfection," which is plotted on the horizontal line of a graph, along with a score for "importance," which is plotted on the vertical. It is a simple matter, then, to calculate the total area of each poem and determine its "greatness." As students take turns reading from this introductory essay in their texts, Keating is drawing a graph on the chalk board, and the boys copy what he is drawing in their own notebooks. This is all very predictable and comforting to the boys, and no one questions the absurdity of rating poems according to a mathematical scale, to arrive at a statistical indication of their "greatness" or excellence. The student's job is simply to follow directions and arrive at predictable conclusions. But suddenly Keating turns on them, parodying a teenager on a popular television show. "I like Byron so I'll give him a 42. But you can't dance to him." As the boys begin to loosen up, he pushes them toward a nihilistic act of rebellion, to tear out the opening essay by Dr. Pritchard and rip it into shreds. "Excrement! That's what I think of Dr. J. Evans Pritchard," he says. Dr. Pritchard represents educators who would classify and measure everything, reducing human understanding and appreciation to a mathematical formula, who would have students follow predictable formulas to arrive at predictable and conventional truths. In this class, Keating tells them, "you will learn to think for yourselves again." But he does much more than challenge them to "think for yourselves," to form their own reasoned judgments as to what is true and good, and what is not. Poetry is not to be read to evaluate it on a scale of greatness. It is to be read and written "because we are members of the human race," he says, a human race that lives for passion, beauty, romance, and love above all else. His job is to convince them that they are actors in a "powerful play," in which everyone is called upon to contribute a verse.

A fellow English teacher who has witnessed Keating's unconventional approach to teaching warns him over lunch that he is trying to turn his students into artists, that is not his job, that his students later will hate him for encouraging them to live unconventional lives. Keating calls the teacher a cynic, although the teacher replies that he is a "realist." This introduces a central tension in the film that undermines somewhat the romantic code that Keating represents. Keating calls upon young people to live like poets. Yet the film suggests that the "realist" teacher may be right, that unconventional people and poetic heroes ultimately get squashed—at least if they push the system too far. Keating may be tolerated in Welton, but his is a type of teacher that does not last long in any school, for he finally ends up calling on students to revolt against their teachers and parents, to subvert the "normalizing" aims of education. Zarathustra the teacher is a journeying teacher, moving from one school to another, never staying long anywhere, and this is only one stop on Keating's journey.

The "Dead Poets Society," it turns out, is a literary society that Keating helped organize when he was a student at Welton. He and a group of fellow students, along with occasional girls from nearby preparatory schools, and supposedly a few daring young teachers, would meet in a nearby cave and read poetry—both the great romantic poets such as Shelley, Keats, Byron, and Whitman, but also poetry of their own. In the cave, Keating remarks, "Spirits soared, women swooned, and gods were created." Here is Zarathustra's cave, with members of the Dead Poets Society transformed into those about to undergo a metamorphosis, emerging as "gods." The name "Dead Poets Society" is taken from a line by Thoreau to the effect that dead poets are dedicated to "sucking the marrow out of life." Dead poets are poets whose poems are treated as corpses to be dissected, turned into studies in rhyme pattern, style, and meter, and scientifically analyzed in poetry textbooks. Poetry is inherently about life, Keating implies, so a living poetry must be killed in order to present it to students as part of the canon of great poetry. To take poetry seriously, and recapture a romantic attitude, one must thus feel and experience poetry more than study it. Poetry is the passageway to the Dionysian release of creativity and thus Nietzsche's will to power. Inspired by Keating, some of his students recreate the Dead Poet's Society and begin to view themselves as artists and adventurers, as extraordinary people. As a result of all this, one young man, whose father has determined that he is to be a doctor, decides for himself that his real calling is acting. When the father finds out that his son has secretly been performing in a production of *A Midsummer Night's Dream* (an obvious symbol of the release of the Dionysian impulse), he withdraws him from the school and transfers him to a military academy, at which point the son commits suicide. Keating emerges as the scapegoat of choice for the suicide, for he encouraged the young man to act. As he is booted out of the school, he receives at least a symbolic victory when his students stand up on their desks in protest when the headmaster attempts to take over his class.

In the end, the Hollywood code of retribution must be affirmed. The rebel poet/teacher may be the hero in the film, but he must not be allowed to upset the delicate balance of order and discipline that supposedly holds society together. He must pay for his transgressions. And what exactly are these transgressions? Keating has encouraged only a youthful defiance, a short-lived rebellion. He has done no more than encourage young men to take poetry seriously and to live for today. This is hardly subversive stuff, or is it?

Keating's message, and his pedagogy, are subversive of the established order at Welton Academy, and of the purpose of the schooling process to control young minds and bodies, to make them submit to a numbing institutional routine and authority structure, to make them what Herbert Marcuse called "one-dimensional" men. The film suggests the power of poetry as one of the pathways to developing a radical critique of the dominant culture, and a radical desublimation of the repressive, over-socialized, modern self. Unfortunately, so long as poetry is only romantic, so long as it romanticizes and individualizes the search for meaning and "extraordinariness," it may not lead toward engagement in socially reconstructive change. At no time does Keating politicize poetry or try to engage his students in the great battles brewing in American public life. He never critiques Welton's elitism, nor its removal from these battles. Nor is gender or race ever made the topic of one of Keating's conversations with his students. The only females in the movie are the girls who participate in the cave rituals, who seem to represent Dionysian sirens; and race is a visible absence in the film. Its absence is legitimated by locating the movie in the 1950s, when schools like Welton Academy were not integrated. But since the film was made in the late 1980s, this "whiteness" could have been made a topic of deliberate reflection and comment. Nor do gay people exist in this film, although some critics have suggested that Keating may be a closeted homosexual. He certainly lives a closeted life. He has no romantic interests other than poetry, so that all of his talk about releasing the Dionysian impulse and the libido seems a bit shallow. Keating's romantic rebellion thus has no overt cultural politics. Poet rebels can be a powerful force for change, but only when their rebellion is more than youthful playfulness. For it to become something more, it cannot be a rebellion set apart from the world, as Welton Academy is, and it must be a rebellion that challenges its own privilege.

ZARATHUSTRA, PUNK, AND HIP-HOP

Perhaps we are looking in the wrong place for Zarathustrian youth in schools like Welton Academy. The youthful poet rebel with a politicized sense of the power of poetry is, perhaps, more likely to be found among the poor and the disenfranchised, among Hegel's slaves. Among progressives, counter-cultural forms of youth culture often have been interpreted as expressions of a Zarathustrian spirit and will to power—in this case a spirit and will to power that express themselves most typically in the form of rock music. In the 1950s, rhythm and blues and rock and roll captivated a generation, and, according to this argument, set the tone for the radical counter-culture of the 1960s. By the late 1960s, a whole mythology had emerged around rock and youth culture that took it seriously as a radical and subversive force for change. Punk and rap artists were represented as young Zarathustras, engaged in their own creative self-production, creating their own space and values out of a language of nihilism, rage, and despair.

One of the writers who helped establish the Zarathustrian mythology of rock music and youth culture is Greil Marcus. As a music critic for the *Village Voice*, Marcus took punk rock seriously. His 1989 book on the British working class punk group, the Sex Pistols, locates the group's music within the context of a history of "dada" art youth culture in America. He writes of Johnny Rotten's first moments in "Anarchy in the U.K.": "A rolling earthquake of laugh, a buried shout, then hoary words somehow stripped of all claptrap and set down in the city streets—I AM AN ANTICHRIST." Rotten is no romantic Zarathustra, but rather Zarathustra the anti-Christ, the nihilist, the one who strips away all illusions. He is someone who is "actually saying something he sincerely believes," according to Marcus, something with "real venom" and "real passion."[27] The connection of certain social facts with certain sounds creates "irresistible symbols of the transformation of social reality." The Sex Pistols were a commercial venture in the late 1970s and early 1980s, but their purpose, Marcus says, always was "cultural conspiracy." They breached hegemonic assumptions about "the way the world is supposed to work," and thus challenged "ideological constructs perceived and experienced as natural facts."[28] There is even a radical political impulse to be found in Johnny Rotten's use of the word "fuck" in his music and public appearances. According to Marcus, Rotten was, without being consciously aware of it, working within the dada artistic tradition—a tradition that also liked to use words and art for shock value.

Is the release of "Anarchy in the U.K." a great moment in the history of the twentieth century? Marcus is inclined to believe it is, even if historians continue to write histories in which political leaders are understood to be the real forces shaping history. In doing so, they miss many of the really big events and extraordinary people, those "events" and people that stir a generation out of its apathy, that give it a new anthem to sing. But what kind of an anthem, other than one of nihilism? When Rotten declares that he is the anti-Christ, Marcus argues, he means that it is his business to level everything and turn civilization into a pile of rubble. "He reduces the fruits of Western civilization to a set of guerrilla acronyms and England's green and pleasant land to a block of public housing."[29] Through symbolic acts of nihilism, dada artists clear a space in the forest, so to speak, so that "creation may occupy the suddenly cleared ground."[30] So it is that Elvis Costello, another punk rocker, could observe, "My ultimate vocation in life is to be an irritant. . . . Someone who disrupts the daily drag of life just enough to leave the victim thinking there's maybe more to it all than the mere humdrum quality of existence."[31] The creative nihilism of punk rock, however, has its limits. This, indeed, is one of Marcus' points. In songs like "God Save the Queen," in which Rotten screams over and over again, "NO FUTURE," Marcus concludes that the Sex Pistols "had damned the past with a curse so hard that it took the future with it."[32]

There are certainly similarities between the nihilism and shock politics of punk rock and that of the dada movement in art in the early twentieth century, although the latter was hardly working class in origins. According to Marcus, the dada movement was based on a belief that modern culture was entering a period of dissolution and decomposition. The art forms and narratives we have used to make sense of the world and affirm existence now begin to implode. They are revealed as no more that "a set of empty gestures, a dead commodity, a thing whose only use value is its exchange value." As the art forms and literary narratives of modern culture decompose, "so does the world—it becomes sterile, inaccessible, worthless, unreal." To some extent, dada art merely reflects this decomposition of forms, making people aware of it. But it does more than this. Through dada art and art commentary, "all words had come loose from their meanings and floated from their owners." Only through a nihilistic act is it possible to make room for creativity and change. Dada is a word purposely chosen to signify nothing. But by reducing a word to its letters, its sound, to a "pure sign," dada artists sought to write a new language. "The letter would be ready to form a new alphabet and a new language, a language that could say what had never been said, in tones that had never been heard."[33] This was godlike work, and so dada artists declared that they sought no less than to become gods.

All of this mythology of the dada movement had been invested in rock 'n' roll and the "beatnik" and bohemian cultures of the early 1950s. But while rock music and the youth culture released desire and shattered conventional bourgeois sensibilities, rock very quickly became a medium of commercialized desires, a testosterone desire for release without fulfillment, for mere release. With punk, Marcus writes, rock desires "were transformed into the conscious desire to make your own history, to abolish the history already made for you."[34] Is this radical and transformative? "There is a hint of transformation here," Marcus concludes, "of resentment, leading—who knows where?"[35] This talk of resentment is overtly Nietzschean, and it indicates that in spite of Marcus' celebration of dada and punk rock as movements that sow the seeds of discontent and even revolution, he also is aware of the limits of a cultural politics of *ressentiment*. It does not, in itself, lead in any pro-active or progressive direction. It is ironic that Nietzsche is often associated in popular culture with the will to nihilism and youthful rebellion. In fact, Nietzsche understood nihilism as productive in a progressive sense only when it cleared the way for the production of new truths and values to replace those associated with domination and control. Neither dada nor punk rock ever really moved very far in that direction, despite their claims. While the resistance expressed in punk rock is more politicized and defiant than the romantic rebellion of the prep school boys in *Dead Poets Society*, it accomplishes little more than reinforce the resentment, nihilism, and cynicism of the oppressed. By the 1990s, at least in the United States, punk had morphed into "grunge," a slightly more middle class and commercialized form of rock, but equally nihilistic—as represented symbolically and literally in the death of Kurt Cobain, lead singer of Nirvana, who committed suicide with a shotgun. This nihilistic Zarathustrian impulse in youth culture is reflected as well in the real lives of alienated youth every day. At Columbine High School in Colorado, those who opened fire on their fellow students did so in the name of Nietzsche, as anti-Christ figures on a mission to bring on the abyss. If only they had been able to make the metamorphosis into the child, then they might have been able to leap across the abyss into a creative engagement in the reconstruction of self and culture. Stuck as they were in a language of nihilism and *ressentiment*, the Columbine killers can hardly be considered Zarathustrian youth.

Punk could not, in the final analysis, undergo the metamorphosis into something beyond *ressentiment* and nihilism. In the ashes of the punk movement among white working and middle class youth, however, a new movement began to emerge that may carry more promise. Rap music and hip-hop culture emerged out of the gritty urban landscape, a production of inner city black youth, although by the millennium hip-hop culture was increasingly multi-racial and multi-ethnic.[36] Hip-hop has become a signifier of class, sexual, and gender identity along with racial identity. It expresses the resentment of inner city youth in general, and much of its politics are more particularly about the assertion of poor black (and poor white and Latino) masculine pride in a culture that has systematically stripped them of power and thus symbolically "emasculated" them. One problem is that this self-assertion typically has been at the expense of female and gay Others. Another problem is that rap and hip-hop culture, more than punk, have been highly commercialized, and in the process of turning it into a commodified, consumable object, its street politics (expressed in rage against police and calls for brotherhood and resistance) have been turned into the politics of making it in a white man's world. Flashy clothes, cars, and women become the commercialized rap icons of success. If there is reason to hope that hip-hop culture, or some variation of it, may still serve as a basis for a progressive cultural politics among the young, it is in the fact that some popular rap artists and groups—such as Outkast—have resisted commercial pressure to be either symbols of nihilism and rage or symbols of making it in a white man's world. Instead, they have seen their work as an extension of the best elements of the civil rights movement, a movement now ancient history to urban youth.

Outkast recently has been sued by Rosa Parks, the civil rights leader, for using her name as the title to one of their songs. She is suing, with the help of big-name lawyer Johnny Cochran, because she claims the rap group is commercially exploiting her name and defaming her character. The song, which appears on the group's 1999 album, *Aquemini*, does not mention Parks directly, but the phrase "back of the bus" is used to show disrespect to rival rap groups. The suggestion is that they should go to the back of the bus and make room for Outkast. More politically, the song may be read as a suggestion that it is time for a new generation of black youth to take over, to move beyond the gains made by Parks and her generation of civil rights leaders.

This is what Michael Dyson argues in his short essay on the controversy over the Outkast song in the epilogue to his popular book on the "true" Martin Luther King, Jr., *I May Not Get There With You* (2000). While Dyson sets out to set the record straight and reclaim the "true" King as a progressive hero with a radical vision of social activism, his perspective is influenced by cultural studies, and by a concern with the various ways in which conservatives and liberals have retold King's story to make it less radical and subversive. He also steers away from an attempt to get lost in the past by dwelling on King's life and deeds. At times he adopts an almost supra-historical attitude, arguing that history is dead and it is useless to get bogged down in the details of setting the record straight. What counts is what King, or Parks, mean today, to today's youth, in terms of their own empowerment. The song "Rosa Parks" is meant, he writes, to be "a cautionary tale against an uninformed obsession with the past," a dwelling in the past rather than the present.[37] It is a way of introducing Parks to a new generation in a language they can "own" and relate to. By interpreting Outkast's song literally, Dyson claims, Parks fails to see that she has become a "metaphor for social change," failed to understand "her symbolic importance to some of today's black youth."[38] In hip-hop groups such as Outkast, Dyson sees many of the same qualities that Parks had—namely, a commitment to the forgotten black poor. He concludes that if Parks' legacy is to survive and prove useful in a rapidly changing world, "it will have to be adapted, translated, and reinterpreted by a new generation," a generation whose words may seem angry and crude at times. What Outkast did in their song "Rosa Parks," was to turn her into a "useful hero, a working icon, a meaningful metaphor."[39]

Dyson makes the case for what Nietzsche calls a "supra-historical" use of history. It is a usage that turns Parks into a convenient symbol, one that informs the present by referring us back to the past. But the supra-historical attitude is not necessarily and always progressive. According to Gregory Smith, the supra-historical attitude manifests itself in the "characteristic postmodernist sortie through past forms, which are combined and juxtaposed in novel and at times purposely bizarre ways." In place of novelty and creation one gets "pastiche, collage, montage," all in a commercialized package.[40] If Outkast is using Parks in this way, it would seem to support Parks' case, and suggest that progressive heroes can very quickly be turned into commercialized icons, symbols in the marketplace of popular culture signs. But that depends upon how this music, and the video accompanying it, are "read" by its youthful followers. Part of the power of commercialization in popular culture has to do with its capacity to allow multiple, even contradictory readings or viewings. "Rosa Parks" can be heard and viewed as yet another celebration of black male bravado and posturing, or it can be heard and viewed more progressively, as (I would hope) Outkast wants it to be. Read progressively, "Rosa Parks" is an announcement that black youth need to connect their own struggles over self-affirmation to the historic struggles of those who came before them, but they also have to go beyond where Rosa Parks and her generation of black leaders have brought them. It implies that black youth, and other marginalized youth, are asserting their rights to be treated as equals on their own terms, and to produce their own cultural identities rather than assimilate into the dominant culture. It implies that they want more than their legal rights to a seat on the bus—the great American symbol of a public space. They want to bring their music, their culture, into the bus, and to affirm their difference within a multicultural society.

SCHOOLING AND DE-SCHOOLING THE OVERPERSON

If there is an "evil empire" in the Zarathustra myth, it is the modern, liberal welfare state, the state that sets itself upon "citizens" to organize, regulate, and discipline their lives, to construct and reconstruct their subjectivities in line with the hierarchical relations of modern society and the demands of the new industrial economy. For Hegel, the modern democratic state serves, or at least can potentially serve, the interests of democratic progress and freedom. The state can play an important role in the freeing of slaves by translating the abstract democratic language of the Enlightenment—human rights, equality, social justice, and community—into a legalistic language that gives these words a specific meaning. The state also, through public education, can play a central role in advancing the democratic story of history. Throughout most of the twentieth century, progressives focused on the state, consistent with this Hegelian mythology, to advance the democratic project. While public schools (particularly in elementary and secondary education) were understood to primarily serve dominant bureaucratic state and corporate interests, progressives always believed that if they could get control of the state, things would be different. I do not mean to imply that this attitude has entirely vanished. Far from it. Many Progressives, perhaps the majority, continue to be very Hegelian in their commitment to working within the state, and using the power of the state to reconstruct public education at all levels as part of a project of social reconstruction. I would count myself among them.

But things have changed over the past several decades in America. The new progressives no longer look to the state with so much hope and desire. The state is understood to be an expression of a disciplinary power, a discourse that circulates and regulates power within a culture, to privilege some and bring various sub-groups and classes of "abnormal" Others under a more complete and totalizing gaze. The modern state is not a "thing" so much as an economy of power that is in the business of "governmentality," governing over people. This is the state as Nietzsche understands it, and as Foucault does. The education of Zarathustra, and Zarathustrian pedagogy, can thus only occur outside the state. But where is this "outside"? Is it possible to be "outside" of this economy of power? Both Nietzsche and Foucault presume that power circulates through discourse or language usage, so that through the production of alternative discourses it is possible to produce different subjects and bodies, to regulate and distribute power in different ways. Thus space is discursive space, a field opened up through different discursive practices. But such space is also material and "real" in the sense that one can presumably only engage in new conversations about what it means to become educated, to become a democratic citizen, outside of the regulatory discourses of the state, along with the social science and psychological disciplines that work together to produce the modern subject of power. The hope for postmodern, Nietzschean progressives thus has been that space can be developed outside the state through which they might engage in other discourses and practices of education and freedom.

This Nietzschean anti-statism began to enter into progressive discourse in the late 1960s and early 1970s, in conjunction with a growing cynicism among progressives about the state, no doubt brought on at least partially by the perceived failure of liberal welfarism in America in the 1960s—as symbolized by the "War on Poverty." The urban school crisis also became more visible in the wake of the Civil Rights Movement and the urban riots of that decade. Public schools that "served" the poor and minority youth were exposed as oppressive institutions in a series of books that chronicled first-hand accounts of teaching in inner-city schools. Charles Silberman's influential bestseller, *Crisis in the Classroom* (1970), sponsored by the Carnegie Foundation, argued that across the nation, a "culture of docility" prevailed in public education. Neo-Marxist scholars and revisionist historians of education, at about the same time, began developing a sophisticated theory of how public schools served overwhelmingly to reproduce inequality. All of this was associated with a growing cynicism among those on the democratic left about using public institutions to advance the interests of a democratic public.

One of the first to link this growing cynicism about public education and corporate state "schooling" to a new cultural and educational politics was Ivan Illich. In *Deschooling Society* (1970), Illich argued that public schools had become the primary state institution charged with "schooling" people. Schooling is something done to people, to make them into consuming citizens, docile workers, and subjects of the corporate state. Illich was concerned in particular with the increasing power of schooling in keeping the poor dependent and thus enslaved in a new way. "The poor have always been socially powerless," he writes. "The increasing reliance on institutional care adds a new dimension to their helplessness." The result of welfare state dependency is "psychological impotence," an inability to assert oneself and take care of oneself.[41] Echoing Nietzsche, Illich argues that the poor do not need pity, and that money is not the answer to their problems. The liberal and leftist concern with eliminating poverty, with an ever-expanding standard of living as a sign of social progress, makes little sense when American welfare recipients already "can count on a truant officer to return their children to schools until they reach seventeen, or on a doctor to assign them to a hospital bed which costs sixty dollars per day—the equivalent of three months' income for a majority of the people in the world." Illich certainly overstates the "privileges" of the poor in America, particularly in an era when the safety net of welfare state poverty programs has been withdrawn. His basic point, however, is well taken. The more programs are established by the welfare state to "help" the poor, the more it encourages "dependence, anger, frustration, and further demands."[42] Meanwhile, "educational reformers promise each new generation the latest and the best, and the public is schooled into demanding what they offer."[43] But reforms only deepen the crisis of schooling, only make the system work more efficiently to turn people into consumer subjects. They only have the effect of creating an educational industry committed to educational reforms the way Detroit is committed to turning out new car models, so that people are dissatisfied with the "old" ones and feel the need to keep investing in planned obsolescence.

Three public myths support schooling, according to Illich. The first of these is the "Myth of Institutionalized Values," the belief that only values and knowledge produced within institutional frameworks, adhering to institutionalized planning processes, employing certified professionals, are worth anything. The result is a transference of responsibility from the self to the institution and the transference of democratic power to cadres of professional educators. Another result is the growth of a credentialing society, in which people mistake credentials for learning and competence. A second myth of schooling is "The Myth of Measurement of Values," the idea that "what cannot be measured becomes secondary, threatening." The "schooled" subject has learned that the world must be ordered, categorized, measured, rank-ordered. Finally, the "Myth of Packaging Values" implies that schools are in the business of delivering to students "a bundle of goods made according to the same process and having the same structure as other merchandise."[44] As the student learns to consume the curriculum, s/he learns to become a consumer of packaged values. The only way to effectively subvert these three myths of modern life is to "deschool" society. But how, precisely, is this to be done?

One response is perhaps most consistent with Nietzsche. According to Illich, "each of us is personally responsible for his or her own deschooling, and only we have the power to do it."[45] This entails unplugging oneself from the diploma and credentialing mill, and organizing reading and study groups with like-minded people. It also entails connecting with others who have particular skills or a particular knowledge that you want or need to pursue your goals. Illich envisioned a future in which individuals would form learning groups or "learning webs" connected by the new computer technology, in which schools and colleges have been transformed into "skill centers" where people come to get connected, in which peer-matching is facilitated so that people can share knowledge and skills. Teachers would no longer be licensed by the state, but rather become free academics who make their services available to those who seek them. While this approach to deschooling may make more sense in the decades ahead, it was not and is not now a politically viable and thus realistic option. A more realistic option or response, and thus politically more controversial, is to use state legislation and investment powers to dismantle state schooling through a voucher system, in which individuals would be paid by the state to pursue their own educations in skill centers or schools and colleges of various sorts. When Illich suggested that progressives should support a voucher system of public education, vouchers had already begun to emerge as a key element of the neo-conservative discourse in education. It has remained so, although never as a top priority. For support for public schools has continued to be strong, and even neo-conservatives, once they get in power, have generally supported reform of the public schools—through more standardized testing, which means more top-down, bureaucratic controls. Meanwhile, among progressives support for some modified voucher or public school choice program has risen in recent years. If a Nietzschean cultural politics prevails among progressives in the decades ahead, we may well see an historic turnaround, with conservatives supporting public schools as a means of producing docile subjects, and with progressives supporting some form of voucher or choice system.

In the academy, the shift toward Nietzschean cultural politics is most closely associated with Foucault, whose work finally began to impact on educational discourse in the 1980s. Foucault directs progressives to think of public education, as Illich did, in fundamentally new ways and to dare to think beyond the reform or even "renewal" of the current bureaucratic state system, to create the conditions for a postmodern form of education. There is, by now, a "discipline" of sorts devoted to the study of Foucault that explores his relevance in addressing educational concerns. Foucault would certainly find this ironic, given that his work may be read as anti-disciplinarian. He understood the academic disciplines as engaged in the regulation and control of knowledge and power, and like Nietzsche he sought to move beyond disciplinary knowledge. I want to limit my comments here to Foucault's notion of "governmentality," which he developed in his late work.[46] The term governmentality does not take on any fixed, uniform meaning in Foucault's late work, but he does use it as a "thought-space" across which he can bridge the domains of ethics and politics, without reducing one to the other. What is a democratic ethics, and from this, what is a democratic cultural politics? These are the questions Foucault raises with this multifaceted concept of governmentality, which he applies both to the governance of self and others. Governmentality is the active process of working on subjectivity, disciplining it, shaping and molding it according to a particular political rationality. It is the self-forming activity, and the techniques by which the self is formed. For Foucault governmentality is neither inherently good nor bad, from a democratic standpoint. Rather, it is an expression of particular forms of political rationality, linked to particular discourses of democracy. It is a rationality that links the micropolitics of power with the macropolitics of power. In this sense, the state is no longer understood as a "sovereign" power, separate and autonomous from the micropolitics of power. Rather, each is an expression of a political rationality embedded in discourse. The state need not exercise direct control at all times over micropolitics so long as politics at the micro level is organized according to a shared rationality. Governance thus does not involve a sovereign state responding to pressure from civil society. Instead, both centralized state and individual public citizens are produced through a particular discourse or political rationality, linked to a particular economy of power.

Foucault follows Nietzsche in tracing the rhizomes of modern governmentality back to a Judeo-Christian tradition of pastoral care. In doing so, he makes it clear that continuities are to be found between modern secular authority and traditional religious authority, and that modernism is only a continuation in new form of something that has a long history in the West. Within the Christian church, leadership and authority began to be organized at a quite early date around the metaphors of a "shepherd" guiding a "flock."[47] This is a mythology very closely related, of course, to Nietzsche's metaphor of the modern subject as a herd animal. Sheep represent sacrifice, innocence, and submissiveness. These are the traits that the clergy projects upon the congregation in assuming the role of shepherd to the flock. Through the confessional, the rites of the sacraments, and other rituals, the clergy symbolically assumes control over the salvation of those under their care, and members of the congregation learn to submit to this care, to become stoical and repentant, to need the shepherd to redeem them. In the development of a culture of "pastorship," or the care of others, Foucault locates many of the institutional forms that later will coalesce within the modern welfare state. The state becomes inextricably intertwined with governmentality over the public flock. It assumes responsibility for the management, surveillance, supervision, and disciplining of the public flock, usurping or sharing these roles with the church hierarchy. In the late modern era, according to Foucault, this pastoral authority, this ethic of care, has organized itself around state health, welfare, and education institutions—all of which are "oriented toward the care of individual life."[48] They express a governmentality that is concerned with the "health" of the "body politic," that seeks to manage populations, to sort and classify sub-groups within the population for special "treatment." Governmentality may be exercised through any number of political rationalities, but in the advanced modern state, it presupposes the existence of state agencies which rule *over* populations, regulating them according to an instrumental calculus, bringing them under a normalizing gaze. For both Nietzsche and Foucault, the modern subject is produced by these institutions and thus loses all sense of agency, of its own will to power. By implication, teaching in public educational institutions is constrained by the dominant discourse of governmentality, in which teachers are made to stand in for the authority of the institution, to participate in disciplining minds and bodies.

For an alternative discourse of governmentality, Foucault turns to ancient Greek culture. Within pre-Platonic Greek culture, according to Foucault, the public is never represented as a body to be administered or governed. Rather the public is understood to be a set of relationships between self-governing individuals and groups. Democratic political community is thus understood to require the heightened development of skills and "truths" associated with self-governance. Governmentality in this sense is associated with "practices of freedom" aimed at establishing an independent relationship between people, a governmentality of "self-self" rather than "shepherd-flock." Practices of freedom require the development, educationally speaking, of a heightened capacity for reflexivity of a certain sort—a reflexivity that allows people to self-monitor and self-regulate their relations with one another. If dominant forms of governmentality in the modern era are predicated on an individualizing surveillance, that surveillance must now become a self-surveillance, not as Freud's superego (the eye of the dominant culture) but as expressive of one's own desire for freedom.

In one sense, what is called for here is little more than what Hegel called for—a form of education that leads in the direction of a self-conscious subject, reflexive citizens who no longer need a master, who are ready—like Zarathustra—to take control of their own lives. Still, one cannot help but wonder just how democratic such a deschooled and deinstitutionalized world would be. It is important to keep in mind that the classical Greek discourse on democratic governmentality that Foucault offers as an alternative to the pastoral discourse is a discourse of freedom that constituted itself around its exclusion of slaves and women, who together were the great majority of the Athenian population. Do the practices of freedom that Foucault celebrates require these Others to endure bondage and servitude? Would a deschooled society provide opportunities for freedom and self-production for some at the expense of others? These are troubling questions, and they point to the very real possibility that Zarathustra's freedom has, throughout the modern era, been made possible only through the act of negation. In his most cynical mood, on the Blessed Isles, Zarathustra comes to believe the overperson needs the "rabble" to be free. But this is not the thrust of Nietzsche's mythology. He, like Foucault, held out the hope that all people can be free, that one person's freedom need not be constituted by dominating an Other. That may be a bit idealistic at this historical juncture. But perhaps we have more freedom than we think.

THE MOON LANDING AND THE MYTHOLOGY OF THE MILLENNIUM

The Zarathustra myth, for all of its debunking of Hegelian idealism, provides progressives with a narrative of possibility and hope, in which the meaning of phrases like "human freedom" take on new and more democratic meaning. Zarathustra stands at the beginning of a new era in history and looks forward more than backward. And he suggests that out of the chaos of late modern culture, a metamorphosis is occurring. Most are still too close to it to see what is in front of their eyes, and many are holding back, afraid of what they see ahead. Some are not ready to make the leap across the abyss of late modern culture into a new era, marked by dramatic shifts in culture. Some are not ready for the postmodern, for the shock of recognition that comes with the awareness of our own freedom to construct and reconstruct self and culture. But the shift is occurring. In recent years, the millennium has been a convenient marker for the growing sense of expectation that we are about to make Zarathustra's giant leap, to become overpersons.

Let me close with a few comments on the mythology of the millennium in popular culture, and its close association with the moon landing. Certainly, one of the most important examples of the Zarathustra mythology in popular culture is Stanley Kubrick's film, *2001: A Space Odyssey* (1968), a screen adaptation of Arthur C. Clarke's novel of the same name. Is it only coincidental that Kubrick chooses to begin and end his film with the haunting chords of Richard Strauss' tone poem, "Thus Spake Zarathustra"? Hardly, when one takes into consideration that this is a story of a series of metamorphoses of human consciousness, and that it ends with the "Star Child" ready, in the year of the millennium, to emerge from his embryonic cocoon. The film begins with a segment titled "The Dawn of Man." Here once again we encounter the image of the cave, and the mythology of leaving the cave (along with the use of "Man" as a universal signifier for humanity). In the opening sequence, a tribe of proto-human apes is roaming the African savannah. As night falls, they seek shelter in a cave and huddle together, fearful of the sounds of wild leopards and lions that pierce the night. As the sun rises they stir from their restless slumber and prepare once more to leave the cave to hunt for food. It is at this point that they encounter one of the film's recurring symbols—a huge rectangular monolith, obviously left by some higher intelligence. Most of the proto-humans are fearful of the monolith, but one overcomes his fear and, hesitantly at first, reaches out his hand to touch it. Soon thereafter, as the group plays with the ravaged bones of an antelope, this ape-human suddenly has an insight. The bones can be used as weapons to kill animals. This is the first great leap in human consciousness—although it is obviously a "giant leap for mankind" that is a double-edged sword. For soon these same bones will be used as weapons to attack and kill a neighboring tribe of apes who infringe on their territory. The segment ends as one of the ape-humans throws an antelope bone into the air. The camera follows it upward as it slowly revolves in the air.

This is where the first segment of the film ends, and the second segment begins. The year is now 2001—the millennium—and humanity has moved from the simple technology of the bone weapon to that of a revolving space station. Four million years have passed and humanity seems, at least on the surface, to have come a long way. A moon colony has even been established; and it is from the moon that earth radio telescopes pick up a strange signal. When an expedition is sent to the moon to investigate the signals, they find that its source is another huge monolith, buried slightly beneath the surface. As the expedition uncovers the monolith, it suddenly begins broadcasting a new signal—this time a signal that seems to be directed at one of the moons of Jupiter. A space ship, in turn, is sent to investigate the source of this distant signal. The ship is guided by HAL—a super-computer that seems infallible, a symbol of how far the technological and scientific revolution has taken humanity. But HAL proves, in the end, to be quite fallible and tries to take control of the ship from the crew, systematically killing everyone on board except for one crew member who finally is able to deactivate it. The computer and the way of knowing it represents, the film suggests, can only take humanity so far. Technical rationality must be transcended if humanity is to make the next giant leap in consciousness.

In the final segment of the film, titled "Jupiter and Beyond the Infinite," the remaining crew member finally approaches and then enters the monolith near Jupiter. It is as if he is entering a "stargate"—a corridor of vibrant colors, a tunnel of pulsating light, rushing faster and faster. When he finally lands, he goes through a highly surrealistic series of events in which he witnesses himself age and grow old. This all takes place in an incubator of sorts. The last appearance of the monolith occurs at the foot of the bed of the dying man. As he reaches out to it, his body is transformed into a glowing, translucent fetus or embryo—a "Star Child." The last image in the film is of the Star Child floating through space on its way back to Earth, accompanied by the chords of "Thus Spake Zarathustra." In the book, however, Clarke continues his story a bit further. "The baby stared into the depths of the crystal monolith," Clarke writes, "seeing—but not yet understanding—the mysteries that lay ahead." All the child knew was that it could not stay where it was. "The direction, though not the nature, of his destiny was clear before him."[49] With superhuman new powers, and new understandings of the nature of the universe and his own infinite possibilities, the Star Child returns to the vicinity of earth. There, viewing the lush green planet from space, he watches as a "slumbering cargo of death"—an ICBM—is blasted into orbit, about to begin a nuclear war that will undoubtedly destroy human life on earth and take much of the rest of the planet's life with it. The Star Child now understands that humans in their current state must transcend what they have been if they are to survive, and so he uses his new-found powers to destroy the missiles. Clarke leaves the child of the cosmos there, "brooding over his still untested powers," and "not quite sure what to do next." But one is left with the sense that this millennial child will do things differently, and that a new age is dawning.

The late, great popular science writer Stephen Jay Gould argues, in *Questioning the Millennium* (1997), that the sense of expectancy that is associated with the millennium has no basis in logic and that the millennium myth needs to be dispelled.[50] All calendars, after all, are based on arbitrary beginning points. Furthermore, the Christian calendar is governed by a purely arbitrary base ten number system, so that decades, centuries, and millennia take on particular importance which they would not have if we used another number base or were Chinese rather than American. Finally, Gould argues that expectations of dramatic events—either for good or for bad—have their origins in religious traditions—in this case a Christian doctrine which looks forward to a second coming and a final battle between good and evil. Gould suggests we abandon such nonsense and recognize that it is nonsense. We should rise above the myth of the millennium.

Unfortunately, while I think Gould and others of a scientific frame of mind who share his perspective raise important concerns, they miss the point about myth. They fall victim to the modernist tendency to understand myth as a falsehood that needs to be revealed as such and then put aside and left behind. The millennium is indeed an arbitrary marker of time, history, and transformation, and it is important that we recognize this. As Gould reminds us, for much if not most of the world's population, the year 2000 is just another year and, in fact, is not even designated as the year 2000. But because the millennium is a myth does not mean it is "false," or should be dispelled, or that it is inconsequential. Its "truth" is in its recognition that modern culture is in the midst of transforming itself in ways we are not yet fully capable of comprehending. The myth of a millennium, like all great myths, needs to be read as a sign of the times, a message we are sending ourselves, a self-fulfilling prophecy. At the same time, myths—by their very nature—come with no fixed meanings or politics. In the language of cultural studies, myths are "floating signifiers" whose meaning may support divergent and even contradictory claims, projects, and practices. For cultural conservatives, the millennium is a sign of the coming collapse of all moral standards and absolute truths, a collapse that can only be prevented by returning to a Eurocentric cultural heritage and resisting the rhetoric of multiculturalism and diversity. Fundamentalist religious groups look to the millennium as a time of Armageddon, the Apocalypse, the Second Coming, the Rapture.

Progressives too have been influenced by a millennial leap in human consciousness, the coming of a new age; and Kubrick's *2001* serves as perhaps the best and most influential example of a myth of the millennium that is basically progressive in its cultural politics. Interestingly, the film locates the monolith that is to guide humans to their next giant leap forward on the moon. So, one year before the Apollo astronauts touched down on the moon, the myth was already waiting for them. "That's one small step for man, one giant leap for mankind." Ironically, the greatest achievement of late modern culture, and the technical rational worldview, was the Apollo moon landing. Apollo, Nietzsche's god of authority, discipline, and rationality, would carry people to the moon, a symbolic passage into a Dionysian age. Since then, the millennium myth of a giant leap has become part of the taken-for-granted "air" we breathe. What will be the effect of this myth? Will it too become self-fulfilling? Will late modern culture be able to make the leap across the abyss, or will it opt for the other myth of the millennium, the apocalypse? These are hardly "academic" questions any more. They suggest that the new progressivism must proceed with a sense of urgency, and that education must prepare people to make the leap across a divide, into a new, postmodern understanding of the world.

The counter-culture myth of a new age, of the release of the child within, was at its height in the summer of 1969, the summer of both Woodstock and the landing of a man on the moon. It is perhaps not surprising that the two would begin to be linked in popular culture. One could hardly help but read the moon landing as a sign of the end of something, and the beginning of a new journey outward. Its proximity to the millennium also lent credence to the idea that the moon landing was the symbolic end of the old millennium, the beginning of a new one. Woodstock, the moon landing, and the millennium all were woven together into a New Age mythology that looked hopefully toward a giant leap in human consciousness. Of course, the New Age myth of the moon landing was not what NASA originally had in mind when it began selling the idea of a moon landing to the American public in the early 1960s. At that time, NASA was able to gain wide public support for the project through the production of the myth of a "space race," a race that pitted the two great superpowers against one another. The space race myth represented space exploration as a way in which the United States could demonstrate once and for all its superiority over the Soviet Union without the need for nuclear confrontation. But with the moon landing the space race effectively ended, having been won. Talk of detente with the Soviets was in the air, and after the moon landing the myth of the space race could not be sustained. In the 1970s, as America entered a period of economic retrenchment and fiscal crisis, people began to question the value of a continued high public investment in the space program. Efforts to introduce an alternative myth, a myth of public economic and technological payoffs for space exploration, failed to generate enough public support. Luckily for NASA, there was yet another myth of space exploration available, one that President Kennedy had first suggested in the idea that space is the "final frontier," and that Kubrick had extended and given new meaning in *2001*. This is the myth of space exploration as a journey into a new stage of human history. Perhaps it is not coincidental, then, that Neil Armstrong's first words upon touching down on the moon were not, "That's a great victory for the American Way of Life over international communism," or "That's the first step in the commercial and military exploitation of the moon," but rather, "That's one small step for man, one giant leap for mankind." The moon landing, from that point on, was transformed into a signifier for the millennium and the "giant leap" in human consciousness.

One of the first examples of such a mythologizing of the moon landing is to be found in Norman Mailer's popular book, *Of a Fire on the Moon* (1969). Mailer's book came out several months after the moon landing, and it represents the first attempt to interpret the significance of the moon landing within a broad cultural perspective. The book is a rambling, personal narrative of Mailer's journalistic coverage of the events leading up to the landing, framed as a Zarathustrian journey of self-discovery and self-awakening, from the pit of despair to a new hope. Mailer had just completed a race for mayor of New York City, he tells us, when he decided to write about the Apollo mission. He had come in fourth in a field of five candidates—his mix of libertarian and progressive politics soundly defeated. Referring to himself in the third person, Mailer writes, "He was weary of his own voice, own face, person, persona, will, ideas, speeches, and general sense of importance."[51] But in speaking of himself, Mailer is also speaking of American culture, and more particularly certain elements of the democratic left. This blending of autobiography—the personal journey of self-discovery—with fiction, with a commentary on American cultural politics in the late 1960s, was characteristic of a new brand of journalism that crossed the boundaries that separate truth and fiction, self and culture, journalistic reporting and spiritual soul-searching. At times Mailer writes in a personal and poetic language, and at other times he is all journalist, reporting on each detail of the launch and recovery efforts. He declares that he has lost faith in scientific, calculating, technological rationality, and so he deliberately seeks to recapture a poetic, a "savage" language, one that is based on "smelling out" the situation rather than analyzing it with a detached eye.

Mailer, as representative of larger currents in American culture, says he is interested in writing a book about the events leading up to the moon landing because it may draw him away from his sense of foreboding, weariness, gloom, and boredom. His last major work, *The Steps of the Pentagon*, chronicled his involvement in anti-war protests culminating in his arrest at a Pentagon sit-in. After that, he dove into the thick of New York City politics. By the early summer of 1969, he is burned out and cynical, made all the more so by the expansion of the Vietnam War and by setbacks in the Civil Rights Movement after the assassinations of Martin Luther King, Robert Kennedy, and Malcolm X. He is also cynical about the growing commercialization of middle class culture, the conformity of the sprawling suburbs, the rise of a "Military-Industrial Complex" that controls more and more of people's lives. On top of all of these problems in the broader culture, and symptomatic of them, his most recent marriage is falling apart because both he and his wife are too busy pursuing their individual careers, too egocentric to spend the time to care for each other or even get to know each other very well. It is as if they cannot connect with each other, only glance at each other in passing, as if they have lost their passion. As a result of all this, but also contributing to his malaise, he is drinking too much. As others turn to drugs to dull their pain, Mailer turns to booze.

This, then, is the point from which Mailer proposes to begin a journey of self-discovery by reporting on the moon landing. His initial intent is to write a book that views the moon landing as the crowning achievement of a scientific and technical mindset—a cold, calculating, efficient, inhumane, sterile mindset. His aim is not to contribute to the glorification of the moon landing, but to debunk the official NASA mythology. The moon landing, he writes, is the first step in the commercial exploitation and colonization of the moon. "The efforts of these colonies would offer no less than the cheap manufacture in the moon vacuum of products of mass consumption—electronics, communications, pharmaceuticals. . . ."[52] A visit to Houston's Manned Space Center only confirms his darkest fears about who is in control. Upon entering the gate, past the guard, "There was no way to determine whether one was approaching an industrial complex in which computers and electronic equipment were fashioned, or traveling into a marvelously up-to-date minimum-security prison."

The geometrically ordered buildings were all white, starkly utilitarian in design, and "severe, ascetic, without ornament."[53] It looked, he reports, like a futuristic college campus, an "all-but-treeless" campus "composed of many windowless buildings."[54] Ominously, he can detect no smell at all in the Manned Space Center. For smell belongs to the sensuous, animal world, and that world has been banished from the sterile environment that is a product of the dominant technological mindset.

Beneath his cynicism and his desire to portray the moon landing as the achievement of a technological, Military-Industrial Complex that now controlled America, however, Mailer is drawn to the moon landing because it has awakened his sense of wonder, because it seems to draw him out of himself toward some new understanding. The landing on the moon he takes as a fitting symbol for the beginning of a new Age of Aquarius. In Greek mythology, Aquarius is the god who traverses the earth and sky, a god composed of solid, liquid, and gas. So Mailer dares to re-christen himself Aquarius, to identity with a growing number of young people forming their own counter-culture, challenging the values of the Military-Industrial Complex, and ushering in a new age. They, like Aquarius, were traversing a space, assuming new and different forms. Slowly, he begins to view the Apollo mission to the moon more complexly, as the defining achievement of the old technological age that ironically helps usher in a new age. "Our voyage to the moon was finally an exploration by the century itself into the possible consequences of its worship of technology."[55] The journey into space calls upon people "to regard the world once again as poets, behold it as savages."[56] President Kennedy, Mailer feels, had said it best: "This is a new ocean, and I believe the United States must sail upon it." Here again is the image of sailing or traversing a space. In sailing upon a new ocean, we symbolically enter a new era in our history, we move from where we have been to a place we do not yet know. Kennedy did not provide a concrete reason why the public should commit itself to this goal. The appeal was not to "payoffs" or specific goals for colonization of the moon. The appeal, rather, was to a long-repressed desire in the public to venture forth again, to face new challenges, to take risks, to—in the language of *Star Trek*— go where no one has gone before.

However, the counter-culture vision of where culture was going was far different than that represented in *Star Trek*. The counter-culture that Mailer celebrates was decidedly anti-technological, anti-modern, and its vision of the giant leap in human consciousness was a leap back to the "primal self" of pure experience and desire. For Mailer the leap in human consciousness was to involve a reconnection to the "savage" within. To recapture the savage within, one had to "get in touch" with experience itself, let the "child within" out, celebrate, create, and "be." The ultimate ritual of the counter-culture was thus the "be-in," a celebration of being here, living life now, engaged in the primal celebration of life, connected to nature. All of this celebration of the "primal" was radically subversive in some ways, since it challenged the repressive discipline and conformity of modern industrial society. Yet, in a contradictory way, the desublimation of desire that the counter-culture represented quickly became commercially exploitable. It also led away from engagement in struggles going on over the course and direction of cultural development toward an inward journey of experience, and towards play. It became anti-intellectual and anar-chistic, and thus unable to formulate a very sophisticated understanding of what it would have taken to forge a broad-based progressive movement that seriously challenged the Military-Industrial Complex. But Mailer does not see these contradictions in the counter-culture, perhaps because he writes from a time when the counter-culture was growing at a rapid rate and followers took it for granted that a revolution of some sort would erupt in America within a few years, pitting the forces of the old order against the new. The century, he feels, has ended in this summer of the moon landing, Woodstock, and the con-frontations at the Democratic convention in Chicago. Things can never be the same again. The battle has begun, the battle over the heart and soul of America, between the forces of Good and Evil, God and the Devil, the counter-culture and the "Establishment." Yet it was to be a war waged by disengaging from the dominant culture to "get in touch" with Nature and the primal self, a war waged against technology and the machine.

Mailer ends his book with a description of his life in the late summer of 1969, immediately after the moon landing. He travels frequently to Province-town on Cape Cod, his own Blessed Isles, to visit friends and participate in a small but growing counter-culture community of artists and writers who live there. The Cape was the end point of the earlier Pilgrims' journey, and it sym-bolically serves as the beginning point for Mailer's own outward journey. And what does he do on the Cape that late summer, as America seems to be coming apart at the seams? He focuses upon on one defining event that late summer, an event that might also be taken as symbolic of counter-culture approaches to education. Mailer's friends decide to bury a car as part of an end of the summer festival, as a symbolic way of separating themselves from a dying technology, a technology upon which they had vowed to become less dependent. So they bought an old junker and drove it until it died, then gave it a proper burial, with its front end sticking out of the ground. A sculptor was put in charge of transforming the piece of junk into a piece of art, to make it part of a play-ground so that children could play around it. Bumpers were twisted around and soldered on the car to look like legs sticking up from the dying body. Some neighbors wrote poems for the burial ceremony, such as "Duarte Motors giveth, and terminal craftsmanship taketh away."[57] After the ceremony, chil-dren were given paints and brushes to transform its dull and rusty car carcass with bright colors, "drawing figures, figure-drippings, and inchoate totems on the vertical roof of the car." Floodlights were placed at the base of the car, so that it could be illuminated at night. Here, Mailer thinks, lies the "first machine to die with burial in the land of the Pilgrims and the cod," the first casualty in the war against technology and the machine.[58]

The Age of Aquarius and Dionysus is to begin, Mailer suggests, with a new form of "ludditism," involving the smashing of machines. But this time, the smashing of machines is to be accompanied by their creative transformation as artistic and political symbols designed to make people more aware of ecological issues. Even more important, the smashing of machines is to involve people directly, in a visceral, bodily way. The road to self-awareness is not primarily intellectual. It is presumed to follow from existential experience, from the experience of actually feeling and sensing the world. Education for the New Age is to proceed through the return to experience and the release of the savage that has been held captive in the unconscious, and this requires a movement away from logical and scientific reasoning. The child, in Mailer's story, is given paints to transform the drab car into a colorful work of art, to lead the adults. Mailer too becomes a Zarathustrian child, caught up in the carnival.

The counter-culture began to be associated with this idea, already there in Mailer, that the dominant culture could be overthrown through a form of ongoing carnival, through a radical desublimation of desire and creative outburst of energy that would send shock waves around the world, and into the heavens. Herbert Marcuse, the popular social theorist of the counter-culture, had argued in *Eros and Civilization* that while the building of modern industrial society may have required a good deal of self-discipline and repression, in which creativity and desire were sublimated or channeled into productive economic labor, the time had finally arrived when the promise of progress could begin to be realized, when people could at last begin to enjoy the fruits of their labor and explore their creative and expressive selves. Individuals could, like Zarathustra, be metamorphosed into the archetypal child, given free rein to fully develop and explore their interests and desires. This was to be the next phase in the conscious evolution of modern culture. The limits of this counter-culture interpretation of the Zarathustra myth are all visible, I think, in Mailer's story. To begin with, Mailer locates his story in the privileged environment of Cape Cod, safely removed from the "real world," among a group of upper middle class artists, sculptors, and writers who are probably all white. The celebration of expression and creativity turns out to be linked to a privileged middle class and white position. The politics of aesthetic self-expression tend to have their origins in upper middle class privilege. So too does the tendency to view artists and intellectuals of the upper middle class as Zarathustras, standing above the morality and beliefs of the herd, viewing themselves as the vanguard of the New Age.

Another problem suggested by Mailer's account of the car burial is that it is an anti-technological story, based on a presumption that the New Age will see a return to pre-modern and very local technologies and products—certainly no mass-produced cars. Implicit here is a rather naive "back to the earth" ideal that romanticizes small agricultural and craft communes, with children educated within the community. This withdrawal from organized political parties and movements is one of the reasons why conservatives were able to reestablish political and cultural dominance, beginning with the election of President Nixon in 1968. But perhaps the counter-culture movement *was* right about one thing. Before Americans could make another giant leap into a new phase of democratic progress, they would need to begin unplugging from much of the dominant culture and simultaneously begin creating something new, organized along quite different principles, right alongside the old. That something new included a vision of personal and cultural transformation that was progressive in many ways, even if the progressive potential of counter-cultural beliefs and values was not fully developed. The counter-culture went underground in the conservative era that followed the cultural rupture of the late 1960s, but it did not really go away. Its celebrations of difference, of finding a space at the borders between "inside" and "outside" the system, of building communities of affinity and difference, its engagement with the moment—all of these are precursors to the postmodern.

CHAPTER 5

A Cyborg's Education

Heidegger and Eco-Progressivism

Gregory Bateson writes that when a person is using a computer, "what 'thinks' ... is the man plus the computer plus the environment." Within this matrix, "the lines between man, computer and environment are purely artificial, fictitious lines."[1] They are virtual borders across which information and difference flow. As we have produced the personal computer, it has been engaged in producing us and "framing" the way we both see the world and inhabit it. If all this is true, it changes everything in education. We are entering an age, for good or bad, in which all education is the education of "cyborgs," human subjects that have ruptured the borders that the modern mind constructed to separate them from animals, nature, and each other, human subjects who are assembling themselves, or being assembled, who seek a limited freedom in the spiral dance between unity and difference.

In this chapter I want to map-out some of the ecological discourses and mythologies that have begun to surface, or I should say resurface, in America over the past several decades, pointing toward some of the new territory that lies ahead as progressivism becomes more ecological, as battles in education have more and more to do with ecological issues. Ecology has no fixed cultural politics, although it is emerging most powerfully as a progressive social movement on the left in America. The basic tension that runs throughout ecological mythologies and narratives is a tendency to emphasize unity, and attribute knowing to the "system" or the "spirit" of the system (on the one hand), and a tendency to emphasize chaos, and the emergence of "cyborgs" who have carved out a limited space on the grid for freedom and self-production (on the other). Once more, the dialectic between modernism and postmodernism is at least partially a dialectic between theories of cultural unity and difference. So the dialectic is, metaphorically, a dialectic between the earth goddess and the freed cyborg. Within this dialectic, one side is not "progressive" and the other

"anti-progressive." Unifying mythologies and practices have their place in democratic cultures, so long as they are countered with mythologies and practices
of difference and freedom. Out of the play of difference and unity, progressive
ecology, I want to argue, is forged and develops. It desires neither a romanticized return to a mythic Garden of Eden in which the earth goddess is now in
charge, nor a romanticized, science fiction fantasy of cyborg freedom in a capitalist, technological, information age.

To a significant extent, when we move into the realm of ecological
mythologies of knowing and becoming educated, we are moving into a terrain
in which the myth truly precedes the reality. Science fiction more than history
must be our guide. At this historical juncture, education is still being organized
according to different mythologies, and ecology calls on us to think about education in fundamentally new and different ways. But why should progressives
care about ecology? The answer, I believe, is that unless we begin to care, our
current technology and technological consciousness will become self-destructive
and suicidal. Beyond this concern for the sustainability of the human species
and the preservation of ecological relationships with the natural world, ecological mythology provides a basis for linking class, race, sexual, and gender issues
in new ways, what we might call a unifying politics of difference. It remains
unclear what the fuller implications of the shift toward ecological consciousness
are for the way we think about education, although it is my intent to engage in
some speculation in what follows. To the extent that I do, it is a speculation that
is based on extrapolating trends which are already visible to all who would look
and see. I move, theoretically and mythologically, from Martin Heidegger to
Donna Haraway, the former expressive of a basically modernist ecology and the
latter decidedly postmodern.

HEIDEGGER AND THE MYTHOLOGY OF *TECHNÊ*

In his essay, "The Question Concerning Technology," Heidegger provides a
compelling argument for a new form of education, one that is organized
around the questioning of *technê*. He means to develop an idea that is embedded in Hegelian mythology, that human consciousness and the material world
are caught in a dialectic, and that the potter is both the maker of the pot and
simultaneously made by the pot. But Hegel never adequately developed a
missing piece in this mythology of pot and potter, although Marx would
later—namely, the pottery wheel, the potter's stone, the technology that mediates between consciousness and the material world, that is in some ways an
extension of the potter. Heidegger thus locates technology, and technique—
both of which are encapsulated in the Greek word *technê*—at the center of
the educational project. It is through questioning the technology we use to
mediate our relations with the natural world that we learn to appreciate the
particular form of "being" that is bringing on the crisis of late modern culture,

that is leading us to the edge of Nietzsche's abyss. And it is only through and with the development of new forms of *techné*, new ways of revealing the natural world and landscape and inhabiting the world, that modern culture will be able to successfully make the transition into a postmodern, ecological age. The aim of education is thus not only to aid in the critique of dominant forms of technological consciousness, but also to promote the use of new technologies and techniques for mediating between consciousness and materiality, based on new forms of consciousness and "being in the world." The computer obviously is one such technology; although Heidegger would have grave concerns about whether or not, at least in its current form, it is a "saving" *techné* instead of a *techné* that further detaches consciousness from the "real" material world.

Heidegger begins by raising the question of what it might mean to "question" technology. He means, he says, to question technology by not taking it for granted. The modern age, and modern forms of education and cultural production, are based on a way of revealing the earth which has become so taken for granted that it can only be made visible by questioning. So it is that an education or philosophy that seeks a "saving" way out of the crisis of late modern capitalism must proceed by questioning. To question is a way of thinking, a way that "builds a way" for truth, a way that seeks to set up a "free" and "open" relationship to a phenomenon, such as technology.[2] For Heidegger, the problem of late modern culture is that people take for granted contemporary forms of *techné* as if they are invisible, part of the air they breath.

He proceeds to question contemporary forms of *techné* by deliberately trying to think from an alternative mindset or "enframing." Of course, one can raise questions as to whether this is entirely possible, particularly since Heidegger chooses to think about *techné* from the mindset of pre-Platonic Greek culture. However, he does suggest that it is only possible to question contemporary culture and reveal what has been taken for granted in it by gazing at it through a different set of discursive lenses. This is why it is so important for Heidegger that he trace back the meaning of *techné* in early Greek texts, to find an alternative meaning and one that would give a different answer to the question, what is technology? Heidegger finds in ancient Greek texts, or at least claims to find, that the subject and the object were not yet split. The knowing human subject did not yet set itself up as an abstract presence, apart from materiality. This means that people did not apprehend the world as "out there" in an objectified manner. To demonstrate his meaning, Heidegger draws upon the example of a silver chalice and asks, how would the ancient Greeks understand its coming forth into presence or existence? Heidegger's answer is based on a reference to Aristotle's four causes—formal, final, efficient or effective, and material. In the modern age, the efficient cause is understood to stand behind the coming forth of something like a chalice, the cause associated with willed actions of individual subjects—Nietzsche's will to power.

For Heidegger, this modern emphasis upon understanding the things people make as expressions of human will, and more particularly as expressions of an autonomous or individual human will, is fundamentally different from the way ancient Greeks saw things. They would see the role that the craftsperson performed in bringing the chalice into existence as only that of binding together three other causes—the material from which the chalice is made, the final cause or ceremony in which it is to be used, and the formal or instrumental cause (people needed something that could hold wine). These other, non-efficient causes, according to the Greeks, were most important in bringing a chalice into appearance. The craftsperson is in no way the producer of the chalice, only the one who helps the chalice appear.[3] Its "essence" already exists in a long tradition of chalices. For Heidegger, serves as an ecological *technê*, and it implies a radical decentering of the human subject as a detached, autonomous will. By questioning how the ancient Greeks, or other ancient people for that matter, understood technology and technique, Heidegger suggests that people can begin to think outside the box of modern forms of *technê*.

If we take this discussion of the chalice as providing a template for a particular type of ecological education, it seems to imply that young people need to locate themselves within a larger becoming, to not see themselves as "center stage," to not think of their own ambitions so much as how they might participate in bringing into being something that is not their own autonomous creation but rather the creation of a "being in the world" that is ancient and supra-human. The individual must learn that s/he is only part of something more, only a handmaiden of creation. This is where Heidegger's work, as it so often does, seems to lapse into a romanticism of a tradition-bound, premodern past, where education involves apprenticeship and mentorship, learning the discipline of a craft, the history of the chalice, and the intricacies of its design over the centuries, the rituals in which it is used, the variations on design motifs. There is no real way of speaking of creativity in such a context, at least the creativity of the individual artist/craftsperson. For creativity would reflect an overabundance of the efficient cause, too much concern for one's own autonomous expression. Instead, education is the slow mastery and modification of the techniques that individuals use to produce something that is more important than they are and that precedes them. When Heidegger poses the ancient Greek form of *technê* as the answer to the problems of late modern culture, he certainly is open to criticisms that he romanticizes the past. But at times he is more interested in using the example of the chalice in a Nietzschean sense, as a supra-historical symbol, a historical phenomenon that is useful in drawing out certain distinctions in the contemporary situation. He means to suggest that here are certain aspects of the ancient Greek approach to technology and technique that may be useful in helping us think beyond the crisis of late modern culture. After all, the future is always made by returning to the past for narratives and myths, and reconstructing them so that they become something new.

What, then, is it about this ancient form of *technê* that Heidegger suggests is important within democratic cultures? For one thing, *technê* in this form is inseparable from what the Greeks called *poiesis*, the language of poetry and aesthetics. The happiness and fulfillment of humans, their destiny, is—according to Heidegger—to "dwell poetically upon the earth." Only through a reappropriation of the poetic voice (and here Heidegger and Nietzsche are in almost complete agreement) will people be capable of making the "leap" into an ecological age. Second, Heidegger sees in the ancient Greek form of *technê* as craft skill an idea that is central to democratic public life. Modernists, he argues, have placed too much emphasis upon a liberal form of democracy that understands progress in terms of the will to power—of either the individual subject and/or the "public" taken as a whole. As I have said, in craft practices such as those involved in bringing the chalice into presence, people learn to be less concerned with their own autonomous freedom and more with seeing themselves as part of a community and history, a broader becoming. Finally, the *technê* that produces the chalice encourages the decentralization of power and production to local craftspersons. There was no central government in ancient Greece precisely because the development of technology and craft techniques was kept in the hands of individuals. Thus, even as the individual is made part of a broader becoming, power is invested in individual craftspersons who have mastered a tradition.

What is the "essence" of technology in the modern era? According to Heidegger, modern technology and technique reveal the earth as a "setting-in-order, which *sets* upon nature." The earth is revealed to be no more than a "coal mining district," a "standing reserve" waiting to be exploited.[4] The sun itself, which provides the power locked in coal, is understood as no more than a supplier of heat, a heat which can be "ordered" from coal and delivered to steam engines, which can be used to keep the wheels of factories running. The irony is that by turning nature into a "natural resource," or into a "standing reserve" waiting until the time when it can be profitably exploited, people are likely to be treated in very much the same way. Heidegger points to talk about "human resources," about the supply of patients for a clinic, as evidence of this.[5] It is at this point that Heidegger introduces the image of a hydroelectric dam across the Rhine River. He is interested in what the dam has to say about nature and about our relationship to the natural world. So he reads the dam as a sign upon the landscape. What does the dam signify? What are the defining features of the modern hydroelectric dam? What *technê* does it embody? In addressing these questions, Heidegger uses a language to describe the dam that is designed to disrupt and trouble the way people usually talk about dams, by making visible what they take for granted in their thinking. He says, for example, that the dam "sets the Rhine to supplying its hydraulic pressure, which then sets the turbines turning." By referring to the dam as an active agent, Heidegger suggests something of the modern attitude toward nature. Nature is reduced to a supplier of natural resources for modern technology. The Rhine appears to be at the command of the dam, to serve the dam's purposes rather than its own. Heidegger writes that "the river is dammed up into the power plant." The river's reason for existing is to be tamed by the dam and the power plant. In turn, the technology of the dam is involved in transforming natural power into human power. The dam sets machines in motion "whose thrust sets going the electric current for which the long-distance power stand and its network of cables are set up to dispatch electricity." The meaning and purpose of the dam, its essence, is located within the context of a whole set of interlocking processes which distribute the river's power in an orderly fashion from a centralized point. It will be argued, Heidegger says, that "the Rhine is still a river in the landscape." But if so, how? "In no other way," he concludes, "than as an object on call for inspection by a tour group ordered there by the vacation industry."[6]

The dam provides, for Heidegger, a concrete example of a particularly modern way of seeing, revealing, and inhabiting the natural landscape. The particularly modern way of revealing the natural landscape, Heidegger argues, is one that assembles and orders the landscape so that it stands at attention, ready to be exploited. It orders and disciplines nature, both in the sense that it orders or commands the earth to give up its resources but also in the sense that it attempts to bring order to what is perceived to be a chaotic natural world. Enframing "entraps nature as a calculable coherence of forces."[7] Nature is made to stand at attention, to obey fixed laws, to be predictable. It is a wasted resource until it is exploited and put to some practical use, until its power is tapped. The efficient cause, the will to power, reaches new extremes in the human folly of damming up mighty rivers, to change their courses and flow, to make them serve human power. The hydroelectric dam, as a symbol that has broader relevance, may be associated with a particular form of modern schooling, in this case with human subjects as the river that must be dammed, the water that must efficiently be turned into units of labor power, ready to be distributed across the labor market power grid. The state must establish a plan for this "challenging forth" of human labor power, based on a statistical calculation of shifts in productivity, employment, and demographics. Hence, humans and majestic redwood trees are no longer in substantial ways different. Both are challenged forth according to an abstract logic of productivity. One is transformed into board feet, the other into "human resources" and "manpower." People are themselves ordered and defined by this mode of revealing and thus are in no sense free from its objectifying power. This is an instance when Heidegger and Nietzsche, along with Foucault, sound very similar alarms. For

Nietzsche and Foucault, modern institutional power is an apparatus of regulatory, disciplining, governmental control over populations and sub-populations, with the aim of increasing their productivity and their docility. In Heidegger, the modern institution, like the corporate/state conglomerate which operates the hydroelectric dam, is part of a challenging forth that orders and channels people and other objectified elements of the standing reserve.

How, then, can we begin to think and act outside of this ordering logic? It is not by attempting to "quit" modern technology and technical, means-ends rationality and returning to some pure ideal—as expressed in the metaphor of the chalice. This will only tighten the noose around our neck. It is not possible to "quit" technology and technical rationality, but it is possible to use an earlier form of *technê* to illuminate some of its problems, with the aim of finding a "saving power." Part of what is called for in finding a saving form of technology and rationality, Heidegger suggests, is attentiveness, attunement, preparedness for seeing and recognizing a saving form when it does flash before our eyes. He concludes by turning to several lines from the German poet Hölderlin: "But where danger is, grows /The saving power also," and " . . . poetically dwells man upon the earth."[8] The first of these passages suggests that the saving path out of the current technological and environmental crisis is to be found by looking into the very core of modern technological ways of knowing, to reveal a transformative new *technê* that will save us. The saving power will come, according to Heidegger, as an intuitive insight or "in-flashing" if we pay attention to the world around us rather than living in our heads, unmindful of what is right before us. Heidegger is vague about what a "saving" technology might look like, for it will only emerge once the modern era begins looking for it in earnest and questioning its own taken-for-granted assumptions about self and nature. By dwelling upon the earth and relating to the natural world according to a poetic attitude, the "saving power" will be revealed. It is less important, Heidegger would say, to worry about what the saving power will be than to be attuned to the world, to question it, to be ready to see a saving power when it presents itself before us. Nevertheless, Heidegger does provide some framework for thinking about a saving *technê*. It would have to be a technology of revealing the world and opening up a space in it that is based on a return to an ethic of caring for the earth, accepting it again as our home, our dwelling, as something we love. Caring about the natural and material world means caring about *conserving* it, that is, not treating the natural world like a resource that is to be used up, then disposed of, like some no-deposit, no-return Coke bottle. Caring also means not trying to reshape nature according to our own changing whims and our own image. When we care people, we allow them to be who they are, we respect their freedom, we resist molding them into who we want them to be. So it should be in our relationship with the natural world of which we are a part, Heidegger says. To conserve the earth is also to preserve it from one generation to the next, making it a home worthy of passing on to the next generation. The other and related caring attitude is *saving*, an urgent attitude of trying to rescue and protect the earth from imminent danger and harm.[9] When people adopt a saving attitude, Heidegger says, they will find a way of saving themselves and the earth. The attitude must come first.

Heidegger would situate education in the context of the crisis of late modern culture, which takes the form of a global ecological crisis. To respond effectively to that crisis, education must begin with the critical questioning of the dominant mode of revealing the world and dwelling in it, to make this "air" visible once again. Then, or simultaneously, education must develop in people the capacities for attunement, engagement, attentiveness to the possibilities within technologies and situations. In a very real sense, Heidegger had come to the conclusion that a saving generation would need to be educated, one that no longer took for granted what its parents had. Heidegger's work suggests, among other things, that the natural and human-made landscape is a curriculum text that may be critically read and decoded. Nature is understood to be a social construct, and we are led to ask what meaning, what myths, we project upon nature. Such a "reading" of the natural landscape actually involves a two-tiered reading of the world. First, it involves a questioning of the visual landscape that surrounds us in our everyday lives—as it has been shaped and framed by technology. How is the landscape ordered, according to what priorities and taken-for-granted assumptions? Whose interests are being served in this organization of the landscape? What *technê* have been used to shape the landscape? How do I dwell within the landscape, according to what attitude, mood, feeling? Do I view the landscape as an instrumental assemblage of parts to be exploited? Do I feel detached from or connected to this landscape? These are the questions Heidegger suggests are the most fundamental and basic questions we must ask as educators and students, before we can ask any other questions. They call for autobiographical and personal reflection on how we experience our everyday lives and what we take for granted in the landscape we inhabit. They call for deliberate and critical reflection on the material landscape of our everyday lives—the buildings, transportation systems, the way space within physical structures is organized, and so forth. Is space and technology within offices, factories, homes, and schools organized to encourage webs of relationships and equitable distributions of power, or is it organized to discipline and confine, to narrowly channel activity and set up hierarchical relationships?

A second form of reading the world is one step removed from the actual experience of viewing the landscape from a position within it. This is the reading of popular cultural texts—fiction and non-fiction, films and photographs, and so on—that represent "nature" and our own place in it in one way or another. If how we see the visual world around us is framed by cultural lenses, as Heidegger suggests, then how people write about the natural and technological world is even more open to cultural framing and re-representation. The reader of a fiction or non-fiction text is seeing nature through the writer's eyes, and according to the writer's framing. When the reader and the writer share a very similar cultural framing of nature—as is often the case—much is typically taken for granted in the writing and the reading process. The task in education is thus to encourage people to be more critical readers of texts, to question texts and how they represent technology and the natural world.

READING THE HYDROELECTRIC DAM

Certainly, as Heidegger recognizes, the hydroelectric dam has been a powerful signifier of modern progress and modern ways of dwelling upon the earth, and as such it has spawned a mythology of its own in American popular culture that was at its height in the 1930s through 1950s. More than any other technological achievement of the twentieth century—except perhaps for putting a man on the moon—the building of hydroelectric dams across the world's great rivers was a sign of progress, a sign of how science and technology could combine to transform the natural landscape. In the United States, the 1930s was the era of giant dams, beginning with Hoover Dam across the Colorado and then the even more monumental Grand Coulee Dam on the Columbia River. A whole popular cultural mythology grew up around dams, beginning with the dams built by the Tennessee Valley Authority (TVA). The TVA was based on a progressive belief that the federal government, in cooperation with local people, could control flooding in the river valleys of Tennessee. Its dams became symbolic of a new kind of project—a public works project, one that served the public and was controlled by the public. The builders of dams were depicted as modern day heroes. There was a certain amount of progressive idealism invested in dams in this era. They served as great symbols of national pride. The Aswan High Dam in Egypt, completed in the late 1950s, was the last of the great monumental dams to be built, and its construction was a feat of immense proportions, even involving cutting out and relocating ancient statues and temples along the river's edge. One can almost imagine that if the great pyramids of Egypt stood in the way, they would have been lifted onto rollers and moved safely out of harm's way. The origins of the myth of the hydroelectric dam certainly are intertwined with the technological and nationalistic mythology forged early in the twentieth century around the Panama Canal project. By the 1930s, the hydroelectric dam was replacing the Panama Canal as the signifier of the power of American technology to "tame" nature.

In the 1930s, at the height of depression era progressivism, even populist songwriters like Woodie Guthrie were caught up in this mythologizing of technology. He paid tribute to the Grand Coulee Dam on the Columbia River in his popular song, "Roll on, Columbia"—a song commissioned by the United States

Army Corps of Engineers that built the dam. As a child growing up in the Northwest in the 1950s, I remember singing "Roll on, Columbia" frequently in music class and at school assemblies. It was at that time the unofficial anthem of the region, part of the official mythology of the Northwest. The song begins with a tribute to the "wild" and "untamed" river that enters Washington State from Canada—"Green Douglas firs where the waters cut through/ Down her wild mountains and canyons she flew." But soon the tone changes. Guthrie writes of "the taming of the West"—the realization of Thomas Jefferson's vision of "an empire he saw in the Pacific Northwest." The building of the Grand Coulee Dam is represented in terms of a "battle" won against the river, and as a monument to that victory. The dam is "The mightiest thing ever built by a man/ To run the great factories and water the land." The song concludes with a tribute to the heroic efforts of the men who built Grand Coulee Dam—the new working class heroes.

> These mighty men labored by day and by night
> Matching their strength 'gainst the river's wild flight
> Through rapids and falls, they won the hard fight.

The river is praised, almost turned into a god, as American Indians once had viewed it. But now it is a god, a power, under human control—a working, utilitarian god. Also a patriarchal god. For the river, as part of Mother Earth, has been tamed by "mighty men."

In Guthrie's song I think it is possible to discern the underlying tension and contradiction within what we might call populist progressivism. Guthrie romanticizes the ruggedness of the American wilderness and relates it to the ruggedness of the American people, their untamed character. Then, only a few lines later, he romanticizes the taming of that wilderness as symbolic of the power and promise of the new technological, industrial, electric age that will make the life of all Americans better, more secure. He never appeared to recognize that there might be a contradiction between celebrating both the "wildness" of the Columbia and "taming" it. Not that being aware of this tension or contradiction will necessarily lead to its resolution. For this may be a basic, underlying tension within progressivism in American culture that cannot fully be resolved. It is easy, but also simplistic and idealistic, to say that we should un-dam all the rivers that have been dammed and return nature to its "natural state"—as if there was a stable "natural state" to nature. Nor can we afford to go on "taming" the natural landscape through technologies that not only degrade the natural environment, our habitat, but are related to ways of knowing that objectify, distance, exploit, dominate, and control. We need a technology and a transformation of the landscape that serve human interests like the dam, but that also reconnect people to the earth and are ecologically non-disruptive, the way the ancient pyramids still do.

One of the most popular books that both established and represented this dominant mythology surrounding the Grand Coulee Dam is Murray Morgan's *The Dam* (1954), a fictionalized journalistic account of the building of the Grand Coulee Dam across the Columbia River in the Northwest United States. Targeted at an adolescent and young adult male audience, the book romanticized the technology of the dam and made heroes out of those engaged in building it. While the book is written in story form, along the way the reader learns many "facts" about the Grand Coulee Dam, all of them designed to emphasize its bigness, its monumental proportions. The reader learns, for example, that the dam was constructed from 12 million cubic yards of concrete, making it the largest concrete structure in the United States. Grand Coulee is the first of eleven dams on the Columbia after the river enters the United States from Canada. Lake Roosevelt, the reservoir created by the dam, contains nine million acre-feet of water and stretches over 150 miles back to the border. The dam has 24 generators providing up to 6.5 million kilowatts of power. Water pumped from behind the dam provides irrigation for over half a million acres of farmland in the Columbia basin—farmland created out of the "wasteland" that was "reclaimed." Initial excavation of the dam site began in December of 1933 under the direction of the Federal Bureau of Land Reclamation. By 1941, the main dam was finished on schedule, demonstrating the effectiveness of new long-range planning methods subsequently used in planning the design and production of military hardware in World War II.

Morgan begins *The Dam* with a remembrance from 1935, when he was a young college student at the University of Washington. At the end of the academic year, his friend Carl tells him, "I won't be back next year."[10] Carl decides to interrupt his college education for a year or two so that he can work on building the dam. He leaves the academic world to engage in what he views as a more important form of public service—a kind of Peace Corps experience. To work on building the dam is to participate in making history, in taking one more step out of the cave and into the light. The dam is represented as a great symbol of democracy, built by thousands of people, each doing their small part, but drawn together in pursuit of a common good. That common good is the "taming" of the mighty Columbia River to make it serve "the people"—to generate power, to irrigate fields, to control flooding. Its purpose is to make nature adhere to rational "land management," to "reclaim" the "wasted" desert land. Nothing quite so grand had ever been envisioned, planned, or constructed. And so Carl thinks of himself as engaged in the building of a new pyramid, but this time a pyramid that "works" instead of just sitting there on the desert doing nothing. Choked up on emotion, Carl says:

> There are parts of our culture that stink with phoniness. But we can do some wonderful things too. That dam is one of them. If our generation has

anything good to offer history, it's that dam. Why, the thing is going to be completely useful. It's going to be a *working pyramid*. I just want to help build it.[11]

The books ends with an account of a conversation between the narrator and an engineer as they take an evening stroll out over the dam and gaze down at its spillways. It is evening, and the great floodlights that illuminate the spillways have been turned on, producing a light show that begins to draw tourists, thus creating a whole new industry in the desert that was not there before. But the engineer is fascinated by another unanticipated consequence of the dam. "We put these lights in here," he says, "and the next thing we knew the moths came, and right after the moths, the spiders. . . . Who would have thought when we built this dam that it would change the insect ecology of the Grand Coulee?" The engineer becomes reflective. The lesson he draws is that this is yet another sign of "just how much this dam has changed things. Now we know what it means to us."[12] This implies much. For one thing, it implies that ecology was being talked about among the public, or at least among engineers, in the early 1950s. But in this context, the ecology of the Grand Coulee region is not viewed as something that needs to be preserved and cared for. Quite the contrary. The dam is designed to change the ecology of the region. Finally, the change in the insect ecology around the dam is taken as a sign of human power, and thus something to be proud of. It is an example of being able to tamper with nature, altering its normal course of development.

Of course, it is simplistic and ultimately not very progressive to go around blowing up all the great dams across the earth's mighty rivers to undo the ecological damage they have done—which is considerable. The salmon may never return to the Columbia River now that the river has been tamed, and an indigenous Indian culture that was dependent upon salmon fishing was effectively destroyed. Power from the dam and irrigation water have opened up the desert to development in ways that are not ecologically sustainable. At this point, it makes ecological sense to stop building more and more dams, and to start undamming some of the streams and rivers that have been "tamed" over the past century. At the same time, a saving *technê* is not to be found by turning backwards to a romanticized pre-modern past. Even the hydroelectric dam is not all "bad." It has helped people move beyond reliance on burning coal to produce power, for example. And the observer who views the Grand Coulee Dam at night, with colored lights playing across the spillways and the roar of the water filling the desert air, is left with a powerful aesthetic experience. At such a moment the Grand Coulee Dam does seem like a kind of "working pyramid." Like the pyramid, it connects the human and nature, it makes one humble in the face of the power of nature and aware of our own place in the natural landscape. But monuments like the Grand Coulee Dam must become monuments to the past in an ecological age, enduring reminders of a form of *technê* that sought, naively, to tame nature rather than join forces with nature, as part of nature.

THE MYTH OF MOTORCYCLE MAINTENANCE

What might constitute a metaphor for an alternative, more progressive *technê*? Robert Pirsig's metaphor of the motorcycle, in the ecological cult novel *Zen and the Art of Motorcycle Maintenance* (1974), points to one possible alternative. Pirsig's novel is a partially autobiographical narrative of a journey across America taken by a father and his teen-age son on a motorcycle, traveling the back roads and feeling the exhilaration of being thrown down the highway, in intimate contact with the pavement, the landscape, and each other. The motorcycle is a metaphor for a relationship or mediation between human consciousness and the earth in which consciousness always finds itself "thrown." It is a symbol of a technology that returns people to an "authentic" relationship to the earth and each other. In one sense, modern technology—like the motorcycle—is the culmination of a detached and analytic rationality. It is designed according to a mathematical precision, and its form can be expressed in algebraic equations. It is a feat of engineering, reliant upon a complex understanding of the laws of physics. But the "essence" of the motorcycle is not encapsulated in this engineering, analytic *technê*. The essence of motorcycle technology is that it provides a way of connecting the human rider and the earth below, a way of bridging subjectivity and a material world and thus disrupting the boundaries that separate and divide the two. "Being," as the interrelationship of will and matter, "air" and "earth," is allowed to come into presence through the experience of riding a motorcycle. The rider, the motorcycle, the earth they traverse, and the purpose of their journey form a continuous feedback loop. The communication circle and relationship that is expressed through riding a motorcycle transforms the human into a communicative relationship in which information flows both ways. The motorcycle rider is a border crosser, staying close to nature and traveling the borderlands.

The narrator in Pirsig's novel is the father, and during the course of the cross-country journey he has a chance to reflect on his own life and also reconnect with his son, from whom he has been estranged. Indeed, his estrangement from his son has been part of his estrangement from the world, his withdrawal into a world of abstract truths. Throughout the journey, the narrator has flashbacks to a time several years before when he had been a philosophy graduate student. His interest in philosophy, it turns out, is intimately connected to his estrangement from life, for he has turned away from engagement to seek a firm foundation for his life in timeless, abstract truths and values—those supposedly available through philosophy. Yet the search for a transcendent Truth to live by has actually led him away from life. Consequently, he feels alienated from philosophy even as it seems to meet some of his needs.

At one point, as he is discussing Plato's *Phaedrus* in a graduate seminar, he has a revelation. They are discussing the famous myth in the first section of that dialogue in which Socrates compares the human soul to a charioteer, driving a chariot drawn by two horses. One horse is always trying to lead the driver down a path towards the True and the Good, while the other—a dark, passionate horse—is forever pulling in the opposite direction. As this metaphor is being discussed in the seminar, the narrator of the novel is suddenly struck with something I have already discussed—the fact that, in the final analysis, Plato always relies on myth and metaphor to separate truth from myth. In a flash, the solid foundation of truth upon which he had sought to build his life is revealed to be grounded upon the not-so-firm foundation of myth—and myth is the very creature from which Plato seeks to separate the truth. This ironic recognition that truth is grounded in cultural myths and metaphors and thus humanly produced, leads the narrator to an existential crisis and a form of madness. In the hospital, he is given shock treatment, which supposedly "kills" the logocentric, philosophical, abstract part of his psyche. What remains is his alter ego, which lives a "romantic reality." By romantic, Pirsig means to refer to that literary and artistic tradition of the nineteenth century in particular, characterized by a dwelling in the landscape, a sense of awe and wonder in nature, and an expressiveness of feeling, mood, and desire. The motorcycle trip is a manifestation of his new awareness of a "romantic reality." At the same time, and during the course of the journey, the narrator begins to become aware of the voice of Phaedrus reawakening within him. Slowly, be struggles to integrate the classical and romantic voices within him, to recognize the need for both an analytic, scientific, and philosophical reasoning and a reasoning that expresses feelings and personal experience, that is connected to here and now and the sights, sounds, and people around us in the concreteness of our lives.

One key to reintegrating the narrator's psyche, bringing an ecological (which Pirsig calls romantic) way of knowing together with an analytic and detached way of knowing, lies in bringing the human together with the machine in a caring relationship. Motorcycle owners, at least of folklore, understand their machines and trust them because they spend many hours maintaining them. They get to know their particular machines, and they care about keeping them in good running order. The machine becomes an extension of the self's authentic mode of caring for the material world. This is a quite different relationship between machines and their owners than is enacted in many commercial chain repair shops for automobiles and motorcycles. One of the recurring images in Pirsig's book is of the motorcycle breaking down along the journey. This time, it will require a new part to repair, and for that the father and son take the motorcycle to a motorcycle repair shop in a nearby town. As the narrator enters the shop, be gets an intuition that something is wrong already, that this is not going to be a pleasant experience. "The radio was a clue," Pirsig writes. "You can't really think hard about what you're doing and listen to the radio at the same time." Of course, it may well be the case that the mechanics do not perceive themselves as engaged in anything that requires a good deal of concentration and focus. They are "just wrench twiddling"—and having the radio play in the background makes this "wrench twiddling" more enjoyable. It makes the time pass more quickly. The narrator is troubled as well by the speed at which the mechanics are working. "They were really slopping things around in a hurry and not looking where they slopped them." A final thing that the narrator notices, as he attunes himself to what is going on all around him, has to do with the facial expressions of the mechanics. "Good-natured, friendly, easy-going—and uninvolved. They were like spectators." Along with education for docility, we must list education for spectatorship as a primary aim of most modern educational institutions. It is all the more ironic, then, that education for spectatorship backfires upon the educational institution. For young people learn to disengage, become outside spectators of the learning process, tuning out while appearing to still be there. The mechanics in the motorcycle shop have the look of students in classrooms. They are trying to make the time go as pleasantly as possible, without really engaging, without really defining themselves as doing something. "At 5 p.m. or whenever their eight hours were in, you know they would cut it off and not have another thought about their work. They were already trying not to have any thought about their work *on* the job."[13] And what is the effect of this kind of schooling to spectatorship? The mechanics never find the sheered pin that is the source of the problem, and the narrator concludes that it was probably a mechanic like these who had sheered the pin in the first place by installing it improperly.

The narrator returns to this repair shop incident again and again throughout the novel, each time finding new meaning in it, framing it in terms of a personal question, one that helps him reflect upon his own work. The narrator is employed as an editor of technical computer manuals, and he begins to see similarities between the work of these mechanics and the sloppy work he gets to edit. "What struck me for the first time was the agreement of these manuals with the spectator attitude I had seen in the shop." Indeed, the detached, analytic, spectator attitude was built right into technical manuals. "It has no relationship to you, you have no relationship to it."[14] He too had been a spectator, not caring about the technical manuals, just doing it to make a living. He too had been a spectator, detached from other people, nature, and technology. Once he believed that it was possible to write a technical manual for everything, for life itself. Now he was beginning to recognize that technical rationality can only take you so far, that without the caring that comes through engagement in the world, technical rationality leads to an erosion of quality and pride in craft—which is one manifestation of the crisis of late modern culture.

Pirsig's story of motorcycle maintenance by "spectator" mechanics has to be interpreted carefully in order for it to take on progressive meaning. After all, the argument that American workers have lost their concern for quality and for pride in craft has been a conservative argument. The 1983 report of the Presidential Commission for Excellence in Education, *A Nation at Risk*, argued that academic standards in public education have been falling largely because teachers and students were no longer committed to excellence, to striving to do their best, to being "world class" workers. Certainly, teachers, students, and other "workers" have not always been as engaged or as committed to quality as they could be. But this does not mean that the answer is for teachers and students to merely will themselves to be more committed to quality and excellence. The roots of the problem lie in the way work has been organized in modern culture, including schools and classrooms, which is also to say in the *technê* that holds sway in modern culture. The problem with motorcycle maintenance lies not so much in the worker as in the rationalization of work, the detachment of the subject from an objectified and distanced world, the hegemony of a technical rationality that reduces everything to a means-ends calculus. Pirsig's story suggests that quality education and quality work require levels of caring and engagement that cannot be mandated. Quality and caring will only return to our lives, and our educational institutions, when the binary oppositions that separate mind and body, spirit and material world, "inside" and "outside," have been ruptured.

BETWEEN THE GAIA HYPOTHESIS AND CHAOS THEORY

To this point I have not had cause to cast a critical eye on Heidegger's work, and on modern ecological mythologies of knowing and becoming. If modern ecological philosophy was able to critique the dominant Western epistemology of technical rationality, instrumentalism, detachment, and objectification, it was not effectively able to reflect back on its own "air," its own taken-for-granted investment in the archetypal image of the unifying circle, in which all difference is eliminated, in which everything fits together seamlessly and everyone serves the common good. Unity certainly is a central trope in Heidegger's work, since he represents "being" as a characteristic of the earth as a whole, with human subjectivity only part of the equation, and assigned the role not of increasing its own power but rather caring for the earth and dwelling upon it poetically. The earth becomes a symbol for a spirit that unites and runs through everything, an ecological spirit that unifies not from on high but by bringing everything within its circle of care, within its boundaries, and by making the system as a whole the sentient being. No longer residing in the heavens as a patriarchal father god, the spirit becomes the earth, with humans part of the web of matter and consciousness that constitutes her spirit, whose meaning is found in caring and nurturing for the nurturer of all life, the goddess. The relocation of the spirit in the earth goddess ruptures the opposition between humans and nature, making both part of a supra-organism and deity. This is a radical relocation that seems to change every-thing, bringing humanity back from its quest to detach from the earth and find god and thus itself in the stars, locating god back on a familiar earthy terrain. But the earth goddess, like the patriarchal god, still represents a being in the world that has a "mind of its own," a spirit who must—at some point—speak with its own voice. Otherwise, in what way is it a spirit? Herein lies the danger for progressives who would see in the earth goddess mythology the basis for a new ecological pedagogy of connectedness and caring. All unifying myths run the risk of investing that unity—that ecosystem, nation, or organization—with a mind of its own. They inject the system with a spirit that transcends the human, even as they make humans part of this spirit, this collective uncon-scious. Then the pertinent questions become, Who is to speak for this spirit? Who speaks in a language that represents the system and its "needs" over human interests?

These are the questions that Derrida raises with regard to Heidegger's work. Is it not curious, Derrida says, that the word "spirit" has been disinher-ited, banished from the vocabulary of Heidegger and Heideggerians? After all, anything that people go out of their way to avoid, to not recognize, must be something that still haunts them and that "magnetizes" their speech from first to last. Like Foucault, for Derrida what is unsaid, what is avoided and "skirted" in discourse, is as important or more important than what is actually said, for what is said depends upon what is not said, what remains unspoken. So Derrida proceeds to question Heidegger about "spirit" and "spirituality." These, he finds, were not always absent presences in Heidegger's work. Once they were quite visible, quite central to his project. There was a time when Heidegger spoke openly of *Geist*. Derrida returns to a 1933 address by Heidegger as he is about to be made rector of his university. Before the assem-bled faculty and students, he proclaims, "To take over the rectorship is to oblige oneself to guide this high school spiritually. Those who follow, masters and pupils, owe their existence and their strength only to a true common rooted-ness in the essence of the German university." This can only come to pass, according to Heidegger, when the "guide" (*Führer*) is guided in turn by "the inflexibility of this spiritual mission," a mission that "imprints the destiny of the German people with its specific historical character."[15] Throughout the 1930s and early 1940s, Heidegger *spiritualized* pedagogical leadership, endowing it with a divinely ordained mission, representing it as the expression of the collective spirit of the German people. Of course, in Heidegger's defense, he always maintained that he wanted to save the idea of National Socialism from its barbarous uses by Hitler and others, that by investing the idea of National

Socialism with a spirit, he was trying to elevate it above what it had become, to turn in more humane and caring directions and away from a politics of blood and national glory. Nevertheless, Heidegger's attempt to establish pedagogical authority on the notion that faculty and institutional authority figures are the voice to a unified spirit is reminiscent of Plato.

The spirit, after all, enters Western mythology as a unified, abstract, rationality and *logos* with Plato; and its project historically has been identified with the interests of those who would be guardians of Plato's Truth, whether they are on the political right or left. Such a mythology works to unify a cultural system around one voice, vision, and supra-human spirit. Whether that voice be represented by a father god in the heavens, an earth goddess, a nation, a "people," or an institution. This should raise serious concerns for progressives. For it means that if the word "spirit" is to be recuperated in a progressive sense (and I think it can and should be), it must first be made the subject of a good deal of questioning. Near the end of his deconstructive reading of Heidegger, Derrida observes that "Nazism was not born in the desert. We all know this, but it has to be constantly recalled." It was born in the rich earth of Eurocentric soil, like a mushroom sprouting out of soil that promotes its growth and nourishes it. And it grew under the "the shadow of big trees," protected by an "immense black forest" of educators, intellectuals, and philosophers.[16] Of course, it is foolish to try to go out of one's way to avoid using the language of "spirit," for that, as Derrida reveals, is part of the problem.

The idea of "spirit" is firmly entrenched in the language, in Western mythologies. It has served an important role, and continues to, in the advancement of democratic struggles, where it is associated with the notion of a struggle of the "human spirit" for freedom, justice, and equality. It is just that progressives need to be very reflexive in their use of this term, troubling its histories of usage and what it takes for granted, and resisting ecological mythologies of the spirit that unify everything into one sentient earth goddess. This is not to dismiss the earth goddess mythology as anti-progressive, or suggest that all talk of unity is part of an authoritarian project to erase difference. Myths of ecological unity and spirit can and have been progressive, but only when they bring mythologies of unity and difference together, into a dialectic relationship. Some basis for such a progressive ecology of unity/difference does exist, particularly among postmodern ecologists (to whom I will return later). However, within much of the ecological discourse that has influenced education in recent years, the emphasis has been on unity, and on the subordination of individuals and cultures to the needs of the system. Let me point to two inter-related examples here, first a version of the "Gaia hypothesis" in the natural sciences and political discourse, and second, a managerial discourse on institutional leadership based on an adaptation of "chaos theory" in the natural sciences and mathematics.

In the natural sciences, the idea of a unified spirit is to be found in the so-called "Gaia hypothesis." In his influential book, *Gaia: A New Look at Life on Earth* (1979), the environmental scientist James Lovelock argued that everything on planet earth is set to the motion of a self-regulating, cynergistic, global weather system which constitutes a sentient being—an idea he called the Gaia hypothesis. Lovelock came to these conclusions through the study of air pollution. His own research led him to realize that any attempt to understand air pollution with looking at the feedback loop or cycle between the atmosphere and the biosphere was doomed to failure. The result of this study was the formulation of a hypothesis that "the entire range of living matter on Earth, from whales to viruses, from oaks to algae, could be regarded as constituting a single living entity," one that was capable of manipulating and regulating the atmosphere to support and sustain its own needs. But Lovelock did not stop there. Gaia, he argued, is "endowed with faculties and powers far beyond those of its constituent parts."[17] Instead of the atmosphere being a biological product, it was more like a biological construction, an extension of a living system, produced by it the way a bird constructs a nest. As for the ocean, it assumes the function and role within the living goddess Gaia of "conveying raw materials to and from the biosphere."[18] Like a plasma system in the body, the oceans and streams are the arteries and veins of Gaia. This means that the worldwide ecological crisis, one aspect of which is the pollution of the atmosphere, is represented as the rape/killing of Gaia. For Lovelock, Gaia is an ecosystem that has evolved, in a Darwinian manner, to maintain the optimal conditions for life, adapting to shifts in solar output, the temperature of the earth's molten core, and a multitude of other variables. The human species, through most of its history, has been part of this "planetary homoeostasis."[19] Humans have slowly adapted to changing climatic conditions and contributed to the overall feedback loop which sustains life at its optimal level. The trouble is that the human species over the past two centuries has become "technological man," alienated from Gaia and consciously or unconsciously engaging in practices that have the effect of killing Gaia by disrupting the fragile homoeostasis. For Lovelock the good news, although it is not good news for humans, is that Gaia is far more resilient and adaptive than we think she is, and that she will survive our own self-destructive efforts—although she will not long put up with a species so self-destructive.

By the 1990s, the "Gaia hypothesis" in the natural sciences was slipping into political discourse—particularly progressive political discourse. None other than Vaclav Havel, president of the Czech Republic and one of the most influential post-Cold War political leaders in the West, was calling for a new global progressivism. On July 4, 1994, when Havel was awarded the prestigious Liberty Medal in Philadelphia's Independence Hall, he told those assembled that democracy would have to be redefined in the new era that was just opening up. Throughout the twentieth century, the democratic project had been almost synonymous with the extension of human freedom. While freedom is still an important concept for progressives, he argued, its meaning would need to be redefined. In the new global village it could no longer mean the unrestricted freedom to pursue one's own interests. To forge a new democratic order out of the chaos of the moment, he suggested that democratic social movements would need to rediscover and recover ways of knowing what our ancestors took for granted—ways of knowing implicit in the new science, "a science producing ideas that in a certain sense allow it to transcend its own limits."

The first of these new scientific ideas or principles, according to Havel, is the "anthropic cosmological principle," an insight as old as humanity itself that makes us aware "that we are mysteriously connected to the universe, we are mirrored in it, just as the entire evolution of the universe is mirrored in us." We are, in effect, part of the mind of god, part of a cosmic connection and unity that is the divine. Havel called for a new reverence, a new humility in the face of the divine revealed by the new cosmological science. Modern progressives had been too full of pride, of *hubris*. Now, what was called for was the humility that springs from seeing ourselves as part of something beyond our capability of grasping. A second and related anchor for a new democratic progressivism, according to Havel, is the Gaia hypothesis, the scientific theory that "brings together proof that the dense network of mutual interactions between the organic and inorganic portions of the Earth's surface form a single system, a kind of meta-organism." Human knowing, and human purposes, are thus inseparable from Gaia's knowing and Gaia's purposes. The Gaia hypothesis reminds us, he said, "of what we have long suspected. . . . What has always lain dormant within us as archetypes." Progress cannot mean merely thinking of new ways we can advance our own power and freedom as individuals, as members of identity groups, or as members of the human species, new ways of putting our own needs above those of Gaia. "If we endanger her [Gaia], she will dispense with us in the interest of a higher value—life itself." Ecological ways of knowing, Havel concluded, hold out the promise of a better future. They open the way for "peaceful coexistence and creative cooperation" based on a common conviction, a common "awareness of our being anchored in the Earth and the universe."[20] Havel also, however, recognized that in a global age, difference is becoming more important, and that a way must be found to balance global needs and concerns with the "new tribalism."

The unifying themes embraced in the early "Gaia hypothesis" discourse in the natural sciences have in recent years been countered somewhat by a growing postmodern turn toward what is most often called "chaos theory." James Gleick was one of those who translated chaos theory in the natural sciences and mathematics into a popular language in his influential book, *Chaos: Making a New Science* (1987). One of the stories Gleick tells to demonstrate how chaos theory has begun to take hold in the natural sciences has to do with weather forecasting. He observes that "the Fifties and Sixties were years of unreal optimism about weather forecasting."[21] The popular media were filled with stories about how science was on the verge of not just predicting but modifying and controlling the weather, so that, for example, hurricanes did not move onto land and areas of drought received needed rain. Perhaps more than any other metaphor, chaos theory is governed by the mythic image and metaphor of the global weather system as a fluid, unpredictable system. Modern science, of course, anchored itself on the myth of predictability, and with predictability the hope of controlling nature. Consequently, beyond its practical value, the goal of long-range weather forecasting had an appeal to the modern scientific mind. It signified that science was on the verge of "taming" that which had so long eluded control. By the mid-twentieth century, most scientists believed that the age-old problem of predicting the weather was about to be solved. Predicting the weather three or four months in advance with a high degree of accuracy was understood only as a difficult project, not a problem of a different sort. It was a problem that presumably could be solved once scientists had a sufficient amount of data and the capacity to process that data rapidly. This was such a powerful myth by the early 1950s, and one with such appeal to the public, that it quickly became one of the primary rationales used to support the space program.

In 1951, for example, an elite group of astrophysicists and rocket scientists working for the Army and for major research universities authored a series of articles in *Colliers* magazine calling for a public commitment to place a permanent space station into earth orbit by the year 2000—at an estimated cost of $4,000,000,000—with one of the "payoffs" to be long-range weather prediction. This series of articles, published in book form as *Across the Space Frontier*, included a concluding chapter by Fred Whipple, chair of the astronomy department at Harvard, who argued that with a space station, meteorologists would be able to "photograph every cloud on the surface of the earth, at least once in 24 hours." With special films, meteorologists would be able to measure moisture in clouds, determine temperatures on land masses; time-lapse photography of cloud formations would reveal emerging weather patterns. Whipple concluded, "Eventually the meteorologists will be able to make forecasts weeks in advance, because it would appear likely that a relationship will be found between the large-scale cloud, moisture, temperature, and wind patterns." When a bit more information is available—such as atmospheric dust levels and fluctuations in the sun's radiation—"long-range forecasting, possibly covering months or years, may be expected." According to Whipple, the answer to processing all of this information was "the huge 'electronic brain' calculating machines which we have today." Whipple concluded that "rain checks at baseball games would become obsolete. We can confidently look forward to such accurate forecasting when the meteorologist has a space observatory at his command."[22]

This myth of long-range weather forecasting was still the operative myth within the scientific community by the 1960s, and the technological breakthroughs that Whipple pointed to—the satellite eye in the sky and the computer—were beginning to be linked in ways that suggested to many that a breakthrough was at hand. Early weather satellites were sending back a stream of data on atmospheric conditions along with photographs, and the "electronic brain" of the post-World War II years was about to reach a "takeoff" point in its development so that it could now process and interpret this stream of data. This is where Edward Lorenz, one of the early computer pioneers at MIT, enters the picture. As Gleick tells the story, Lorenz had pieced together in his office at MIT in the early 1960s a computer that seemed on the threshold of this takeoff point, this "giant leap" in capacity to process information. Lorenz's computer was "primitive" by the standards of even a few years later. The machine, Gleick observes, "was a thicket of wiring and vacuum tubes that occupied an ungainly portion of Lorenz's office, made a surprising and irritating noise, and broke down every week or so."[23] It also printed out information in series of numbers that had to be decoded and then graphed. But Lorenz did have enough power to design a computer model that would predict changes in the earth's weather system, given twelve variables which were entered at the beginning of the program. He found that with these twelve variables, he could generate complex, computer-simulated weather systems over a several-month period, with patterns emerging and then dissolving again. The era of long-range weather forecasting, it seemed, had finally arrived. But one evening, so the story goes, Lorenz decided to run a program over again to check some data. This time, however, he accidentally changed one of the twelve variables by rounding off to the nearest thousandth rather than ten-thousandth. This almost infinitesimally small change in one variable produced a weather pattern after only two weeks that was totally different from the original. Lorenz was struck with an inescapable conclusion. Long-range weather forecasting would never be possible. One small change in a fluid system, as its effects ripple throughout the system, is amplified so that the whole system is fundamentally altered. Lorenz characterized this as the "butterfly effect." One small butterfly flapping its wings over Beijing today will affect the weather over America within two weeks. In place of the fantasy of long-range weather forecasting, Gleick observes that, "the simplest systems are now seen to create extraordinarily difficult problems of predictability. Yet order arises spontaneously in those systems—chaos and order together."[24] It was just that this order was not a predictable, controllable order. From now on, Gleick said, scientists would need to view nature in terms of process more than structure. They could no longer afford to be captives of the "fantasy of deterministic predictability" that was the norm in the modern era.[25]

Gleick defined chaos as "a science of the global nature of systems," bringing together scientists from widely distinct fields. What all of these scientists had in common, according to Gleick, was "an eye for pattern" and "a taste for randomness and complexity."[26] Aside from the butterfly effect, Gleick paid particular attention to two other images and concepts in the new science. *Fractals* are geometric branching structures, the best examples being snowflakes and other crystalline structures. While each snowflake develops according to a mathematical logic, the particular branchings on a snowflake are each unique and can never be predicted. Irregularity and difference, according to fractal theory, are built into the very structure of even mathematical systems. The notion of *strange attractors*, another idea Gleick relied upon to define chaos theory, comes from quantum physics—the physics of the subatomic world. According to quantum physics, the behavior of subatomic particles appears to be completely random or arbitrary. If we know the location of a particle at one moment in time, there is no basis for predicting where it will be the next, or the next after that. Only by computing all of its locations over a period of time does some order begin to emerge out of the chaos. The random motion of subatomic particles is seen to adhere to a trajectory or path, and also a central point. It is almost as if the particles are attracted to these patterns, paths, and points—held in a kind of force field. It is almost as if they adhere to some larger, emerging order in nature.

Gleick never applied this science of chaos to an understanding of social systems and organizations, but that was the next step, and one that was taken very quickly. Within several years after Gleick published his book on "chaos science," the ideas he and other popularizers of the new science explored were being taken up and incorporated into a "new paradigm" in business management theory. And within a few years more, this "chaos theory" in business management was finding its way into the discourse of educational reform and renewal. In making the translation from the natural science to first business and then public service organizations like schools and universities, one book has played a particularly important role—Margaret Wheatley's *Leadership and the New Science* (1992). The new organization, Wheatley argues, is moving away from the "old paradigm," the "mechanistic" metaphor that characterized the "age of bureaucracy," to metamorphose into a "learning organization," an organization that is always in process of change as it adapts to an ever-changing, chaotic, fluid environment—both within the organization and outside, in the larger ecosystem. Under such conditions of unpredictability, the primary managerial (or pedagogical) virtue becomes flexibility. Control from a "command central" simply will not work, at least not if the organism/organization is to grow and evolve in response to its environment. Wheatley thus encourages corporate executives and educational leaders to let go of the need to control everything, to trust that order will emerge out of apparent chaos. According to Wheatley, chaos theory in the new physics demonstrates that if we look at a system long enough, it always demonstrates an underlying and unifying orderliness, a force that brings order out of chaos. This is related to a theme that runs throughout Wheatley's writing. Leadership involves a spiritual element, and being part of an organization means being part of something bigger and more important than ourselves. The organization, for Wheatley, has a "spirit" and is a living being. When workers feel that they are part of an organization with a spirit, something bigger than themselves, something with a mission, then they are better able to integrate their own goals with those of the organization. Their "deep longings" for community and love can be met within the organization. This organizational spirit is like a "strange attractor" in quantum physics that draws phenomena toward a central tendency. The organizational spirit is thus a "meaning attractor." Once a meaning attractor is in place in an organization, "employees can be trusted to move freely, drawn in many directions by their energy and creativity." There is no need for management to regiment or even supervise employees. "We know they will be affected and shaped by the attractor, their behavior never going out of bounds."[27]

When this form of chaos theory is applied to the organization of educational institutions, it involves a two-tiered borrowing. It borrows a corporate managerial language and mythology that in turn borrows its metaphors and mythic themes from a new postmodern science. This means that in questioning the usefulness of chaos theory in forging a new progressivism, we must question the validity of both of these borrowings. The first borrowing (from the natural sciences) is linked to the second borrowing (from management and administration theory) in that the natural sciences are understood to provide a firm foundation for establishing a "science" of organizational development and management. The effect is to depoliticize the way organizations are organized and run. Chaos theorists like Wheatley say, in effect: this is the way things are in the natural world; and since this is the way "nature" works, then we certainly should run our businesses and schools along similar lines. We should learn from nature and adopt the "natural" way of doing things. From this perspective, "nature" provides the key to understanding both how culture is organized and how it *should be* organized. Historically, this depoliticization of social order and institutional organization, by drawing upon natural science metaphors and myths, has served some very undemocratic causes; so we need to be more than a bit suspicious of the use of natural science to ground chaos theory. Perhaps the best example of the social application of natural science metaphors in the twentieth century was Social Darwinism, which was used— and still is used—to legitimate inequalities as the result of natural differences in ability or competence. We also need to question whether there is one "natural" way of doing things in nature, or whether we are not involved in projecting our own myths onto the natural world. In the modern era, nature was represented as a source of stability and authority. It operated according to fixed and unchanging laws. Now nature is represented as a more chaotic place. This suggests that there are many faces to nature, many metaphors we can use to describe nature, and that none of them are "natural." Why compare society to a global weather system rather than the much slower, more predictable, if still somewhat chaotic movements of the earth's tectonic plates? Or why not compare society to an ant colony, or to the behavior of chimpanzees in the wild? From a social constructivist perspective, "nature" can be said to be a human, cultural production.

In this case, chaos theory may be appreciated as a variation on ecological mythologies that, in the final analysis, end up taking for granted a "systems" theory of society. Systems theory was influential in the social sciences and the business world throughout the 1950s and 1960s. Its governing metaphor was that of the biological organism. Society was said to be like a "whole" organism. Each organ in the body played its part in the overall health of the organism, just as each institution (the family, the schools, the church, the workplace, and so on) played its part in keeping the organism alive and well. For example, as Talcott Parsons and other early systems theorists argued, the role of education as an institution is to prepare young people to perform their expected functional roles in other social institutions. The trouble with this 1950s version of systems theory is that it tended to take for granted that the organism—society—was good. The only question was how to socialize young people to fit in, to play their expected roles in a relatively stable society. Not only was conflict ignored, but also change. The emphasis was upon equilibrium in the system, although minor adjustments to changes in the environment were acknowledged to be necessary. Chaos theory revises this systems theory of society and institutions by shifting from the metaphor of a mature organism, in which everything fits together in a relatively fixed structure, to the cybernetic metaphor of the earth's weather system, in which everything fits together in a chaotic and fluid order. This treatment of Gaia as a sentient, knowing being—as a meta-organism that unifies all life and all knowing on earth—is another example of applying a system's theory to "nature." If we think of the organization as Gaia, for example, it implies that the organization is what matters more than the individuals in it, that we all need to bow down to the new god—the organization—whose purposes guide us in our everyday lives. So chaos theory may, in Foucault's language, actually be associated with a shift towards a more "totalizing" form of control. Democratic forms of progressivism always have been based on the idea that people are the makers of meaning and purpose, not systems; and their needs need to prevail over those of "the system," whether that system be understood as stable or chaotic.

When natural systems metaphors are invoked within a basically managerial discourse, progressive educators should be even more suspicious of the "real" interests and purposes they serve. Democratic progressivism cannot ultimately be governed by metaphors and mythologies borrowed from the corporate managerial world—as chaos theory has been. Indeed, the wholesale borrowing of models and ideas from business management theory to apply to the organization and operation of the nation's schools is part of what progressivism will need to challenge in the new century. Should we be concerned that Wheatley established her reputation as a consultant to the CEOs of Fortune 500 companies, or that her book was named "Best Management Book of 1992" in *Industry Week*? I think we should be. For if corporate elites think chaos theory is so great, one begins to wonder just how threatening it is to the powers that be, just how much democratic and progressive potential it contains. Staying adaptive and flexible, decentralizing power within the organization, giving up on the need to control everything from the top with five-year plans— all of these are valued in chaos theory not because they are consistent with democratic values, but because they are consistent with rising worker productivity and corporate profits—always the "bottom line" in corporate mythology.

So it is that "chaos theory," in this corporate managerial form, turns out to be a theory that returns to themes and myths that have long been part of managerial discourse—order, unity, a common vision or mission that all who work in institutions are to revere. It is about the internalization of this vision so that employees never go "out of bounds," regulating themselves to meet the overall needs of the organizational spirit. Direct management through the rationalization of procedures (the "old" management) is to be replaced by an ecological management (the "new" management) in which procedures are kept flexible and management's job is to set the tone, hold out a vision, and speak for the spirit of the organization. Needless to say, this is a mythology that is consistent with a benign, human relationist theory of corporate management that has quite a long history. But this should only give progressives cause to raise some serious questions about the cultural politics behind the new ecological management and leadership discourse. Who, in the end, will speak for this living organism, this spirit of the organization or institution? If those someones are top managers and administrators, or senior faculty members and deans, do they claim that the spirit of the organization is speaking through them, that they are mediums for the spirit? Must the spirit speak with one voice of a unified knowing? Or is it possible to think about the spirit in a less unifying way? These are the kinds of questions that lead in the direction of a postmodern ecology of difference and limited freedom, in the direction of the cyborg.

EDUCATING CYBORGS

By the late twentieth century a new postmodern ecological discourse was being articulated that promised to overcome these problems. I will take Donna

Haraway as a representative of this postmodern, eco-feminist discourse, and more particularly the Haraway of *Simians, Cyborgs, and Women: The Reinvention of Nature* (1991). In the metaphor of the "cyborg," Haraway find the possibility of a radical new myth of ecological freedom, although she also recognizes that this is only one possible cyborg future, one that must be actively "made." Haraway acknowledges Heidegger's "Question Concerning Technology" as informing her myth of the cyborg subject; and one might even interpret the myth of the cyborg as an attempt to imagine a "saving power," a new *technê* constructed out of modern *technê*. The cyborg is a subject that now knows it cannot separate itself from its own technology of self-production and self-knowledge. The cyborg, Haraway writes, "is a cybernetic organism, a hybrid of machine and organism, a creature of social reality as well as a creature of fiction."[28] She invokes the cyborg as a myth, one expressed in various forms in popular culture. But as our myths, our science fictions, are self-fulfilling, Haraway treats the cyborg as a metaphor for a new type of postmodern subject. If this postmodern cyborg still is represented as inhabiting a science fiction world, it speaks of our future, even our present condition. The cyborg is the "postmodern collective and personal self."[29] Science fiction is peopled with cyborgs, and modern life increasingly is about a tight coupling between organism and machine. This means that the cyborg is to be viewed as a "fiction mapping our social and bodily reality," but also as an "imaginative resource suggesting some very fruitful couplings." By this time we are all cyborg subjects, Haraway argues. "The cyborg is our ontology; it gives us our politics."[30] So the real questions have to do with what kind of cyborgs we are becoming.

The age of the cyborg subject is ushered in, according to Haraway, by the breakdown of three boundaries in late modern culture, those that separate the human and the animal, the organism and the machine, and the real and the virtual. The breakdown of these borders is merely a fact of life in postmodern society, and the cultural politics attached to such a breakdown remain open. Modern science and forms of education, ironically, have been responsible for policing these borders and also setting the stage for their disruption. As for the binary opposition between the human and the animal, biology and the science of evolution produced the human subject as an organism and thus participated in rupturing the lines between the two. The opposition between humans and animals, Haraway writes, has been reduced to "a faint trace re-etched in ideological struggle or professional disputes." It is precisely here, where the boundary between the human and the animal is transgressed, that the cyborg is born. Thus, the animal rights movement cannot be dismissed as "fringe" politics, as taking the idea of human rights too far. Instead, it represents a "clear-sighted recognition of connection across the discredited breach of nature and culture."[31] Educationally, this calls for a critical reading of the representation of "animal" as Other to "human." As Alexander Wilson observes, "the presentations of baboons in zoos or movies as members of 'families,' or as 'aggressive' or 'territorial,' tell us far more about our own culture than they do about captive or performing animals."[32] And what it tells us is that we understand ourselves no longer as abstract subjectivities, as pure consciousness without body. As animals, we also inhabit the world in a non-detached, connected fashion, attuned to the world around us and the possibilities of the moment. And as animals, our understanding is limited by our situated position on the landscape and directed by our desires. The "human" implied a space outside of such a limited landscape, outside of desire, toward a pure and autonomous reason and truth. Now that the borders have been breached, we are beginning to realize the situatedness of our own knowledge, and the limits of a science that claimed to rise about human interests and desires.

The second border that is being breached separates organisms or living beings from machines. Haraway observes that "in the traditions of 'Western' science and politics . . . the relation between organism and machine has been a border war."[33] Modern science, once more, served to erect and maintain the boundary between organism and machine, even as it continuously disrupted that boundary through biotechnologies. So too did science fiction. The old myth of the robot was about a machine that at times seemed haunted by a ghost. Still, according to Haraway, "basically machines were not self-moving, self-designing, autonomous. They could not achieve man's dream, only mock it." Those robots or Frankenstein's monsters who dared to think they were human, or those computers like HAL in *2001* who dared to think themselves superior to their masters, their creators, were represented as paranoid. "Now," she writes, "we are not so sure." The computerized technology of the postmodern age has blurred the difference between natural and artificial, mind and body, programmed and self-generating. Indeed, "our machines are disturbingly lively, and we ourselves frighteningly inert."[34]

Thirdly, and related to these other breakdowns in boundaries, we are witnessing a rupture of the physical and the representational or non-physical. Haraway relates this to the popular fascination with quantum physics and Heisenberg's uncertainty principle in physics, which implies that the knower and the known are somehow inextricably interconnected, that our expectations influence what happens, that (ultimately) all we are, and all the cosmos is, is a vast web or grid of electromagnetic waves. Reality is never directly accessible. It must be assembled and represented, and it can be assembled and represented in different ways. Furthermore, the assembling and representing is nothing more than the manipulation of a series of digital codes. Haraway writes, "The silicon chip is a surface for writing; it is etched in molecular scales disturbed only by atomic noise." She predicts that computers will become more like "sunshine," light and clean because "they are nothing but signals, electromagnetic waves, a section of the spectrum"—a prediction that became closer to reality with the current generation of Apple "see through" computers.[35] All of this is an expression of a movement from representation to simulation. To speak of representation, after all, still presumes that there is a "real" world "out there" that the text or image represents. If this is indeed the case, it makes sense to ask which representations distort more than others, which represent the "real" more accurately or "truthfully." If, however, representations have no referent other than other representations, if there is no direct access to reality, if the simulation precedes reality, then we are in a whole different ballgame and playing field. This is the ironic world of the postmodern cyborg, a world in which the idea of a "realist" narrative is giving way to imagined and virtual "realities."

The cyborg is being assembled in the borderlands between these boundaries that separate human/animal, organism/machine, and physical reality/virtual reality. This means that we are entering a cyborg age, when cyborg technologies and *technê* become powerful forces in shaping and reshaping culture and self. It remains to be seen, however, what kind of cyborg will prevail in this "brave new world." If we are all to be cyborgs, who is to be our role model? Within science fiction, we can identity two quite different and oppositional cyborg fantasies, each of which provides a role model, or template, for educating cyborg subjects. The first, and dominant cyborg fantasy in the modern era has represented the cyborg as a product of a totalizing, centralized, technological power and rationality, as an extension of what Foucault called "disciplinary power" and "bio power." If this cyborg fantasy becomes our collective and individual reality, then the language of human freedom, social justice, and agency or will must all be abandoned as relics of an era now past. The second, postmodern cyborg fantasy, in which Haraway finds hope, represents the cyborg as more free and creative than the modern human, as ushering in a new era of democratic cultural politics, as a representative of a "higher" type of human. We might think of this as the myth of Zarathustra the cyborg. Haraway pins her hopes on this second cyborg fantasy, although as I indicated in the last chapter, the postmodern mythology of freedom and self-production is undermined by its own contradictions and limitations. Haraway remarks, "Though they are caught in the spiral dance, I'd rather be a cyborg than a goddess."[36] So I mean to view these two cyborg myths or fantasies as caught in the "spiral dance," the dialectic out of which each has been formed and continues to develop. We need a myth of unity, although in order to prevent unifying myths from becoming totalitarian and totalizing, we also need myths of difference and freedom, myths of human agency and will.

We might take the "Borg" in *Star Trek II: The Next Generation* as an example of the totalitarian and totalizing form of cyborg, a sentient *technê* in which every unit thinks only of the good of the whole, where everyone is plugged into the central brain or spirit that does the thinking. Borg units are all interchangeable, all egoless. To the extent that these Others to the crew members of the *Enterprise* represent an alterity, a negation of what it means to be "human," they are also a tacit reminder of what the human could become, a projection of a discourse on the human. The viewer identifies with the borg units as wired and programmed subjects and objects of power. The viewer also gains vicarious pleasure out of witnessing the freeing of a former borg unit, so that it becomes "one of us"—human, and thus supposedly free. Haraway views the borg and other cyborg fantasies as a "fiction" that is actively engaged in mapping social and bodily reality in ways that are similar to what Foucault has in mind in the idea of "biopolitics," an individualizing apparatus of control that is totalizing, from cradle to grave.[37] The borg units cannot (supposedly) desire a freedom they have never experienced. They exist only as they are programmed, and those programs do not recognize autonomy and have no word for "freedom." Their very thoughts are not separable from the central computer program that links all borg units on a power and information grid. This myth of the borg raises some troubling questions about how computer technologies are being used in educational institutions, and in popular culture, about whether they might be used in ways that program people to become good cyborg citizens, units without any real autonomy or independent judgment.

Could the cyborg represent a saving power rather than an oppressive power? To address that question, I turn now to Haraway's alternative cyborg myth, one she also identifies with science fiction. She notes in passing that Rachel, the escaped cyborg in Ridley Scott's film, *Blade Runner* (1982), represents "a cyborg culture's fear, love, and confusion."[38] *Blade Runner* is by now one of the most written-about movies of the late modern era, and not only reflects a particular cyborg fantasy but has played a part in making that fantasy a reality. So I want to discuss the alternative cyborg myth by returning to this film that Haraway only mentions in passing, to explore it in a bit more detail. The year is 2019, and the place is Los Angeles, represented as a dark, rainy, borderland space, a *film noir* space, in an age after the earth has been scorched and irradiated by a nuclear war. Life is hard here, and chaos prevails as the infrastructure of society continues to decay. Yet the technology of control has continued to advance, and people are kept under continuous surveillance. Global capitalism is more solidly in control than ever before, and air ships float through the hazy night sky flashing neon advertisements and seductive images, luring tourists to an "Off-World," a Disneyesque vacation land on a planet colony. If the "real" earth has been despoiled, there is still a Disney replica of it waiting for the tourist who can afford the journey. Even as the streets of Los Angeles are transformed into a chaotic and violent no-man's-land of street vendors, homeless people, and outlaws, technology has continued to develop to turn more and more of the real work over to cyborg robots called "replicants." The narrative begins with a bloody revolt by a new line of advanced replicants, virtually identical to humans in every way ("superior in strength and agility, and at least equal in intelligence"). When several of the replicants escape to earth from the "Off-World," where they have been enslaved, they are hunted down by a special police squad called the Blade Runner Unit.

Blade Runner implies that education is about the implanting of memory, and the only questions are what memories, who does the implanting, and for what purposes? This is the postmodern recognition. When Deckard, the "Blade Runner" who has been assigned to round-up and terminate run-away replicants, meets their maker, a man named Tyrell who represents all master programmers of public and private memory, he is informed that the latest generation of replicants has been programmed with a past so that "we can control them better." Deckard replies, "Memories. You're talking memories." Education is about memory, and through both public schooling and popular culture modern subjects have been programmed with a collective memory of the past, one that makes them more controllable and that depoliticizes their lives. But it is not a question anymore, if it ever was, of choosing not to program memory. History is always a construction, a memory that helps us make sense of our own lives. If we are to be free, it is not a freedom outside of the programming of memory, but rather a freedom in choosing between a proliferation of programs and possibilities, a freedom to become our own programmers.

This does not mean the end of the human, at least the human as that expressive, life affirming spirit. But it does mean giving renewed meaning to the human. In another conversation with Tyrell, this one with the rebel replicant Roy, Tyrell declares, "You are doomed to live your programmed life as a simulated human being and your feelings are all false." The effect of these disclosures is crushing at first, but not disabling. For if replicants have no essential being, no fixed essence, then they are radically free to begin re-programming themselves, assembling and disassembling their own memory banks. In the modern discourse of the Enlightenment, this self-consciousness makes Roy "fully human." He is now ready to accept responsibility for his own freedom. Ironically, as replicants take on human qualities, the "real" humans are becoming dehumanized and objectified, no longer fully human. The replicants have become what their human makers set out to build, something that, as the Tyrell Corporation brags, is "more human than human." As he is about to die, Roy cries out that he has seen things humans would not believe, "Attack ships off the shoulders of Orion." Then he grasps for a final poetic metaphor. "All these things will be lost in time, like tears in rain." In the great cosmic ecosystem, Roy imagines himself being reabsorbed and reassembled, recycled like rain from the sky.

Blade Runner suggests that we are all cyborgs. The only question is whether we are aware of it or not, and which type of cyborg we are. Postmodern cyborgs understand that they have no firm foundation for their sense of who they are. They recognize that they have been produced and programmed, assembled in schools and universities, that their memories, their innermost thoughts, the way they present themselves and perform identity, are not their own. The very foundation upon which they have built their lives turns out to be nothing more than myth, and a myth designed to keep them in their place. Such replicants are without anchor, but this makes them freer to assemble themselves, to decide who they want to be, to carve out a limited space for themselves outside of the commercialized, commodified, and objectified identities they have learned to perform. Norman Denzin writes of *Blade Runner*: "The simulation has become the real, but it outdistances the real, for what the androids have, no human appears able to find."[39] What the simulations/androids/replicants have is a capacity to engage in the kind of reflexivity that allows one to be free, although that word "free" must now be understood in a new way. What they have is a heightened capacity to engage in their own self-production, to adapt and grow, to control who they are and who they are becoming, to regulate their relations with others in ways that do not require negation and domination. The freedom they claim is that derived from the openness of the moment, the openness of all discourses and practices, and the existence of alternative discourses and practices of freedom. They also are armed with a new awareness that they are a "simulacrum," a copy for which there is no original.[40] As such, they feel no need to reproduce themselves according to a master plan.

How does the education of Rachel, Roy, and other replicants proceed? Haraway's "Cyborg Manifesto" suggests that the development of ironic consciousness is one key element in the education of free cyborgs. In order to affirm one's freedom, one must learn to live with contradictions that remain unresolved and unresolvable, with dialectics that have no clear or unified direction, with believing two mutually incompatible "truths" because both seem to be necessary in adapting to the situation at hand. For Haraway, "Irony is about humor and serious play. It is also a rhetorical strategy and a political method."[41] It undermines those who would find stable, fixed meaning in the world and highlights the extent to which all our truths are situated, partial, and contingent. Irony also is associated with the state of having no firm foundation under our feet, no place of origin or authentic selfhood to which we can refer or return. "An origin story in the 'Western', humanist sense," Haraway writes, " depends on the myth of original unity, fullness, bliss and terror." The cyborg "does not expect its father to save it through a restoration of the garden."[42] It cannot find itself by attempting to recover an imaginary utopian past or future, or an original and supposedly authentic self. The ironic self is thus cut free, able to become more creative and improvisational. Ironic discourse and practice is associated rather closely with another element in the cyborg's education, the development of the capacity for "shape-shifting." In Haraway's language, the subject is "stitched together imperfectly" and always being restitched, without a master plan. Rather than expect internal coherence and unity, educated cyborgs learn to live with pieces that do not quite fit together neatly or form a whole.

The education of the cyborg occurs at the borderlands, that new hybrid space being constructed around the major national boundaries that divide peoples and cultural identities. Thus, for Haraway the cyborg par excellence is the "Third World" woman of color, who is engaged in information processing in a global labor force, part of a new cyborg working class learning how to use the new information technologies, but also increasingly working on their own, contracting out their services. Postcolonial and "Third World" peoples also, more than most, now inhabit a cultural landscape in which cultural identities are blurred, multiple languages are spoken, cultural traditions and rituals rub against one another. Their writing blurs the lines between genres and registers and ironically plays with language in ways that shock the reader into a new recognition. We might take Gloria Anzaldua's writing in her influential book, *Borderlands* (1987) as an example. For Anzaldua, a Chicana lesbian, marginalized from the white, middle class women's movement, marginalized within a still patriarchal Mexican culture, and marginalized as a sexual rebel by a normalizing culture, the borderlands are a permanent state. The geographical borderland Anzaldua inhabits is that which separates Mexico from the United States, marked by "this thin edge of barbwire." If this barbwire is symbolic of cultural hegemony and violence, it is a barbwire that does not frighten some—in fact many—from crossing over it every day. Those who are border crossers are not a new homogeneous blend of Mexican and Anglo cultures, but rather people who shift back and forth from one culture to the other, speaking in diverse tongues, surviving by interweaving and juxtaposing ideas, literary forms, linguistic styles. The "new mestiza" represents a new type of educator/intellectual, whose aim is no less than drawing humanity back from the edge of ecological crisis and human exploitation and oppression by breaking through all dualisms, binary oppositions, borders that artificially separate and divide. She writes of the U.S.-Mexican border that it is a place where "the Third World grates against the first and bleeds." Out of this bleeding, a scab has formed and hemorrhaged again and again, and a new borderlands people is being created in the process. Who now lives in the borderlands? The "prohibited" and the "forbidden" find it their home. In short: "the squint-eyed, the perverse, the queer, the troublesome, the mongrel, the mulato, the half-breed, the half dead." This is a territory, in short, for those who "cross over, pass over, or go through the confines of the 'normal.'"[43] Gringos consider mestizas to be "aliens"—interestingly a term that refers to both those of Mexican descent and extraterrestrials. But these "aliens" are, increasingly, "us," as more and more people inhabit borderlands, where hybridity is taken for granted rather than uniformity and homogeneity.

The postmodern cyborg that Haraway and Anzaldua imagine is a subject who maintains "limited freedom" within a chaotic system characterized by difference and in which there is no center of cultural politics. Cyborgs come together around their differences, as moments in a fluid, cybernetic system that will soon reabsorb them and turn them into something new. Their politics is thus pragmatic rather than utopian, and they are not seduced by myths of an "organic wholeness" or politics that is aimed at a "higher unity." In particular, they are not seduced by Hegelian and Marxian mythology of a dialectic that defines one's politics and one's sense of self. Haraway borrows a phrase from the Vietnamese filmmaker and postcolonial theorist, Trinh T. Minh-ha—"inappropriate/d others"—to refer to the cyborg as one who does not engage in self-definition through reference to dominant categories of "self" and "other," the kinds of identities offered to the late modern subject by identity politics. To the extent that cyborgs define themselves by identity labels it is always for strategic purposes. Politically, cyborgs prefer a politics of personal communicative freedom and strategic political mobilizations over a politics of welfare state progressivism and reformism. Haraway looks to forms of politics that allow cyborgs to "join with another, to see together without claiming to be another."[44] Cyborgs are neither master nor slave, but "multiply heterogeneous, inhomogeneous, accountable, and connected human agents."[45]

Rather than view gender, class, race, and sexual identities as the basis for a proper progressive politics, Haraway seeks to liberate progressivism from the taken-for-granted character of these categories. The cyborg is not accustomed to thinking about "race" or "gender" or "class" or "sexual orientation" as if these were naturally given and meaningful categories. In fact, the rise of a post-identity politics is very much associated with the rise of networks of connections that cross borders and begin to see these identity borders as more oppressive than as potentially liberatory.[46] Cyborgs begin to view gender, race, class, and sexual orientation, among other markers of identity, as forced upon them by patriarchy, colonialism, and capitalism. In the subversion of identity in the new borderlands of culture, Haraway sees the possibility for weaving together a new progressive politics of hybridity. This is, in most respects, the cultural politics of Nietzsche and Foucault, and of Butler and other postmodern feminists. Haraway is keenly aware, however, of the problems of building a cyborg cultural politics around difference if no one ever wants to come together around any unifying principles or strategies. So, as a partial and contradictory cyborg, she embraces the myth of the earth goddess as well as that of the cyborg, although she much prefers the latter and feels the former has to be used carefully.

Both the myth of the earth goddess and the cyborg are caught in the "spirit dance" of the dialectic. The cyborg society can only be imagined as the negativity of a unifying mythological logic. If this seems to violate Haraway's claim that dialectics are not really possible in a cybernetic system, she makes no claim to be non-contradictory. Progressives have to draw upon both the myth of unity and the myth of difference when appropriate and cannot do without either. Cyborgs, she says, "are wary of holism, but needy for connection." This need for connection draws them towards a unifying politics, although one without a vanguard party or a determining dialectic. A cyborg unifying politics is not unified around identity so much as affinity, a strategic drawing together based on choice and common interest that dissolves again when it is no longer useful. Affinity politics is the only kind of politics that makes sense in a postmodern, cyborg world, in which "none of 'us' have any longer the symbolic or material capability of dictating the shape of reality to any of 'them.'"[47] It is the only politics, Haraway would say, that has the chance of saving the future for democratic modes of global public life, the only politics that might challenge the apocalyptic vision of *Blade Runner*.

TOWARD ECO-PROGRESSIVISM

Ecological education typically has referred to a study of "nature" or the "environment." To the extent that technology gets talked about within this dominant form of ecological education, it is as the despoiler of the environment. Ecology means making efforts to save sections of the earth from being despoiled, safe zones where "nature" is allowed to reign. "Man" and his technology are to be kept out as much as possible. We can now see that this ecological discourse is actually anti-ecological in the sense that Heidegger, Haraway, Bateson, and others use the word. It sets up a dualism or binary opposition between "man" and "nature" that does not actually exist in ecological systems. From this "deep ecology" standpoint, technology is the interface between mind, body, and world, a tool of communication with the world much like language and thus ultimately inseparable from cultural discourses and mythology. Education is, inevitably, technological education. "Schooling" we might define as a process of socializing young people into the dominant *technê*. In contrast, eco-progressive forms of education we might define as those that question the taken-for-granted character of technology and the way the dominant technology frames the way we dwell upon the earth and relate to others. Eco-progressivism also needs to be about introducing young people to counter-narratives and counter-technologies, ones that can be used to help stitch together a new *technê*, a saving *technê*. Haraway and other eco-feminists share with Heidegger and Nietzsche the belief that the currently dominant form of *technê*, with its objectifying, commodifying, and ordering logic, has a destiny of its own making, its own projection.

Modern science fiction fantasies imagined a future in which robots would serve their masters' whims and fancies, freeing humans to realize their fuller potentials as artists and adventurers. Yet, this modern fantasy was always just that. The destiny of the modern *technê*—a corporate capitalist, technical-rational, instrumental *technê*—always has been and continues to be apocalyptic, nihilistic, the final reduction of humans to cyborg slaves. At the same time, films like *Blade Runner* imply that the "human spirit," the desire for freedom and self-production, can never totally be extinguished. Eco-progressivism thus proceeds with a good deal of urgency, knowing that the hour is late, but also hopeful that, in these unsettling times, the saving power will emerge, people will not allow themselves to become cyborg slaves, that we can make the leap across Nietzsche's abyss. If that hope is to be realized, a new eco-progressivism will need to develop out of late modern culture, attuned to postmodern ways of knowing, global in its awareness and concerns, finding its strength in difference and localism, but also able to come together with other strands of progressivism in the mobilization of political power. It must question technology and what stands behind technology, that is, what interests it serves, what power relations it is involved in organizing, and what boundaries between human, animal, machine, and world it constructs or deconstructs.

Perhaps the November, 1999, mobilization of a protest movement to confront the World Trade Organization (WTO) in Seattle might serve as an example of an emergent eco-progressivism. As a movement, it coalesced around the actions of individuals and small groups increasingly connected on a global internet grid. In effect, word went out on the worldwide grid to come to Seattle to participate in the protest. Who came? Mostly white, middle, and upper middle class young people, living on the fringes and the borderlands of power and technology, a reserve army of cyborg youth ready to be mobilized by itself. But others also came. Third world peoples and indigenous peoples came, the new global information-age working class who feel increasingly exploited and colonized by global capital, along with the "old" working class of organized labor, upset about what the globalization of the labor force means to American workers. Anti-racist groups came, as did lesbian, gay, bisexual, and transgendered rights groups, eco-feminist groups, socialist and green party groups, and animal rights groups. All began to find a common ground of affinity, an admittedly unstable and provisional space to come together amid their differences. Interestingly, C-Span broadcast portions of a pre-march meeting, led by Starhawk, the popular eco-feminist novelist and activist. Here was a perfect blending of science fiction and cyborg reality, with Starhawk admonishing the young people to go into the protest with love rather than hate, to refuse appeals to violence and nihilism, to find their own space and decide for themselves what they are going to do. And so the protests and marches went off in their own chaotic way. People differed as to tactics and objectives, but little effort was made to paper over or erase these differences. Instead, they were made visible, as signs of the strength of the movement. Meanwhile, everyone participated in the web or communication that was the movement, the e-mails and web site information, the technology and *techné* that brought them all together. The "event" itself was also understood from the very start to be about a battle over signification. As a media event, it was designed to be turned into a signifier of oppositionality, to be read in popular culture and the seats of power around the world as a sign of things to come. So too was the cyborg cop reaction by the police department to be read as a sign of power, and a sign that the battle will be hard fought and long, that the revolt of the cyborg has just begun.

If there is a growing awareness of the importance of developing new ecological mythologies of knowing, and growing signs of the revolt of ecological cyborgs, there is also growing awareness in popular culture and philosophy that the hour is late for modern culture, unless it can transcend its current *techné*. In popular culture, as Mike Davis observes, there are a growing number of Hollywood movies and television shows that are apocalyptic, that suggest Mother Nature is about to take her revenge. "Could these be the Last Days," Davis writes, "as prefigured so often in the genre of Los Angeles disaster fiction and film?"[48] Films such as *Day of the Locust* are reflections of our own sense of impending ecological doom. Los Angeles, the symbol of the technical rational, market-driven epistemology of late capitalism, is symbolically destroyed again and again in movies about flood, fire, earthquake, nuclear, and asteroid disasters. Davis argues that this popular culture fascination with disaster films, and particularly those, including *Blade Runner*, that feature the destruction of Los Angeles, are both a reflection of public fear, but also a sense that Los Angeles is getting what it deserves. In this sense, natural disaster films are either self-fulfilling prophecies or, more hopefully, messages we are sending ourselves warning of what will happen unless we finding a saving *techné*.

CHAPTER 6

Leaving Safe Harbors

In his short novel *Nausea* (1938), Jean Paul Sartre examines bourgeois French culture on the eve of war. Before the narrator leaves Bouville, the provincial harbor town where he has grown up, a town that represents the bourgeois desire for security and predictability, he takes a tram to a hill overlooking the town—to step outside of the town's taken for grantedness, to view it from a more detached distance. It is Sunday, and he watches as the good people of Bouville flow out of the churches and into the streets, to take their after-church promenades along the bay. "All they have ever seen is trained water running from taps," he says, "light which fills bulbs when you turn on the switch, half-breed, bastard trees held up with crutches." They are given proof, over and over again each day, that the world obeys fixed and unchanging laws, that everything is controlled mechanically. Objects fall at the same rate in a vacuum, lead melts at 335 degrees centigrade, the public park is open until four p.m., the final street-car leaves the Hotel de Ville each evening at precisely 11:05 p.m. All of this gives the good bourgeoisie of Bouville a sense of security. So they are peaceful and law-abiding, if a bit morose. Every day is pretty much like the others. People go about their business. Nature, as an unpredictable force, has been banished to a realm outside the city gates. Or it has been rounded-up and placed in parks and zoos within the city where it can be carefully supervised. Yet, this security and predictability are an illusion. "What they take for constancy," the narrator observes, "is only habit and can change tomorrow." He questions what it might take to wake the fine people of Bouville from their sleep of reason and speculates that it might take some natural catastrophe. "Then what good would their dykes, bulwarks, power houses, furnaces and pile drivers be to them?"[1]

Democracy cannot be sustained from a position of detachment, by a people who no longer are attuned to the world around them or engaged in real struggles going on in the world, in which real human bodies are on the line, real people are being discriminated against, real battles are being waged in local communities over commitments to human freedom and equity. Sartre was critical of the French middle class before World War II for becoming desensitized to what was going on around them in their own back yard, so to speak, for remaining detached and uninvolved, captives of the illusion that their routine would not be shattered, prisoners of Plato's cave. It turned out that because they would not see what was before their very eyes, in the form of fascism, because they valued security, predictability, and order above all else, the French bourgeoisie was paralyzed in the face of the Nazi invasion. And their detachment meant that it was easier not to care what happened, easier not to feel responsible for doing something to stop it, or at least stand up defiantly in its path. They let others make decisions for them while they waited, secure that their predictable routines would go on without change, that they would not need to confront the necessity of acting in the world and choosing one future over another. Or they participated in blaming Others, projecting their *ressentiment* upon the Huns, or the Jews, or the communists, or the anarchists. Or they secretly admired the Nazis for bringing law and order to the streets and making the trains run on time.

Ironically, Sartre began to feel that the Nazi invasion and occupation were the natural disaster the French needed to wake up from their detachment and disengagement, their preference for order over democracy. In his epic trilogy, *Roads to Freedom*, written in the years following World War II, Sartre ends with the beginning of resistance, as a group of French prisoners huddle together in a train car headed for Germany, where they are to be slowly worked to death. The train is a metaphor for yet another journey, and one which they seem to have very little control over. They are prisoners in dark trains, unclear where they are going or what will happen when they get there. Like Plato's prisoners, they systematically mistake the passing landscape for signs that they are returning to the French countryside of their origins. Here, in a moving train, Sartre begins a story of resistance, of the building of democratic community. In the train together they begin to feel what it means to be denied freedom. They feel it to the core of their being. They also feel the intimacy of their fellow prisoners, body rubbing against body, the sights and smells and sounds of the moment, of here and now. Slowly, they begin to talk among themselves about what they might do. With no apparent order or direction to their spontaneous comments, the group begins to develop a sense of collectivity, and they begin to think about what they are going to do, no longer harboring any illusions. They become fully absorbed in the here and now of living and planning their resistance. A young political activist in the train car comments to himself that in this hour of darkness, "the game's won." The war against fascism was won at the moment when people, groping around in the dark, began to become reengaged, to realize they were involved in common if also separate journeys, and that they have some control over what happens to them, over who they will be. The train and its prisoners become, in an ironic and contradictory manner, symbols of democratic education and public life, and of progressivism "grinding, bumping, shuddering its way onward."[2]

In one way or another, all of the new progressive mythologies I have examined in this book share this common narrative of education and cultural development as a journey away from safety zones and safety nets, away from what is comfortable and secure, away from the predictable habits and commonsense wisdom of our routine, everyday lives. In *Moby Dick*, Melville speaks of the new urban workers, of various strata, as increasingly "landsmen," men and women who have allowed themselves to be "tied to counters, nailed to benches, clinched to desks."[3] He is led to ponder about what has become of the democratic spirit, about the capacity of Americans to demand that the promise of democracy be realized in a much fuller sense, to change and adapt, to take on the challenge of building a new, post-slavery America, of re-building the nation around the diversity of its peoples. Still, Melville observes that these "landsmen" who have become so thoroughly domesticated and controlled also spend their lunch hours as "water-gazers," leaning against the rails of peers, striving to catch a glimpse of life beyond land, beyond safe harbors, caught up in the desire to begin a new journey. This may be a form of romantic escapism, but it also speaks, Melville suggests, to deep desires and needs for something more than what modern, instrumental business culture has to offer. It also speaks to an orientation toward change, toward striving after important goals. Progressives tend to believe that everyone has such strivings within them, strivings which are an expression of what Hegel called "yearnings"—yearnings toward freedom, equity, and community, and for recognition of others outside of the need to "other" anyone.

Progressives must resist the desire, born out of insecurity and fear, to "fix" the world under a clarifying gaze, to offer students and "the public" ready answers to perceived problems, to stay with what is comfortable and safe. For one thing, there are no safe harbors, even if we may like to pretend there are. There is no one, unified, unchanging truth that we can rest our feet upon, no firm foundations that we can use to define who we are. Beyond this, one could say that the current cultural terrain of late modern or "postmodern" culture is one in which truth and value are more un-fixed than ever before. A number of changing are rippling through postmodern culture. Shifts are occurring in the natural sciences, philosophy, and popular culture associated with the notion that "ways of knowing" play a part in shaping and organizing what we see and how we relate to others and the natural world. The critical shift here is away from an understanding of knowledge or truth as something that exists prior to and independent of the language that describes and represents it. The postmodern shift is to a recognition of the formative or generative role of language in producing the world both symbolically but also materially. All of this is linked to a language of paradigm shifts, transformative thinking, and the importance of learning to "think" the world differently. Of course, this can be and often is taken very simplistically, and there is much talk these days in education of "new paradigms" and "transformative" new models of curriculum development or school leadership. These typically are only variations on the same old reform models. They do, however, point to an awareness that is quite important and central to what is happening in postmodern America: people are beginning to move beyond mythologies that represent education in terms of the transmission of a corpus of knowledge to receptive students, and more in terms of the process by which knowledge or truth is actively constructed— that is, the reasoning process. Furthermore, this reasoning process is now understood to be culturally and historically-bounded, and also specific to one's location or position within society. If not everyone would agree with this "constructivist" theory of knowledge, it is increasingly accepted in the academy and in wide sectors of popular culture.

In such a new and unsettling time, the new progressivism shifts its orientation from "correcting" history, from countering "distorted" ideological truths with a "politically correct" truth. Such an orientation can only play into the sense that progressives are still living in the "old" modern world, that they have not understood the profundity of the shift occurring in human consciousness. Language, and the mythic core of language, are now understood to play a generative and formative role, to shape both our reading of texts and the texts themselves. Language thus becomes the central concern of a new progressivism in education, and the role of language in constituting the world along particular lines. Furthermore, I have argued throughout this book that until people are able to "re-think" self, world, and Other, they have not really changed, no matter how much more information they have access to, no matter how many textbooks they read. They also are not able to reconstruct self and culture to meet the challenges of unsettling times. A core theme that runs throughout this text, consequently, has to do with the importance of a progressive education that encourages reflection of the mythologies that frame and organize the production of truth. These include our own mythologies as well as those mythologies embedded in both popular culture texts and official school texts.

In using a language of myth, I realize I am subverting the normal meaning of this word among progressives, so part of my interest is in troubling this taken-for-granted treatment of myth. I do this with the realization that it is risky to talk about myth in new ways, and to suggest that progressives take another look at myth. But this is precisely what I think is called for, and precisely what a cultural studies of education offers. At the same time, I think progressives will need to be careful in talking about myth in a positive sense, as I have. I want to distinguish myself, for example, from one current of discourse on myth in popular culture that bemoans the loss of myth and associates myth with a the security of firm foundations for individual development. According to the humanistic psychologist Rollo May, for example, there is a "cry for myth" in modern American society, and particularly among the young. "Many of the problems of our society," he writes, "including cults and drug addiction, can be traced to the lack of myths which will give us as individuals the inner security we need in order to live adequately in our lives."[4] May's argument is that modern culture has lost its vitality, its sense of purpose and direction, because it has lost touch with its founding and governing myths. As a result, the individual experiences meaningless and alienation, a loss of values and purpose. Now I do not necessarily want to disagree with such an assessment of the modern age. In some ways, it is quite insightful. There is a cry for myths that stir people to face life's challenges, adversities, and opportunities, to uphold ideals that are worth living and even dying for, other than making more money and moving on up the organizational hierarchy. At this beginning of a new century and a new age, one that will call upon us to face unexpected challenges, to keep the democratic vision alive in unsettling times, people are looking for myths to live by, both individually and collectively. So I think Rollo May is right when he says that contemporary society is marked by a cry for myth. As the dominant culture has become more scientific, rational, technical, and practical, it has ignored the importance of myth in sustaining the vitality and creativity within a society. Myth has been ignored, de-bunked, and left behind. Or so it would seem. But it is not quite that simple, of course. The truth is that there is myth all around us, and that modern culture is itself governed by a core set of myths and metaphors. Furthermore, the myths progressives have to offer are not ones that will re-establish a firm foundation of social and moral order. They will not offer security to people who feel they are being tossed about at sea. Nor will they hold out the illusion that all we need to do is to reconstruct the world is to "re-think" it.

FROM THE PHOTOGRAPH OF THE COSMOS TO *THE MATRIX*

To leave the safe harbors of modern, scientific rational mythologies, progressives need only pay attention to certain developments occurring quite rapidly that have do to with visual representation and cosmology. Throughout the twentieth century, "normal science" was grounded on the modernist hope of obtaining an ever more accurate and detailed "picture" of the cosmos—the idea of capturing the truth about the world on film, to fix it, to reveal it from above the distorting effects of the earth's atmosphere. Photographs were presumably "objective" facsimiles of the "real thing." They were not, it was said, like paintings, in which the painter always puts something of her- or him-self into the painting, even in attempting to "realistically" depict a landscape. A good photographer, of course, appreciates the extent to which photography is an active framing and enhancing of the landscape much as painting is. But the idea that the photograph was a mirror image representation of reality gave a certain stability to the modern world. The world could be photographed, fixed, revealed under the light of the flashbulb, and made to reveal its truth. Photojournalists from *Life* magazine went out to record "snapshots" of every-day life in America, snapshots that presumably spoke for themselves, revealing the truth about life in America in a direct, accessible, objective, undistorted way. Unlike words, it was said that the "camera does not lie." At the same time, Americans were urged to document their own lives on Kodak film. No need to keep a journal or write letters, for those accounts of life are subjective. Instead, one only had to record one's life on film with a Kodak Instamatic. It is almost as if the modern age created the myth of the photograph first, then went about inventing the camera.

It was only "natural," consequently, to presume that the way to finally clear up the mystery about what the cosmos looked like would be to build a powerful enough telescope, put it in orbit, and take a picture of it. In 1990, this modernist myth of taking a picture of the cosmos finally seemed within reach with the launch of the Hubble Space Telescope (HST)—a joint venture of NASA and the European Space Agency. Unfortunately, the long-awaited first pictures from the new orbiting telescope were disappointing. The Hubble Telescope had a spherical aberration in the mirror, so pictures came back fuzzy rather than distinct. In 1993, this problem was corrected during a dramatic spacewalk repair job by shuttle astronauts, and the world sat back to wait for the new pictures to begin to arrive. When they did arrive, they lived up to expectations. When the Hubble Telescope looked into deepest space, at the very edge of the universe, it was actually looking at the cosmos of 13 billion years ago, as if space were its own time machine and we were watch-ing the early childhood of the cosmos only two billion years or so after the Big Bang. At the edge of the universe, Hubble saw embryonic galaxies glow-ing in gaseous clouds, with cosmic winds blowing the galaxies outward at an enormous and accelerating speed. The new cosmos revealed by Hubble is one of "black holes," of "walls" of galaxies, of warpage in time and space, of unimaginable complexity, of unimaginable wonder, of (ultimately) unknowa-bility and unintelligibility. The cosmos itself acts as a "lens" that magnifies and distorts the light from these deep space galaxies, so it is impossible to see them as if through an empty space. In the end, the photographs from deep space only further undermine the modernist belief that it is possible to reveal the cosmos "clearly," without distortion.

In fact, NASA did not even use the word "photograph" to describe the images released to the public. They were acknowledged to be computer generated and enhanced images, produced by an "imaging team." They were images constructed in a virtual, electronic world, digital displays of binary data assembled by computers and human information "artists" to produce an image that the people could make some sense of. They were colorized and enhanced images, even three-dimensional images—constructed by a new breed of NASA computer "geeks." According to a NASA spokesperson, computer imaging is the "art" of dividing the world into digital codes, "and then playing computer games with them to release their potential."[5] A scientist on the Hubble imaging team is quoted in a *New York Times* story as saying, "the color does not represent anything physical but is simply a way of contrasting different brightness levels. This is far from snapping a photo. We have to have computers and high technology to do this stuff."[6] NASA "imaging experts" also made it clear that Hubble was able to detect only a very small part of what was "out there," since it was designed to see what humans can see—which is a very small part of the "big picture." Hubble misses entirely the "background noise" of the universe consisting of radiation left over from the Big Bang—which may be more than 90 percent of the mass of the universe. Hubble cannot "see" the greatest pieces of cosmic architecture at all—the black holes at the centers of galaxies— because these holes absorb all light. All of these qualifications by NASA officials lead *New York Times* science columnist Gustav Niebuhr to observe, "The brain paints its pictures with a paltry palette. We are surrounded by a world we cannot see." The Hubble images, he wrote, are "somewhere between a photograph and an impressionist painting." Such images suggest that "there are many different ways the world can be mapped inside a brain or a computer. The mental pictures we take for the real world are just as much constructions as the enhanced infrared images or Van Gogh's 'Starry Night.'"[7] This is a quite astonishing statement. To compare the Hubble images with a Van Gogh painting is to link the scientist with the artist and suggest both are in the business of producing images or representations of the world, investing it with a coherent shape and reading meaning into it.

The idea that the cosmos must be represented, and that it is therefore not directly accessible to the senses and reason, began to enter the scientific community in a rather dramatic way with the publication of Thomas Kuhn's *The Structure of Scientific Revolutions* (1962)—certainly one of the most influential books of the twentieth century. Kuhn was an historian of science, and a member of a new breed of historians of science who were beginning to ask some very fundamental questions about scientific models of the cosmos. Traditionally, historians of science had examined "older science" to find out what its contribution was to modern science's knowledge of the world and the physical and mathematical laws which hold the world together. So, for example, historians of science asked what the contributions of Galileo were to modern astronomy or physics. But Kuhn was more interested in "the relation of Galileo's views to those of . . . his teachers, contemporaries, and immediate successors in the sciences."[8] That is, he was interested in Galileo as an historical actor, but also as expressive of a shift in thinking about the cosmos and about scientific models and "pictures" of the cosmos that was circulating in the scientific discourse of the age. Galileo, according to Kuhn, was one of those who began to see the cosmos through new lenses, according to a new "paradigm" or conceptual framework. For Kuhn, science historically has advanced not through the accumulation of more and more data, more and more facts, but rather through paradigm shifts—fundamental shifts in the way the universe is represented or imagined. When an old paradigm no longer serves to adequately explain phenomena, there is a crisis in "normal science." This crisis leads to "scientific revolution"—the emergence of a new scientific theory or discourse that overcomes the limitations of the old. At no time, consequently, are scientific explanations or models "objective." Kuhn concluded that we may have to "relinquish the notion, explicit or implicit, that changes of paradigm carry scientists and those who learn from them closer and closer to the truth."[9] We must give up the pretense that there is "some one full, objective, true account of nature."[10] The cosmos may be known and represented in far more elegant, sophisticated, and complex ways than it now is. Science should not be content with its current truths and ways of knowing. But Kuhn argues that no matter how elegant our theories and detailed our "pictures" of the cosmos, they must always be representations, and rather poor ones at that. What Kuhn was proposing was itself a scientific revolution, a new way of thinking that fundamentally challenged the "normal science" of the early 1960s.

The postmodern world is one in which all we have is images, representations of reality, virtual realities constructed by computers with an eye to the artistic. The effect of all of this has been that scientists and the general public are beginning to view "truth" and "reality" in a much different way, to begin to focus on the linguistic and conceptual lenses used to produce a particular picture or representation of the "real," while "reality" itself remains elusive, never accessible to any direct, unmediated reason. Donna Haraway writes: "Twentieth-century people are used to the idea that all photographs are constructs in some sense, and that the appearance that a photograph gives of being a 'message without a code,' that is, what is pictured being simply there, is an effect of many layers of history." Interestingly, Haraway observes that the first pictures of the planets radioed back to earth by planetary probes such as Voyager in the 1970s, "up the ante on this issue by orders of magnitude." Such pictures have "gone through processes of construction that make the metaphor of the 'eye of the camera' completely misleading."[11] Not only are the images virtual, so too are we, as we become "virtual spacemen" on a tour of the cosmos, revealed before us in a computer-generated fly-by of the planets. In these virtual images and virtual voyages, Haraway sees the boundaries between Outer Space and Inner Space eroding. Without those boundaries firmly established, the cyborg is beginning to be aware of the power of its visions and imaginings to change self and world.

The film *The Matrix* (1999) provides a good case in point. On one level, *The Matrix* is yet another re-telling and re-scripting of Plato's cave analogy, set in a dystopian future. The Zarathustrian hero of *The Matrix* is a computer hacker who has begun to suspect that the ostensibly "real" world he and others inhabit is really a computer simulation. Reality, it turns out, is much harsher. People are actually prisoners in a great underground chamber, kept plugged into machines and fed a programmed reality, even as their bodies are being used as batteries to sustain the Matrix—that master computer program, that information grid, that virtual reality that has taken over the world. The "real" world has been ecologi- cally devastated in a great war between humans and robots, but the virtual world has gone on, and is now the one people inhabit, along with certain sen- tient beings who control the Matrix. Some humans have begun to wake up to what is going on (to literally unplug themselves) and have chosen to live in the "real" world, with all of its shortcomings. There they lead a resistance against the Matrix.

Morpheus, the spiritual leader of the rebel humans, tells Neo, the computer hacker hero of the film, that he has been living a dream, "a world that that has been pulled over your eyes to blind you from the truth." What is that truth? "That you're a slave." Thus, the rebellion is that of the oppressed, against their oppressor, and in this case it takes the form of preferring the "real" world, with all its limitations, over the Matrix that has been programmed by the master. But this choice of the "real" world over the virtual is also problematized. As Morpheus leads Neo around a computer program world, he asks, "What is real?" Real, he says, is only a series of electrical signals that are interpreted by the brain to produce and image. So this virtual world is, in one sense, only a variation on a theme, and one that offers people great new powers if they learn to use it in certain ways. The film ends not with the destruction of the Matrix, but with Neo returning, like Zarathustra, to tell people that they can use the Matrix to make a giant leap in consciousness, in the direction of understanding their own role in the construction and reconstruction of "reality."

THE CURRICULUM AS A REPRESENTATIONAL TEXT

This shift taking place in the understanding of "reality," in both the sciences and popular culture, may seem interesting but also a bit dangerous, and not very closely connected to a progressive cultural politics. It may seem danger- ous because it threatens to take progressives down the rabbit hole, to borrow a phrase from *The Matrix*. It threatens to lose us in a mirror game, or to make us think that there is nothing substantial to the world, that it is all some elaborate simulation. It seems unconnected to a progressive cultural politics because it gets "lost in the stars." It has relevance, perhaps, to the study of the cosmos, or the quantum world, and thus to science and mathematics education. But what does it mean in terms of democratic struggles going on in contemporary American society? It means, I think, that progressives need to focus on curriculum as a representational text, and upon forms of critical literacy that involve asking: How does this text represent the world and particular identity groups in the world? What mythologies and narratives framed the representation process? What mythologies and narratives frame my own reading and interpretation of texts? How might various narratives be parodied, subverted, and re-scripted to give them new meaning?

Let me offer a few examples that point to some of the ways textbooks might be read, and thus de-authorized as "the" truth, by focusing upon the underlying myths and narratives that frame the representational process. In my work with teachers, I have often found it useful to do deconstructive readings of textbooks from the past, for we are able to place some distance between ourselves and the past, and it becomes easier for us to approach the text from the outside. Then we can see how the "truths" it affirms, and the values it takes for granted, are very much truths and values that are related to the particular consciousness of the age, to a particular way that the author and others of that time "thought" the world into existence. We can see that to "think" the world anew it is necessary to "un-think" some of what was part of the commonsense mythology of an earlier era; and we can see similarities and continuities between the present and the past that remind us how much we are still living according to some of the same old myths.

A good text to begin with, one that places itself within a particular strand of progressivism early in the twentieth century, is Ellwood P. Cubberley's influential book, *A Brief History of Education* (1922), a standard textbook in many teacher education programs beginning in the 1920s and continuing through the 1940s—a book that was lauded for its progressive philosophy. Cubberley concludes with a chapter on "New Tendencies and Expansions," in which he points to some of the progressive ideas and model programs that were lighting the way to a better future—the public schools and colleges leading the way. And what is this way? One path being opened by the new progressives Cubberley writes about under sections titled "The Education of Defectives" and "The Education of Superior Children." Of the "defectives," Cubberley observes, "Today the state school systems of Christian nations generally make some provisions … for the training of children who belong to the seriously defective classes of society." Since "defective" children cannot be expected to serve productive economic roles, their education is an expression of the altruism of the modern state. Note, however, that this secular concern is not fully separated from the religious yet. Secular authority is, in these ways, only an extension of religious authority; and both supposedly are grounded upon altruism. Presumably, non-Christian nations would not do as much for their "defectives." And how are these "defectives"—who include large numbers of illegitimate children and those who populated orphanages, along with those who have very low IQ scores—to be cared for? How are their needs to be met? According to Cubberley, their needs are to be met within the modern, specialized state institutions being built "on a large scale" to house, care for, and educate them. Within the new state institutions, a new cadre of specialized professional educators is being created, specially trained to work with "defectives."

Surely, Cubberley concludes, all of this that is being done for "defectives" must be taken as another sign of "the rise of humanitarianism, altruism, justice, order, morality, and civilization itself." Yet he cautions that we should not let our altruism be the only guide in educating "defectives." They are, after all, not going to be productive citizens, and we must approach their education with a pragmatic and utilitarian concern as well as with an altruistic spirit. These are the people from whom "society may expect the least. They are at the same time the most costly wards of the state." Cubberley writes of a brave new world of standardized testing to identity "defectives" so that they can be put in institutions built just for them, institutions that are to be run according to scientific management principles of cost effectiveness, in which they get the care and education they need, but at a cost kept strictly under control. The rise of these specialized institutions for the education of "defectives" is linked, in Cubberley's text, to the rise of other "child welfare" agencies and institutions, including juvenile courts, disciplinary classes, parental schools, classes for mothers, visiting home-teachers and nurses, and child-welfare societies and officers.

What about the education of "superior" children? According to Cubberley, the new intelligence tests not only could identity "defectives." "We are now about to sort out, for special attention, a new class of what are known as superior, or gifted children." The very future of democracy "hinges largely upon the proper education and utilization of these superior children." Democratic societies are unlike aristocratic and monarchical societies, because in a democracy the intellectually superior who lead society are selected "from the whole mass of the people, rather than from a selected class or caste." In Cubberley, the tension between democracy and meritocracy is dissolved and in the process modern America is transformed into Plato's utopian republic. Democracy is about survival of the fittest and governance by an intellectual elite. Cubberley concludes his discussion of "superior" children by returning to a utilitarian language, one based on assigning an educational dollar value to young people according to their "return on investment." "One child of superior intellectual capacity," he writes, "may confer greater benefits upon mankind . . . than a thousand feeble-minded children upon whom we have recently come to put so much educational effort and expense."[12] One is led to presume that perhaps it would be wise for the public to invest resources in young people's education based on the return that can be expected on the investment. But is this a democratic rationale or an economic one? Behind Cubberley's democratic language is a mythology that is hardly democratic. Furthermore, he takes for granted the idea that standardized intelligence tests measure something called "intelligence" that some people have a lot of and other people have little of. The fact that middle class white males of northern European descent just happened consistently to outscore everyone else on such tests only confirmed the truthfulness of the patriarchal and Eurocentric mythology of the day.

It seems sometimes that not much has changed in the years since Cubberley wrote his hymn of praise to the new progressive approaches to meeting the special needs of both "defective" or "feeble-minded" children as well as "superior" or "gifted" children. The language now is different, to be sure. No one would dare use a language of "defective" and "superior" children in public education today. But one suspects that much the same thing is implied when professional educators and policy-makers talk of identifying and meeting the special educational needs of "developmentally handicapped" and "low ability" students one the one hand, and "gifted and talented" and "high ability" students on the other, or the "cognitive elite" and the "cognitive underclass." Furthermore, the standardized testing movement continues to support a conservative cultural politics and the mythology of meritocracy is more hegemonic than ever. Tests not only serve a central role in the social construction of inequality in contemporary America, they also serve a central role in legitimating inequalities as the result of "natural" differences in ability.

I want to move ahead now to the late 1930s, and a progressive textbook designed for junior high and high school students rather than teachers, a textbook that claims to be "social reconstructionist," and indeed in some ways is. I am referring to *America Today* (Nichols, Bagley, & Beard, 1939). The cover of the textbook represents the mechanical wonders of the modern, industrial age through a set of soaring smokestacks over huge factories. This is a class conscious textbook, with the working "man" no longer left out of history. The textbook includes sections on the rise of a system of selling people items they do not need, about "conspicuous consumption" among the new rich in the 1920s, and about the attempt by "robber barons" to place their own interest above the public good. This is the standard social reconstructionist mythology of American history, framed as a struggle between private self interest and the public good, and indeed it is progressive in a democratic sense. Within a decade, this social reconstructionist mythology would be purged from the textbooks as un-American, but in 1939 it was part of the "official knowledge" of textbooks like *America Today*. At the same time, even this progressivism was limited by its failure to see beyond class. The section on the great wave of American immigration in the late nineteenth and early twentieth century is a good case in point. Of

German and Scandinavian immigrants who ended up in the Midwest, the text notes: "They developed prosperous farms, built schools and churches, and founded colleges. No immigrants to our shores have proved to be more worthy of their new privileges and responsibilities than these newcomers from northern Europe."[13] In contrast, we learn that Chinese immigrants arriving on the West Coast "were willing to accept low wages because they were willing to live in cheap houses among poor surroundings. In this way the Chinese took work away from native Americans or forced them to work for lower wages in order to hold their places."[14] Notice what is going on here. The Chinese are blamed for allowing themselves to be exploited as cheap labor and for taking jobs from "native Americans." And something else is going on. The "native Americans" are understood to be from Europe, and the "real" Native Americans are invisible in the text. In a map of the United States along side this text, Mexico is represented by a man sitting cross-legged, wearing a huge, wide-rimmed sombrero, taking a siesta. None of this is understood to be racist or Eurocentric. It simply never questions the Eurocentric "air" that was still largely invisible in the late 1930s in America. If other narratives of immigration to America were to be found in American culture, they were deeply repressed.

Let us shift in time once more, to 1976, the year of the American bicentennial. Now, it would seem, much has changed. A new breed of textbooks is beginning to circulate in school and college classrooms associated with the newly emerging field of "multicultural education." The dominant culture is by now more sensitive to historic patterns of discrimination and prejudice American public life, and "minorities" are suddenly becoming much more visible in history and in contemporary society. *Minorities: USA*, first published in the bicentennial year, is a good example of textbooks designed for use in "minority studies," multicultural education, and social studies classes at the high school level. In some ways, the textbook represents a breakthrough in its willingness to acknowledge the oppression of "minorities" in American history. But, looking back from a contemporary standpoint, the word "minorities" is troubling. There is the "normal" white culture, and then there are all of those "minorities" that are demanding to be heard and recognized. According to the authors, "this book was written to help you understand the story of our country's minorities."[15] As if "minorities" were possessed or owned by the country— meaning white America. Now, the authors conclude, "minority group problems are national problems." Crime, unemployment, poverty, illiteracy, welfare mothers, drug and other problems are, through this linguistic trick, reconstituted as "minority problems," problems that since the 1960s have begun to affect everyone. The only way to "solve minority group problems" is through new laws and policies. However, "your greater understanding of minority problems will make you a better citizen." The Other has certainly changed in this mid-1970s text, becoming many Others.

But behind the liberal rhetoric of ending prejudice and discrimination, the text still positions the Other as "the problem," the one who needs to be better understood so as to be more effectively controlled and regulated by the welfare state, no longer a threat to the dominant culture. If "minorities" must still struggle against the vestiges of discrimination in society, they now enjoy rights for which "so much of the world must still struggle."[16] Here is yet another version of the "our minorities have it good" myth that has been so central to the legitimation of racial domination in American history since the Civil War if not before. Even when the authors seem radical—as in their use of the word "genocide" to refer to the destruction of the Native American people— this radical language becomes incorporated within a hegemonic Eurocentric discourse. Thus, in a sidebar box we learn that "genocide was not new." Throughout history, people have engaged in genocide. "The list of those who have been guilty of genocide could go on and on." In fact, genocide is one of the ways groups have "controlled conquered peoples" on all continents and every historical era.[17] By universalizing genocide, naturalizing it as part of the human condition—albeit an unfortunate part—its sting is lost. In its place is something that comes very close to legitimating the genocidal treatment of American Indians and other colonial peoples. This is a prime example of what Roland Barthes calls "innoculation," a form of the dominant mythology that acknowledges oppositional discourses and movements in culture by rendering them harmless.[18] It is an admission designed to innoculate the reader against being influenced by those who would use the word "genocide" in a more subversive and troubling manner.

All of this indicates that while things have changed in the curriculum, continuities with the past persist. The 1930s and 1970s textbooks mentioned above are narratives designed, overtly or tacitly, to legitimate a Eurocentric mythology of American history. The implication is that it will do little good to add on more pages to the history textbooks referring to the contributions of "minorities," or "exceptional" children for that matter, so long as these basic colonial narratives do not get interrogated. We certainly should try to "correct" the history textbooks to better reflect the reality of difference in America. But this is not where we should be placing all of our attention. If young people do not learn how to critically read texts, they are not being prepared to be democratic citizens, no matter how "politically correct" we may make the textbooks.

In this regard, the work of Edward Said points to some of the parameters of a critical, deconstructive reading of Eurocentric texts in particular, but with implications for gendered and classed texts as well. In *Orientalism*, he begins with the observation that "the Orient was almost a European invention," a space of romance, exoticism, of "haunting memories and landscape," a cultural landscape upon which the West painted its Other—an Other of both fear and desire. This Other, Said says, this Orient does not exist in quite the same way for the American as it does for the French and British. This is because the French and British look upon the Orient with historical eyes, as "the place of Europe's greatest and richest and oldest colonies," so that it assumes the status of a sign, representing the Other.[19] By projecting its alterity, its "contrasting image" upon the Orient, Europe also came to know itself and define its mission. The Orient as an image of otherness thus assumed a critical role in the construction of European material culture and its institutions of colonial domination. Said coins the term "Orientalism" to refer to a complex set of discourses, narratives, mythologies, and apparatuses and technologies of power that are involved in producing both the colonizer and the colonized, and that created the conditions for the rapid expansion of industrial capitalism and European military and economic hegemony. Orientalism is "a style of thought" that has changed and evolved over time, and that has taken on somewhat different meaning in different European contexts. It is a hegemonic discourse that "unilaterally determines what can be said about the Orient."[20] It is a discourse of identity that has made European culture very powerful by disempowering the Oriental Other. While the era of direct colonial domination of Third World peoples is almost over, Said raises questions about the extent to which Orientalism, or something like it, might still be part of the dominant cultural hegemony in Europe and America (in a somewhat different way).

One way Eurocentric mythology works is by making Europeans the narrators and subjects of history, who claim the right to speak for and represent colonial Others. Said finds this attitude everywhere in French and British literature and popular culture during the height of the colonial era, this sense that colonial people are like the Egyptian courtesan Flaubert describes, someone who "never spoke of herself," who never represented her own feelings or self-presence. "He spoke for her and represented her."[21] Of course, Said is also pointing to another aspect of Eurocentric mythology, its treatment of woman as Other along with Africans, Asians, and Arabs. The Eurocentric gaze is particularly patriarchal, associated with a form of domination that is ritualized in the home and workplace in the domination of women. To be European, wealthy, and male has put one in a position to not only possess and dominate people, as Flaubert possessed the Egyptian courtesan, but to speak for them as well, to tell their stories, to make them represent the exotic Other. But why is this othering process so central to the Eurocentric, colonial mindset? For Said, the answer is quite simple. The major thrust of European culture over the past several centuries has been to make that culture hegemonic on a world scale, to affirm the idea of European identity "as a superior one in comparison with all the non-European peoples and cultures." So, the "scholar, the missionary, the trader, or the soldier" knew where they were going before they arrived in the Orient.[22] They were going to an inferior land of inferior people. Colonial peoples were the subject of study by anthropologists, who understood them as representatives of the "primitive," and who placed them and their "artefacts" in museums. And they were made the subject of study by developmental economic theorists who questioned how (or indeed whether it was possible) to "modernize" them, to bring them up to a developmental parity in some distant time with "civilized" Europeans.

Said is primarily interested in turning a critical gaze on Eurocentrism, and on Orientalism as a particular expression of Eurocentrism. But he does not dismiss European culture outright. He looks for a time when Europeans and European Americans can begin to un-think their own Eurocentrism. One way to do this is through a critical, deconstructive reading of histories, documentaries, and movies in which East meets West. How do they mythologize the meeting? Ella Shohat and Robert Stam suggest a form of multicultural education organized around such a post-colonial pedagogy. Let me point to one example, their reading of a seven-part 1991 PBS documentary titled "Columbus and the Age of Discovery." On the surface, the program seems balanced in its treatment of Columbus, asking at the outset, "Should we celebrate Columbus' achievement as a great discovery ... or should we mourn a world forever lost?" This is a highly dubious choice, one that Shohat and Stam observe leaves "no room for contemporary indigenous identities or for activism in the present." The series is also organized as a voyage of discovery into Columbus' mind, so that he is always the focus, always the center of knowing. Indigenous people are merely a backdrop to his story, to his journey out. Why are so many people obsessed with replicating Columbus' journey of "discovery"? It is, Shohat and Stam suggest, because his voyage speaks to them "in quasi-mythic terms."[23] It is part of a Eurocentric mythology of origins around which European identity has been constructed. Can European Americans begin to construct their identity around a non-Eurocentric mythology in the decades ahead, or will the mythology of Orientalism come back with a vengeance? These are open questions, but questions meant to point to the critical role that public educational institutions might play in reconstructing the mythology of American public life and retelling the stories of American history.

THE END OF HISTORY MYTH

In order for progressivism to supersede itself and become a powerful force in American cultural and educational politics, progressives will have to learn how to deconstruct their own taken-for-granted myths about progress. What mythologies of progress frame the way we think about change in education and society? A new progressivism can only rise from the ashes of the old when the myth of progress has been confronted, when the most cherished and taken-for-granted myth that progressives live by has been deconstructed and revealed for what it is—a myth that has served the interests of establishing power over populations, in establishing the boundaries that separate the normal from the abnormal, in relegating the Other to the margins as the symbol of deviance and deficiency. For progressives to dare to use the name progressive, this history of the term's usage must be critiqued, and the new progressivism must be disassociated from it.

But the need for a myth of progress is as strong as ever, and perhaps particularly now that conservatives are invoking a counter-myth of the "end of history." The conservative social commentator Francis Fukuyama argued in his popular book, *The End of History and the Last Man* (1992) that Hegel was right about history. It does lead progressively, through a series of transformations, to a happy ending—and that end has finally come. There may be a bit of mopping up to do here and there, a few more groups brought into the liberal-pluralist consensus. However, there can be "no further progress in the development of underlying principles and institutions, because all of the really big questions have been settled."[24] These really big questions, in his view, have to do with granting full recognition to everyone as equal before the law, and not granting "special rights" to anyone because of their race, sexual orientation, or gender.

Fukuyama borrows the mythology of an end of history from Hegel, but he rejects Hegel's description of the good society at the end of history as a society of complete equality. The good society, Fukuyama says cannot be a society of complete equality, for then no one could excel. This, of course, is a familiar conservative myth—that equality drives out excellence; and here Fukuyama draws upon Nietzsche for support. If we push the Hegelian story of history any further, he suggests, we will soon reach a point where everyone will be like Nietzsche's "last man"—the citizen of modern liberal democracies who has given up the desire to excel and has settled into a "comfortable self-preservation."[25] The good society must be a society which rewards those who "seek to be recognized not just as equal, but as superior to others."[26] Fukuyama's interpretation of both Hegel and Nietzsche points to the fact that philosophical mythology has no fixed meaning or cultural politics. Its meaning is constantly being struggled over. I think this is where progressives have to affirm a different meaning of excellence, based on a different interpretation of the Zarathustra myth of the overperson. Fukuyama is right on one count. The good society cannot be a society of uniformity, of everyone merely looking and acting alive, of everyone mouthing the same politically correct language. The good society must be creative and it must be a place where people feel they can develop their full potential, explore their possibilities, and think "outside the box" (to use the lingo of the day). We need a society of more Zarathustras. But they cannot be a privileged few whose motivation to excel is that they want to feel superior to others. Excellence is not "naturally" tied to inequality. Indeed, it is only when all youth are treated as "gifted and talented," as young Zarathustras, that excellence in its fullest sense can develop.

To close his book, Fukuyama turns to the wagon train as a useful metaphor for thinking about history, and where it ends. He suggests that we think of history as a wagon train leading West, across the Great Plains toward a community on the West Coast—the end of the trail. He writes that at any given time, "some wagons will be pulling into town sharply and crisply, while others will be bivouacked back in the desert." Others with get stuck in ruts while crossing the Rocky Mountains. Some wagons, "attacked by Indians, will have been set aflame and abandoned along the way." Still others will lose their way and head in the wrong direction, or "decide to set up permanent camps at particular points back along the road." Here, in another form, is a Social Darwinian myth of a "great chain of being," this time with the chain laid out across the desert floor in a long wagon train. As in Plato's cave analogy, not everyone is expected to make it all the way, or arrive at the same time. The peoples of the world take their place in the wagon train, from less advanced to more advanced. Those societies led by strong-willed, assertive, Zarathustrian types lead the way. But in the end, all are headed in the same direction, toward the same destination. There is little doubt what Fukuyama believes that direction and destination to be. Something else is worthy of note here. Fukuyama positions Native Americans outside the wagon train, as representatives of the natural world that is being traversed and domesticated. He borrows freely from the mythology of the opening up of the West in American history, with the presumption that Nature stood in the way of the settling of the continent, the taming of the continent, the civilizing of a savage land. Nature and Native Americans stand outside the story of history, as those who, at best, test the strength of those on the wagon train, picking off the weakest of the lot. If Fukuyama sees the wagon train as those nations and peoples still on their way to where we have supposedly already arrived, then he suggests that their journey will involve many hardships, and that only the strongest will make it— Social Darwinism applied on a worldwide scale.

One of the ironies of Fukuyama's myth of history as a wagon train is that it celebrates both the individual who excels, the Zarathustrian personality that hitches its wagon to a different star, and the conformist personality that hitches its wagon to the wagon in front of it. While Fukuyama talks about Nietzschean types who stand above the herd at one point, he ends his little story of history by observing that all the wagons, as they pull into town, look pretty much alike. After all, the wagon is a functional technology, and its design represents the result of reason rather than whim or cultural tradition. Ultimately, "each has four wheels and is drawn by horses." Some may be painted in different colors than the norm, Fukuyama says, but each is based on the same design and serves the same function. Can the same be said for the people inside the wagons? They too are pretty much all the same, according to Fukuyama. Inside each wagon "sits a family hoping and praying that their journey will be a safe one."[27] So the journey of history is about universal themes, like looking out for the security of one's family. It is about "family values"—a major theme in the new conservative mythology. All around the world, Fukuyama argues, people want the same thing, safety and security for themselves and their immediate families. Certainly, there is nothing wrong with supporting families. But by focusing on individual achievement in the world of work, tied to a "private" family life organized around consumerism, Fukuyama and other cultural conservatives limit the meaning of progress and direct people away from engagement in a public sphere, in a public dialogue, in building a diverse and inclusive community. They present us with a myth of progress to a good society in which the public is no more than a collection of individual nuclear family units. Like the superhighway that has replaced it, the wagon train is represented as a place of private journeys, with each family safe in its own minivan. These journeys are not only private but also universalistic, journeys that wash away cultural difference in the process of modernization.

The conservative "end of history" myth provides not only a limited but a *limiting* vision of the future. This means that it is all the more important that progressives begin to articulate new visions of cultural development, new myths of progress. This will not be an easy task. Another irony of the times in which we live is that it is precisely among those groups and movements in American culture who potentially constitute a new progressive movement that the idea of progress has been most discredited. Cultural conservatives argue that progress has reached its end point, but many progressive-minded people argue that progress has been a hoax all along, that we can do without the myth of progress. Once progressives took the myth of progress for granted, as part of the natural order of things. Progress seemed inevitable, and not just technological progress. Progress in advancing the democratic vision of a "good society" seemed almost inevitable in the upbeat mood of the early twentieth century. Not so anymore. The power of the myth of progress has been substantially deflated as we enter a new century, and for some very good reasons. For one thing, progress never adequately delivered on what it promised. The good society, like President Johnson's "War on Poverty," had to be deferred indefinitely because other matters proved more pressing. The myth of progress also got mixed up with some very undemocratic politics in the twentieth century. In the name of progress, education and other public institutions have been brought under much greater top-down bureaucratic control, using corporate managerial models.

The case against progress is a compelling one, and the current questioning of the mythology of progress may be taken as a good sign. It means that people no longer take this modernist myth for granted, that they are increasingly suspicious of what interests it serves. But questioning should not lead us to abandon the myth of progress so much as re-mythologize it, give it new meaning in a decidedly new time. Without a myth of progress, and some fuzzy vision of a good society to guide us, democratic movements in American culture will not, I believe, be able to effectively develop a cultural politics that is equal to the challenges we face.[28] The beginning of a new century and a new millennium provides a window of opportunity. At a time when people are looking for new answers and compelling new visions of progress, progressivism faces a unique opportunity.

LEAVING SAFE HARBORS

I have argued in this book that a new progressivism is beginning to organize itself, preparing to leave safe harbors. It is a progressivism armed now with some very powerful counter-narratives and mythologies, some powerful new mythological lenses. One element of a new progressivism is associated with a shift from the myth of Ammon-Ra to Theuth/Hermes as a guiding narrative. Ammon-Ra is *logos*, a unified truth and autonomous reason that stands "outside" of human culture, above the distorting effects of "air." Ammon-Ra as educator/intellectual is the keeper of truth and reason, the final authority as to what is true and false or right and wrong, the one who judges with an objective standard. Logocentric education and pedagogy embody all of these aspects of Ammon-Ra. One pictures Ammon-Ra as a patriarchal pedagogue who stands behind a podium, on a stage—preferably elevated—addressing a silent and silenced audience, much like a fatherly priest at the altar. The lecture is not overtly religious or ethical. Instead, it is a scientific tale, moving step by step, counterpoint by counterpoint, from one truth to another. Yet, along the way values will be taken for granted, values that are inextricably intertwined with the truths being produced. Those students who are the audience record these truths in their notebooks, and then submit to learning them in a disciplined fashion, making their bodies and its desires submit to the mind, the ego, the "reality principle." At the same time, their bodies will grow to resent this disciplining of desire, and their minds will inevitably begin to resist having to submit to Ammon-Ra's truths.

The days of Ammon-Ra seem numbered as we move into postmodern times, although his power remains strong and much has been invested in the idea that faculty, and educational institutions, are the keepers of authoritative truth. The challenge to Ammon-Ra has come from within the mythological family, from Theuth/Hermes, the son of the sun god. It represents the negativity of the one authoritative truth and of an autonomous reason. Hermeneutic education offers only the play of difference within diverse texts, in which the meaning of words must be indefinitely deferred, their rhizomes of meaning leading back in diverse directions. Hermeneutic pedagogy takes pleasure in the "textuality" of meaning, in using words in ways that reference their usages in various other texts, making subtle distinctions between one's own usage and these others, playing with the differences produced by language. Hermeneutic educators disrupt all attempts to regulate and discipline language usage, to "normalize" it according to a prescriptive standard. Writing is a form of human expression rather than a mechanical tool used to derive truth statements. Fiction and non-fiction, myth and science, poetry and autobiography—all are valued equally, all understood as ways of expressing and representing truth. In place of a unified "common good" or an authoritative truth, hermeneutic education offers only incommensurability and unintelligibility, the impossibility of every arriving at a consensus on the truth or the meaning of words.

In the language of Plato's cave analogy, hermeneutic education takes place in the cave, which is also the sight of a Dionysian education. This is the way the cave is represented in the film *Dead Poets Society*. For the members of the Dead Poets Society, the cave is the place of wine and dancing and sensuality, of creativity and imagination, of poetry, just as Welton Academy is the site of a disciplined reason. But must we continue to choose between one or the other of these two choices: *logos* or *mythos*, the cave or Welton Academy? Is there a basis for a reconstituted education and scholarship that crosses borders, that occupies a hybrid ground? To move beyond this binary we must supersede it, moving to a more complex understanding of the relationship between truth and myth. The dialectic between Ammon-Ra and Hermes, *logos* and *mythos*, is leading, slowly but surely, to the development of what I have called *dialogic reflexivity*, the capacity to reflect upon our own myths and truths in dialogue with others. Through the reading and interpretation of popular culture texts in an inclusive dialogue, a new democratic education is being constituted. Unfortunately, the dialogue is as yet quite limited and far from inclusive, and a "text" is still understood in a very limited and limiting sense.

We cannot deceive ourselves either into believing that the dialogue can be equitable, or that it will lead to consensus. For it takes place within a world in which there are still masters and slaves, in which oppression still exists, in which those who have been marginalized and silenced still feel resentment and anger. The words "master" and "slave" may seem too extreme and provocative to describe relations between different identity groups in modern American society. They grate on the ear, invoking images of the antebellum American South, when these words were not absent from discourse and practice, but at the very core of that discourse and practice, governing the production of all truth and value. In contemporary America, "master" and "slave" have been exorcised from public discourse. They are words that cannot be spoken, that have been assigned to the dustbin of history. Yet they remain visible absences in contemporary America. The basic modes of consciousness that Hegel describes, the dependent consciousness of the slave and the independent consciousness of the master, are still very much with us. So too are representations and stereotypes that construct the Other as deficient, exotic, deviant, sinful, and lacking in intelligence and moral character. A Hegelian pedagogy aims at increasing self-awareness of how people construct their identities in relation to various Others. Education is a journey of the subject, in which the traveler never travels alone. The Other always precedes us, holding up a mirror, allowing us to see and know ourselves. Can we get along without these "doubles"? In a society in which master/slave relationships still exist in various forms, we cannot really walk away from identity, either as students or teachers. But we can push the dialectic a bit, and direct it toward reconciliation, and we can become more self-consciously aware of "othering" discourses and practices in popular culture and everyday life.

There is no road back to a "first nature" suggested by the Garden of Eden mythology, in which consciousness is not yet self-consciousness, in which self and Other are not yet separated, in which the self does not yet need an Other to know itself. The dialectic does not offer unity and transcendence, the final communion of self and Other. But it does offer the shock of self-recognition, the irony of inversions of power, the possibility of more equitable relations. The dialectic is for those who live in an imperfect and imperfectable world. It offers a long twilight battle over power, truth, values, and identity, recognizing that there is no escape from struggle but also that through struggle it is possible to see ourselves in ways that supersede our previous understandings and that open up the potential for the fuller development of human freedom. These struggles are more multifaceted than ever as we enter a new century, and one of the challenges for a new progressivism will be to recover some provisional basis for a counter-hegemonic cultural politics that is based on some commonly-held mythologies. Class can no longer serve as the glue that holds such a cultural politics together, as the meta-narrative that unifies all progressives. Yet we dare not ignore its importance, as some postmodernists do in their rush to move beyond Marx. Otherwise, the world depicted in the film *Blade Runner* may not be too unrealistic within a few decades.

In this regard, *Blade Runner* is Nietzschean. Hegel still looked to the state, and to public education, to bring people together across their differences and serve as the mechanism for making social progress. Nietzsche sees the slave's hope in an education that is outside of direct state control. He also would have the slave see through the Hegelian promise of reconciliation and equality, of progress towards a good society. The "Last Man" is Hegel's subject as it arrives at the end of history, now no longer divided, reunified in the human spirit, with all inequalities between people erased. The trouble with this vision is that it ends up erasing all difference as well. Zarathustra is thus the former slave who wants his freedom now, who will not wait for a supposed happy ending to history, and who no longer seeks unification. Zarathustrian education is about learning to construct and reconstruct the self by troubling binary oppositional identity categories. We might think of Nietzschean progressives as constituting two rather distinct types, at least at this point in times. First, there are those who are "effective" educators, in the sense that they are interested in power and intentionality as causal agents in individual and cultural development. "Effective" educators and intellectuals are interested in how power historically has been exercised through the construction of binary oppositions and dualisms that privilege some and disempower others, that bring the human subject under a disciplinary power that regulates, labels, ranks orders, and thereby "produces" subjectivity and docile bodies. A second type of Nietzschean educator/intellectual is the child/artist, speaking in new tongues, creating new narratives, always changing and growing.

The mythology of Zarathustra, the overperson, continues to be a subtext throughout popular culture, in various heroic forms—only some of which are progressive in the democratic sense. But if we take Zarathustra's story as a narrative of metamorphosis and self-production, then a film like *Tootsie* represents a particular contemporary version of the story. Michael overcomes who he has been, and is "reborn" as Dorothy/Michael, as someone who has superceded the "old" Michael with his need to dominate, his failure to take other people into consideration except as objects of his desire. In order to advance himself, to move to the next higher step in his conscious development, Michael had to undergo a metamorphosis, to become a hybrid creature with no fixed gender identity, able to draw upon both "masculine" and "feminine" aspects of his personality. Gender, for Michael/Dorothy, is a mere performance, and s/he will subvert the "normal" performance of gender from now on. Dorothy/Michael is less dependent on the Other to complete her/his subjectivity, thus more autonomous in a sense, more free to make her/himself according to his/her desires. At the same time, Zarathustra's freedom is limited so long as it is not extended to all equally. Hegel's Last Man still serves as useful metaphor for this commitment to equity, this realization that without equity human freedom is always limited to a few.

Zarathustra the child is also ecological, tied yet to the earth, its body, and other people through a web of connectivity that does not detach and objectify. The "flower children" of the 1960s had an ecological cultural politics. They were critics of the dominant cyborg mentality of the age, replicants who had decided that the most radical politics was a return to the natural landscape and their bodies, to attempt to reconnect to something that used to be called "spirit" in the pre-modern world, although by now no one really knew what this term meant. One thing it did not mean to the counter-culture, was the disembodied spirit. If the spirit was back in the world, it was not an ethereal world of abstract and timeless truths, but rather a "real" material world of human subjectivity, inseparable from human bodies, and ultimately inseparable from everything in "nature" and in the "cosmos." Ecological progressivism has continued to quietly grow over the past several decades, caught in its own dialectic between the earth goddess and cyborg mythologies. Now, the trick will be to bring Heidegger and Haraway into dialectic dialogue with Hegel and Marx. The basis for such a dialectic certainly exists. For the Hegelian subject of history is also a cyborg, one who comes to fuller self-consciousness only in shaping the clay of the earth, rupturing the borders that separate consciousness, body, and world. Eco-progressivism still proceeds through a pedagogy of pot-making, mediating self and world. For Heidegger, Haraway, and other ecological progressives, that mediation *is* the self, and its "authentic" destiny is to shape and reshape self and nature simultaneously in ways that sustain both and relate one to the other through love and caring. And underneath love and caring, may we not find desire? Is desire for reunification with "nature," the ultimate other to modern "man," but another form of the desire that leads to recognition and communion with the human other? In both cases, humans are "subjects of desire," constituted through and around the willing of that desire.[29] So desire, more than reasoned judgments of what is socially just, is still in the driver's seat of history, and progressivism continues to be the long movement of a desire, now no longer bordered-off from reason, truth, and value.

Notes

NOTES TO CHAPTER I

1. Herman Melville, *Moby-Dick* (New York: Penguin Books, 1992 edition), 66 and 116.
2. Antonio Gramsci, *The Prison Notebooks* (New York: Lawrence & Wishart, 1971), 328.
3. William Doty, "Silent Myths Singing in the Blood: The Sites of Production and Consumption of Myths in a 'Mythless' Society," in *Picturing Cultural Values in Postmodern America*, ed. W. Doty (Tuscaloosa: University of Alabama Press, 1995), 187–220.
4. Jacques Derrida, *Disseminations* (Chicago: University of Chicago Press, 1981), 73.
5. Page DuBois, *Centaurs and Amazons: Women and the Pre-History of the Great Chain of Being* (Ann Arbor: University of Michigan Press, 1982).
6. G. W. F. Hegel, *Phenomenology of Spirit*, trans. A. V. Miller (London: Oxford University Press, 1977). Hegel's *Phenomenology* was originally published in 1807. I do not mean to conflate Marx and Hegel or overlook the significant differences between the traditions associated with each. Marx presents a comprehensive theory of modern capitalist society that Hegel, with his abstract philosophy, virtually ignores. Nevertheless, I think the differences between Hegel and Marx have been much exaggerated, and I view Marx as one of the young Hegelians, his most radical and subversive son. In seeking to reappropriate Marx as a Hegelian, I am in general agreement with the position of Tom Rockmore, *Marx After Marxism: The Philosophy of Karl Marx* (Oxford, UK: Blackwell, 2002).
7. Paulo Freire, *Pedagogy of the Oppressed*, trans. M. Ramos (New York: Seabury Press, 1970).
8. Hegel, 131.
9. Nicholas Burbules and Suzanne Rice, "Dialogue across Differences: Continuing the Conversation," *Harvard Educational Review* 61, (1991): 264–271.
10. See Judith Butler, *Gender Trouble: Feminism and the Subversion of Identity* (New York: Routledge, 1990).

11. Antonio Gramsci, *Selections From the Prison Notebooks*, ed., trans. Q. Hoare and G. Smith (New York: International Publishers, 1971).

12. Friedrich Nietzsche, *Thus Spake Zarathustra*, in *The Portable Nietzsche*, ed. and trans. Walter Kaufmann (New York: Penguin Books, 1982), 139.

13. See Michel Foucault, *The History of Sexuality, Vol. 3: The Care of the Self*, trans. R. Hurley (New York: Pantheon, 1986).

14. James Lovelock, *Gaia: A New Look at Life on Earth* (Oxford: Oxford University Press, 1979), vii.

15. *Ibid*, 148.

16. Martin Heidegger, *The Question Concerning Technology and Other Essays*, trans. W. Lovitt (New York: Garland, 1979).

17. *Ibid*, 21.

18. Donna Haraway, *Simians, Cyborgs, and Women: The Reinvention of Nature* (New York: Routledge, 1991).

19. *Ibid.*, 146.

20. *Ibid.*, 157.

NOTES TO CHAPTER 2

1. Maxine Greene, *Releasing the Imagination: Essays on Education, the Arts, and Social Change* (San Francisco: Jossey-Bass Publishers, 1995), 63.

2. *Ibid.*, 114.

3. *Ibid.*, 114–115.

4. See Gregory Vlastos, *Socratic Studies* (Cambridge: Cambridge University Press, 1994); and Vlastos, *Socrates, Ironist, and Moral Philosopher* (Cambridge: Cambridge University Press, 1991).

5. Plato, *The Republic*, trans. H. L. Harmondsworth (London: Penguin Books, 1955), 278–279.

6. *Ibid.*, 281.

7. *Ibid.*, 281.

8. *Ibid.*, 278–284.

9. Charlene Spretnak, *Lost Goddesses of Early Greece; A Collection of Pre-Hellenic Myth*. Boston: Beacon Press, 1984, 20. The "facts" of the Gaia myth as related by Spretnak and others are open to dispute, although it is surely the myth, not the exact facts, which are important. See Merlin Stone, *When God Was a Woman* (New York: Harcourt, Brace & Co., 1976). According to Stone, there is historical evidence that the first oracle at Delphi was built by women, and that in later years the priests of the male god Apollo took over the shrine. She writes: "The many sculptures and reliefs of women, generally described as 'the Amazons,' fighting against men at this shrine may actually depict the initial seizure" (p. 203).

10. *Ibid.*, 18.

11. *Ibid.*, 25.

12. *Ibid.*, 18.

13. Derrida, "Plato's Pharmacy," *Disseminations*, 93.

14. Plato, *Phaedrus and Letters VII and VIII* (London: Penguin Books. 1973), 96.

15. *Ibid.*, 97.
16. Dinesh D'Souza, *Illiberal Education: The Politics of Race and Sex on Campus* (New York: Macmillan, 1991), 239.
17. Page DuBois, *Centaurs and Amazons*, 4.
18. *Ibid.*, 6
19. P.M. Grand, *Prehistoric Art: Paleolithic Painting and Sculpture* (Greenwich, CT: New York Graphic Society, 1967), 24.
20. Georges Bataille, *Lascaux or the Birth of Art*, trans. A. Wainhouse (Switzerland: Albert Skira, 1955), 38.
21. *Ibid.*, 130.
22. *Ibid.*, 15.
23. *Ibid.*, 24.
24. *Ibid.*, 28.
25. *Ibid.*, 115.
26. Carl Jung, *Memories, Dreams, Reflections*, 158–159.
27. *Ibid.*, 160.
28. *Ibid.*, 269.
29. Michel Foucault, *Madness and Civilization: A History of Insanity in the Age of Reason* (New York: Random House, 1965).
30. See Merle Curti, *The Social Ideas of American Educators* (Paterson, NJ: Littlefield, Adams & Co., 1959), 396–428.
31. Granville Stanley Hall, *Adolescence: Its Psychology and Its Relations to Physiology, Anthropology, Sociology, Sex, Crime, Religion and Education* (New York, D. Appleton and Company, 1904), 200.
32. Richard Herrnstein and Charles Murray, *The Bell Curve: Intelligence and Class Structure in American Life* (New York: The Free Press, 1996), 389.
33. *Ibid.*, 417–418.
34. *Ibid.*, 520.
35. *Ibid.*, 526.
36. *Ibid.*, 528.
37. *Ibid.*, 551.
38. See Joe Kincheloe, Shirley Steinberg, and Aaron Gresson eds., *Measured Lies: The Bell Curve Examined* (New York: St Martin's Press, 1996).
39. Plato, *The Republic*, 126.
40. *Ibid.*, 127.
41. *Ibid.*, 120.
42. William Bennett, *The Book of Virtues: A Treasury of Great Moral Stories* (New York: Simon and Schuster, 1993), 211.
43. *Ibid.*, 212.
44. Albert Camus, *The Rebel* (New York: Alfred Knopf, 1956), 29.
45. Quoted in Camus, *The Rebel*, 26–27.
46. Michel Foucault, *Discipline and Punish: The Birth of the Prison*, trans. A. Sheridan (New York: Vintage Books, 1979), 186.
47. Plato, *The Republic*, 310.
48. *Ibid.*, 614.
49. Gyomay Kubose, *Zen Koans* (Chicago: Henry Regnery, 1973), 17.

50. Franz Kafka, "Before the Law," in *Franz Kafka: The Complete Stories*, ed. N. Glazer (New York: Schocken Books, 1983), 3–5.

51. Jamake Highwater, *The Language of Vision: Meditations on Myth and Metaphor* (New York: Grove Press, 1994), 117.

52. Michael Apple, "Whiteness, Education, and Cheap French Fries." In *Off White: Readings on Race, Power, and Society*, ed. M. Fine, L. Weis, L. Powell, and L. M. Wong (New York: Routledge, 1997), 127.

53. Mary Daly, *Gyn/Ecology: The Metaethics of Radical Feminism* (Boston: Beacon Press, 1978), xiv.

54. *Ibid.*, 23.

55. *Ibid.*, 20.

56. *Ibid.*, 109.

57. *Ibid.*, 38–39.

58. *Ibid.*, xiii.

59. *Ibid.*, 400–401.

60. Murray Bookchin, *The Philosophy of Social Ecology: Essays on Dialectical Naturalism* (New York: Black Rose Books, 1990), 4–5.

61. Gloria Ornstein, *The Reflowering of the Goddess* (New York: Pergamon Press, 1990), 106.

62. Peter McLaren, *Schooling as a Ritual Performance: Towards a Political Economy of Educational Symbols and Gestures* (Boston: Routledge, 1985).

63. Denise Levertov, *Light up the Cave* (New York: New Directions Publishing Co., 1981), 82.

64. *Ibid.*, 83.

65. Virginia Woolf, *To the Lighthouse* (New York: Harcourt, Brace & World, 1927 [Harvest Book edition, 1955]), 240.

66. Helene Cixous, "Sorties: Out and Out: Attacks/Ways Out/Forays," in *The Newly Born Woman*, ed., H. Cixous and C. Clement (Manchester, UK: Manchester University Press, 1986), 67.

67. *Ibid.*, 78.

68. Luce Irigaray, *This Sex Which is Not One*, trans. C. Porter and C. Burke (Ithaca, NY: Cornell University Press, 1985), 215.

69. Luce Irigaray, "Divine Woman," in *Women, Knowledge, and Reality; Explorations in Feminist Philosophy*, eds., A. Garry and M. Pearsall (New York: Routledge, 1996), 481.

NOTES TO CHAPTER 3

1. Paulo Freire, *Education for Critical Consciousness* (New York: Seabury Press, 1973), 81.

2. Freire, *Pedagogy of the Oppressed*, 80.

3. *Ibid.*, 111–112.

4. Judith Butler, *Subjects of Desire: Hegelian Reflections in Twentieth-Century France* (New York: Columbia University Press, 1999), 17.

5. *Ibid.*, 17.

6. *Ibid.*, 21.

7. *Ibid.*, 24.

8. *Ibid.*, 52.

9. Hegel, *Phenomenology of Spirit*, 115.

10. *Ibid.*, 115.

11. *Ibid.*, 117.

12. *Ibid.*, 118–119.

13. *Ibid.*, 117.

14. Omar Khayyam, *Rubáiyát of Omar Khayyám in English Verse*, trans. Edward Fitzgerald (New York: Houghton, Mifflin, 1988), 87.

15. Freire, *Education for Critical Consciousness*, 73.

16. Butler, *Subjects of Desire: Hegelian Reflections in Twentieth-Century France*, 57.

17. Freire, *Pedagogy of the Oppressed*, 75.

18. Molefi Kete Asante, *The Afrocentric Idea* (Philadelphia: Temple University Press, 1988), 60.

19. Hegel, *Phenomenology of Spirit*, 124.

20. Audre Lorde, "The Master's Tools Will Never Dismantle the Master's House," in *Sister Outsider* (New York: Crossing Press, 1984), 110–113.

21. sante, *The Afrocentric Idea*, 13.

22. *Ibid.*, 60.

23. *Ibid.*, 46.

24. *Ibid.*, 50.

25. *Ibid.*, 98.

26. Wil Haywood, "Rethinking Integration: On Schools Many Blacks Return to Roots," *Boston Globe* (Nov. 16, 1997), A1.

27. Asante, *The Afrocentric Idea*, 8.

28. *Ibid.*, 41.

29. *Ibid.*, 13.

30. *Ibid.*, 17.

31. Quoted in Mikkel Borch-Jacobsen, *Lacan: The Absolute Master*, trans. D. Brick (Stanford, CA: Stanford University Press, 1991), 43. See Sigmund Freud, "The Uncanny," in *Standard Edition of the Complete Psychological Works of Sigmund Freud, Vol. XVII*, ed. J. Strachey (London: Hogarth Press, 1958).

32. Hegel, *The Phenomenology of Spirit*, 131.

33. Butler, *Gender Trouble*, 175.

34. Butler, *Subjects of Desire*, xiv.

35. *Ibid.*, 13.

36. Barbara Quart, review in *Cineaste*, Vol. XII, No. 4, 1983, 40, republished in *Film Review Annual*, 1983, 1219–1223.

37. Bob Strauss, "*Bamboozled* is Lee at His Angriest," *Cincinnati Enquirer*, Weekend section (October 20, 2000), 11.

38. Freire, *Pedagogy of the Oppressed*, 28.

39. Butler, *Subjects of Desire*, xix.

40. *Ibid.*, xix.

41. Hegel, *Phenomenology of the Spirit*, 121.

42. Epictetus, *Handbook of Epictetus*, trans. Nicholas White (Indianapolis, IN: Hackett Pub. Co.), ch. 8.

43. Michel de Montaigne, *The Autobiography of Michel de Montaigne*, ed. M. Lowenthal (New York: Houghton-Mifflin Company, 1935), 98–99.
44. Hegel, Phenomenology of the Spirit, 125.
45. Cornel West, "The Making of an American Radical Democrat," in *The Cornel West Reader* (New York: Perseus, 1999), 8.
46. *Ibid.*, 14

NOTES TO CHAPTER 4

1. Richard Rorty, "Education Without Dogma," *Dissent*, Spring, (1989), 199.
2. *Ibid.*, 200.
3. *Ibid.*, 200.
4. Luce Irigaray, *Marine Lover: Of Friedrich Nietzsche*, trans. G. Gill (New York: Columbia University Press, 1991), 50.
5. Joseph Campbell, *The Power of Myth, With Bill Moyers.* (New York: Anchor Books, 1988), 53.
6. See Arthur Danto, "Some Remarks on *The Genealogy of Morals*," in Robert Solomon and Kathleen Higgins, eds., *Reading Nietzsche* (Oxford: Oxford University Press, 1988), 13–28.
7. *Ibid.*, 143.
8. *Ibid.*, 227.
9. *Ibid.*, 126–127.
10. *Ibid.*, 126.
11. See Gregory B. Smith, *Nietzsche, Heidegger, and the Transition to Postmodernity* (Chicago: University of Chicago Press, 1996), 123–127.
12. Nietzsche, *Zarathustra*, 137.
13. *Ibid.*, 138.
14. See Walter Kaufmann, *Nietzsche: Philosopher, Psychologist, Antichrist* (Princeton, NJ: Princeton University Press, 1974), 144.
15. See Mitchell Dean, *Critical and Effective Histories: Foucault's Methods and Historical Sociology* (New York: Routledge, 1994).
16. Michel Foucault, "Nietzsche, Genealogy, History," in *Language, Counter-Memory, Practice: Selected Essays and Interviews by Michel Foucault*, ed. D. F. Bouchard (Ithaca, NY: Cornell University Press, 1992), 154.
17. Nietzsche, *Zarathustra*, 139.
18. Nietzsche, *Zarathustra*, 139.
19. Smith, *Nietzsche, Heidegger, and the Transition to Postmodernity*, 100.
20. See Kaufmann, *Nietzsche: Philosopher, Psychologist, Antichrist*, 145.
21. *Ibid.*, 128.
22. Richard Schacht, "Zarathustra/*Zarathustra* as educator," in *Nietzsche: A Critical Reader*, ed. P. Sedgwick (Cambridge, MA: Blackwell, 1995), 226.
23. Nietzsche, *Zarathustra*, 190.
24. Leslie Thiele, *Friedrich Nietzsche and the Politics of the Soul: A Study of Heroic Individualism* (Princeton, NJ: Princeton University Press, 1990), 165.
25. Kieran Egan, *Romantic Understanding* (New York: Routledge, 1990), 1.
26. *Ibid.*, 241.

27. Greil Marcus, *Lipstick Traces: A Secret History of the Twentieth Century* (Cambridge, MA: Harvard University Press, 1989), 1.

28. *Ibid.*, 2.

29. *Ibid.*, 7.

30. *Ibid.*, 9.

31. *Ibid.*, 200.

32. *Ibid.*, 11.

33. *Ibid.*, 247–248.

34. *Ibid.*, 441.

35. *Ibid.*, 447.

36. See Greg Dimitriadis, *Performing Identity/Performing Culture: Hip Hop as Text, Pedagogy, and Lived Practice* (New York: Peter Lang, 2001), for an educational study of black youth's textual reading and use of hip-hop culture and rap music to empower themselves.

37. Michael Dyson, *I May Not Get There With You: The True Martin Luther King Jr.* (New York: The Free Press, 2000), 308.

38. *Ibid.*, 308–309.

39. *Ibid.*, 310–311.

40. Smith, *Nietzsche, Heidegger, and the Transition to Postmodernity*, 10.

41. Ivan Illich, *Deschooling Society* (New York: Harper & Row, 1970), 3.

42. *Ibid.*, 4.

43. *Ibid.*, 42.

44. *Ibid.*, 41–42.

45. *Ibid.*, 47.

46. See Dean, *Critical and Effective Histories* , 174.

47. Michel Foucault, "Politics and Reason," in *Politics, Philosophy, Culture: Interviews and Other Writings 1977–1984*, ed. L. D. Kritzman (New York: Routledge, 1988), 67–70.

48. *Ibid.*, 147–148.

49. Arthur C. Clarke, *2001: A Space Odyssey* (New York: New American Library, 1968), 218.

50. Stephen Jay Gould, *Questioning the Millennium: A Rationalist's Guide to a Precisely Arbitrary Countdown* (New York: Random House, 1997).

51. Norman Mailer, *Of a Fire on the Moon* (Boston: Little, Brown, and Company, 1969), 5.

52. *Ibid.*, 465.

53. *Ibid.*, 8.

54. *Ibid.*, 9.

55. *Ibid.*, 161.

56. *Ibid.*, 171.

57. *Ibid.*, 463.

58. *Ibid.*, 464

NOTES TO CHAPTER 5

1. Gregory Bateson, *Steps to an Ecology of Mind* (Northvale, NJ: Aronson, 1987), 491.

2. Heidegger, *The Question Concerning Technology and Other Essays*, 3.

3. See Smith, *Nietzsche, Heidegger, and the Transition to Postmodernity*, 239.

4. Heidegger, *The Question Concerning Technology and Other Essays*, 15.

5. *Ibid.*, 18.

6. *Ibid.*, 16.

7. *Ibid.*, 21.

8. *Ibid.*, 34.

9. See Bruce Foltz, *Inhabiting the Earth: Heidegger, Environmental Ethics, and the Metaphysics of Nature* (Atlantic Highlands, NJ: Humanities Press, 1995).

10. Murray Morgan, *The Dam* (New York: Viking Press), xviii.

11. *Ibid.*

12. *Ibid.*, 162.

13. Robert Pirsig, *Zen and the Art of Motorcycle Maintenance* (New York: William Morrow, 1974), 23–25.

14. *Ibid.*, 24.

15. Jacques Derrida, *Of Spirit: Heidegger and the Question*, trans. G. Bennington and R. Bowlby (Chicago: University of Chicago Press, 1989), 34.

16. *Ibid.*, 109.

17. *Ibid.*, 9.

18. *Ibid.*, 11.

19. *Ibid.*, 128.

20. Vaclav Havel, "Our Changing Times, and the New Measure of Man," *New York Times* (July 10, 1994).

21. James Gleick, *Chaos: Making a New Science* (New York: Penguin, 1987), 18.

22. Fred Whipple, "The Heavens Open," in Cornelius Ryan, ed. *Across the Space Frontier* (New York: Viking, 1953), 140–14.

23. *Ibid.*, 11.

24. *Ibid.*, 6–7.

25. *Ibid.*, 6.

26. *Ibid.*, 5.

27. Margaret Wheatley, *Leadership and the New Science: Learning about Organization from an Orderly Universe* (San Francisco: Berrett-Koehler, 1992), 136.

28. Donna Haraway, *Simians, Cyborgs, and Women: The Reinvention of Nature* (New York: Routledge, 1991), 149.

29. *Ibid.*, 163.

30. *Ibid.*, 150.

31. *Ibid.*, 152.

32. Alexander Wilson, *The Culture of Nature: North American Landscape from Disney to the Exxon Valdez* (Cambridge, MA: Blackwell, 1992), 13.

33. Haraway, *Simians, Cyborgs, and Women*, 150.

34. *Ibid.*, 152.

35. *Ibid.*, 153.

36. *Ibid.*, 181.

37. Michel Foucault, *Discipline and Punish: The Birth of the Prison*, trans. A. Sheridan (New York: Vintage Books, 1979), 150.

38. Haraway, *Simians, Cyborgs, and Women*, 177–178.

39. Norman Denzin, *Images of Postmodern Society: Social Theory and Contemporary Cinema* (London: Sage, 1991), 34.
40. See Jean Baudrilliard, *Simulations*, trans. P. Foss, P. Patton, P. Beitchman (New York: Semiotext(e), 1983).
41. Haraway, *Simians, Cyborgs, and Women*, 149.
42. *Ibid.*, 151.
43. Gloria Anzaldua, *Borderlands/La Frontera: The New Mestiza* (San Francisco: Aunt Lute Books, 1987), 25.
44. Haraway, *Simians, Cyborgs, and Women*, 193.
45. *Ibid.*, 150.
46. *Ibid.*, 160.
47. *Ibid.*, 157.
48. Mike Davis, *Ecology of Fear*, 8.

NOTES TO CHAPTER 6

1. Jean-Paul Sartre, *Nausea* (New York: New Directions, 1964), 158. First published in 1938 by Librairie Gallimard, Paris.
2. Jean-Paul Sartre, *Troubled Sleep* (New York: Bantam Books, 1964), 330. First published in 1949 by Librairie Gallimard, Paris.
3. Melville, *Moby-Dick*, 4.
4. Rollo May, *The Cry for Myth* (New York: Bantam Doubleday, 1991), 9.
5. John Sanderson, "NASA Technology Looks Down to Earth," *Living Planet* no. 3 (2001), 43.
6. Gustav Niebuhr, "On the Furthest Fringes of Millennialism," *New York Times* (March 28, 1997).
7. *Ibid.*
8. Thomas Kuhn, *The Structure of Scientific Revolutions* (Chicago: The University of Chicago Press, 1962), 2.
9. *Ibid.*, 170.
10. *Ibid.*, 171.
11. Haraway, *Simians, Cyborgs, and Women*, 221.
12. Ellwood P. Cubberley, *A Brief History of Education: A History of the Practice and Progress and Organization of Education* (New York: Houghton Mifflin, 1922), 450–451.
13. Roy Nichols, William Bagley, and Charles Beard, *America Today* (New York: Macmillan), 55.
14. *Ibid*, 56.
15. Milton Finkelstein, Jawn Sandifer, and Elfreda Wright, *Minorities U.S.A.* (New York: Globe Book Co., 1976), viii.
16. *Ibid*, 9.
17. *Ibid*, 27.
18. Roland Barthes, *Mythologies*, trans. Annette Lavers (New York: Farrar, Straus & Giroux), 150.

19. Edward Said, *Orientalism* (New York: Random House, 1978), 1.
20. *Ibid.*, 2.
21. *Ibid.*, 6.
22. *Ibid.*, 7.
23. Ella Shohat and Robert Stam, *Unthinking Eurocentrism: Multiculturalism and the Media* (New York: Routledge, 1994).
24. Francis Fukuyama, *The End of History and the Last Man* (New York: The Free Press, 1992), xii.
25. *Ibid,*, xxii.
26. *Ibid.*, xxiii.
27. *Ibid.*, 339.
28. See Dennis Carlson, *Making Progress: Education and Culture in New Times* (New York: Teachers College Press, 1997).
29. Butler, *Subjects of Desire.*

Index